D0002659

Contents

Foreword

As a scientific field matures, there is a natural tendency for problems in that field to become increasingly focused. The aims of the field become better defined, and the open problems, while not necessarily easier to solve, with each generation of researchers acquire a structure that matches the emerging orthodoxy of the field. And so we develop a common language, a shared methodology and research "culture" that becomes a signature of the field. This makes working within a given field more efficient, but it might make it more difficult to link two fields together.

In artificial intelligence, particularly in knowledge representation, a goal is to develop compact, discrete representations of intelligent behaviour. The methodology involves defining states, situations, and intentions, fixing transitions among them, and reasoning in a computationally tractable way about the behaviours that can be achieved. One research thread of this work, cognitive robotics, involves reasoning about objects that move and mechanisms that perform activities involving motion.

In computer animation, the quest for realistic synthetic motion blends our fundamental models of everyday motion, namely Newtonian mechanics and kinematics, with control systems that make objects move according to those models. The preoccupation in this area has largely focused on getting objects to move realistically. The large number of degrees of freedom of real objects makes this a difficult problem.

Computer animation has made sufficient progress to allow us to imagine that we will eventually have systems that can make complex objects move in interesting ways. There has thus been a growing interest in getting objects to "behave" realistically. This can be seen as a natural evolution of the field of computer animation, but a systematic study of this involves constructing a bridge between the fields of computer animation and artificial intelligence, particularly cognitive robotics.

John Funge's book is about building such a bridge. He does it by developing a language that on the one hand allows activities and behaviours of computer-animated creatures to emerge, but that on the other hand has crisp formal semantics. The range of applications for this notation is as wide as that of computer animation itself: computer-based games, distributed avatars, and production animation may all benefit from a notation that describes not just the motion of a creature, but why it wants to move.

This book makes a convincing case for a notation that permits the compact specification of behaviours of dynamical creatures. Based on the situation calculus, the notation has a clarity that permits both human understanding and machine execution. But the contribution is greater than this. By developing useful abstractions such as an axiomatisation of interval arithmetic within the situation calculus, Dr. Funge has made significant strides toward linking two fields together. This bodes well for future interaction between the fields of artificial intelligence and computer animation. It also means that we have a language that we can use in the here and now. I invite you to read this book and use the language.

As virtual creatures develop, simulated perception such as speech acquisition and vision, and other kinds of "intelligent" behaviour such as natural language understanding, will also find their way into computer-animated environments. This book establishes a link that will allow others to follow.

Eugene Fiume
June, 1999

Preface

This book investigates the provocative but as yet largely unexplored interface between computer graphics (CG) and artificial intelligence (AI). The CG/AI interface is on the verge of explosive growth as a new breed of highly autonomous, quasi-intelligent graphical characters begins to populate the domains of production animation, game development, and multimedia content creation, as well as distributed multi-user virtual worlds, electronic commerce, and other web-enabled activities.

The modeling of graphical characters is a highly multifaceted endeavor, progressing from geometric modeling at the bottom of the hierarchy, through intermediate level biomechanical modeling and higher level behavioral modeling. The primary focus of this book is to pioneer an area near the apex of the character modeling pyramid, an area I call "cognitive modeling". Cognitive models govern what a character knows, how that knowledge is acquired, and how it can be used to plan actions. Cognitive models can also play subsidiary roles in controlling cinematography and lighting for computer games and animation. Moreover, cognitive modeling addresses a challenging problem that is closely related to mainstream AI and robotics research.

The enthusiasm and openness to new ideas I have found in the games industry has been a continual source of encouragement to me over the past few years. It is also interesting to note that revenue from the computer games industry is fast overtaking that of the movie industry. In spite of this trend and the fact that computer games raise many challenging research problems, the games industry has until recently remained largely ignored by the academic community. In contrast, computer animation research has close ties with the movie industry and many special effects companies boast an impressive list of researchers. As the computer games industry matures it will hopefully form a similarly symbiotic relationship with receptive academics. In this regard, this book makes an important contribution to building that link, as well as reestablishing connections to more traditional applications for AI in computer animation.

On a personal note, ever since I was an undergraduate my two main academic passions have been for computer graphics and mathematical logic. Naturally, I wondered if I might find a field within which I could combine the two. To begin with, the prospects for applications of logic in computer graphics looked bleak. My attempt to find an application began in earnest while I was doing my Master's degree at Oxford. Unfortunately, it was still not clear at the time how the two could fit together and, as bizarre as it sounds, I ended up using a formal specification language to specify a pool break!

Soon afterwards I realized that intelligent computer characters were a more natural application. Heady to put this new found synergy to good use I immediately conceived of a television program in which autonomous computer gladiators would meet on a weekly basis for a fight to the death. My hope was that, by giving the characters enough "personality", viewers would develop an emotional attachment to a character that survived more than a few weeks in a row. I dreamed that, by making the characters genuinely autonomous, these virtual sporting contests might eventually come to be thought of in viewer's minds in much the same way as a real sporting event. Once people came to see think of the computer characters as "alive" they might develop the same bloodthirsty enthusiasm audiences had displayed thousands of years ago for the Roman gladiator contests, but this time, without anyone really getting hurt.

The initial support from Channel 4 television in 1991 could not compensate for the fact that my idea was too ambitious. I came to realize how naïve I had been about the problems involved in developing intelligent computer characters. While pursuing my Ph.D at the University of Toronto, I took a course with Raymond Reiter on Cognitive Robotics that had a heavy emphasis on mathematical logic. Although the course was geared toward robotics, the applications to computer games and animation were obvious to me.

Please note that additional support material (e.g., source code, animations, images) is available at: www.dgp.toronto.edu/~funge/book/

Acknowledgments

This book is based on the course notes of my 1998 Siggraph course. Those course notes were, in turn, derived from my Ph.D. thesis. I am therefore indebted to my Ph.D. committee members Bruce Blumberg, Eugene Fiume (supervisor), Bruce Francis, Hector Levesque, James Stewart, Demetri Terzopoulos and Michiel van de Panne. All funding for my Ph.D. was provided by the Commonwealth Scholarship and Fellowship plan.

There are also some specific contributions that I would like to mention:

- The case study described in Chapter 9 was suggested by Eugene Fiume. Eugene made many helpful suggestions on the text of the book and the work described therein. He also kindly agreed to write the foreword.

- Building a merperson as a vehicle for displaying the results of my work was suggested by Demetri Terzopoulos. Demetri also made many helpful suggestions on the text and taught me a great deal about technical writing. Over the years he had provided invaluable advice, support and encouragement for my work.

- The prehistoric world API used for Chapter 9 and Chapter 10 was provided by Angel Studios (Carlsbad, CA). Steve Rotenberg and Andy Styles of Angel Studios, and Steve Hunt of Intel Corporation, were all extremely helpful in tailoring the API to our requirements.

- For the two case studies described in Chapter 10, and Chapter 11 I am by far the most indebted to Xiaoyuan Tu 涂晓媛. Over the years she has helped out in countless ways with programming, and producing animations. Working with Xiaoyuan has been both a privilege and a pleasure. Some of her larger and more specific contributions are listed below.

The low-level predefined behavior system used as a substrate for the cognitive layer in Chapter 11 was originally provided by Xiaoyuan Tu. Xiaoyuan also helped modify the predefined behaviors to incorporate a new visibility testing algorithm and a new collision avoidance mechanism.

The low-level predefined behavior system used as a substrate for the cognitive layer in Chapter 10 was custom built by Xiaoyuan.

Xiaoyuan also provided the biomechanical and physical model used in Chapter 11. The biomechanical model was modified only slightly to incorporate the geometric model of a merperson.

- Steven Shapiro helped proofread earlier versions of the book and was by far my single most valuable source of technical assistance on the situation calculus and mathematical logic.

- The idea to use intervals to represent a character's knowledge of its world came about through discussions with Jeffrey Tupper, against the backdrop of an advanced course on Knowledge Representation given by Hector Levesque at the University of Toronto. Jeffrey also provided invaluable technical assistance on interval arithmetic, mathematical logic and computer graphics.

- Ramesh Subramonian provided technical assistance on many aspects of machine learning and, as my direct manager at Intel's Microcomputer Research laboratory, he has been as kind and understanding as possible about my desire to write this book.

- Meng Sun 孙萌 provided numerous technical insights and stylistic advice. Her much needed encouragement, at a pivotal stage in my research career, inspired me to write numerous technical papers and, just as importantly, gave me the self-confidence to be successful in getting them published. This led directly to my being asked to write this book.

Finally, I would like to thank all the people at A K Peters, for their help and encouragement.

John David Funge
Mountain View, CA
USA

Introduction

Figure 1.1 depicts a computer character situated in some virtual world. More precisely, it shows one of the dinosaur characters that we will meet later on in one of our case studies. For now, the specifics of the particular character are not important; all we need to notice is the balloon overhead. The balloon is meant to represent what is inside the character's head. In particular, we can see that the character possesses its own internal model of its virtual world. We refer to a character's internal model of its world as a *cognitive model*. Cognitive models are applicable to controlling the new breed of highly autonomous, quasi-intelligent characters that are beginning to find use in animation and game production. Cognitive models are what this book is all about; they govern what a character knows about its world, how that knowledge is acquired, and how it can be used to select actions.

1.1 Cognitive Characters

We define an *autonomous character* as a character that, during the course of a computer game or animation, can decide how to behave on its own. To build an autonomous character, we therefore need a computational model of the character's behavior. An autonomous character also needs to maintain an explicit representation of some knowledge about its world. In the simplest

Figure 1.1. Cognitive models.

case, this knowledge can amount to just a few variables that indicate the current state of the character's world.

A more interesting, and elaborate, alternative is that the character can maintain an explicit representation of how its world can change. We refer to this knowledge about the world's dynamics as the character's *domain knowledge*. In order to distinguish them, we will refer to characters that have domain knowledge as (autonomous) *cognitive characters*.

1.2   Domain Knowledge

Unless we are extremely careful about how a character's domain knowledge is represented, it can be hard for it to reason effectively about the effects of a sequence of actions. The problem is that, when we think intuitively, about the effects of an action, we make a lot of implicit common sense assumptions. For example, we assume that the things we did not mention as being affected by the action are indeed unaffected. Unfortunately, computer characters typically do not come with built-in common sense and so they might be unable to draw the conclusions we would expect when they reason about their worlds. The solution we present in Chapter 3 is to build some of our own common sense notions into the underlying framework a character uses for representing knowledge about the dynamics of its world.

1.3 Character Instruction

In Chapter 5, we discuss the problem of instructing an autonomous character on how to behave. We will assume that a character's behavior is completely determined by the sequence of actions that it executes. This is a slight simplification because the result of those actions may also depend on factors outside of the character's control. For example, in a computer game, two characters might both decide to run toward a mountain, but if one gets shot in the leg *en route* then the resulting behavior of each character will look quite different.[1]

For regular autonomous characters, that do not posses domain knowledge, we must decide in advance on which actions they should perform in all of the different situations they might find themselves in. In this case we say that the character's behavior is *deterministic* or *predefined*.

In computer games, players soon tire of the predictable nature of non-player characters whose behavior is deterministic. Similarly, in computer animation deterministic behavior leads to characters that are tedious to direct. In both cases, what we need are characters whose behaviors need not be completely determined in advance. That is, we want characters that can choose their own behavior depending on the task or high-level direction they are given. When a character's behavior is not completely determined in advance we refer to its subsequent behavior as *nondeterministic*. The simplest example of nondeterministic behavior is behavior that is completely undefined, but of course such random behavior is generally not particularly useful. Instead, the character needs to choose its behavior in a task-specific way. In particular, a cognitive character can use its domain knowledge to reason about what it believes will be the effects of possible action sequences. Some of the action sequences will have desirable effects and others will have

---

[1]It is interesting to note that in the real world it could be hard to realize (unless we are able to ask) that a person or animal scrambling around on the floor with an injured leg actually has the same intention as another person or animal happily running around. In a virtual world we can always find out a character's true intention by simply looking inside their heads to see what action they are trying to execute.

Deterministic Behavior   Nondeterministic Behavior   The Middle Ground

Figure 1.2. Relative trade-offs of various behaviors.

undesirable effects. We can tell the character which effects are desirable by giving it *goals*. The character can then search for action sequences that it believes will result in it attaining its goals. When a character nondeterministically selects actions based on a goal it is trying to achieve, we refer to its subsequent behavior as *goal-directed*.

Deterministic behavior and nondeterministic behavior have different advantages and disadvantages. Figure 1.2 contains three illustrations that depict the relative trade-offs of using nondeterministic goal-directed behavior versus deterministic predefined behavior. In particular, predefined behavior is fast to execute because the programmer has done all the work in advance. Goal-directed behavior can be a lot easier to specify, but can take longer to execute as the character has to do a lot of the work itself at run-time. The relative value of the programmer's extra time spent developing efficient predefined behavior, versus the user's extra time spent waiting for a character using goal-directed behavior, will depend on the application. For a one-off animation, and for rapid prototyping, the trade-off may well be weighted in favor of reducing the programmer's effort.

It turns out, however, that there is an important middle ground between the two extremes of predefined and pure goal-directed behavior. The idea is to give characters domain knowledge *and* instructions.

knowledge + instruction = behavior

The domain knowledge can be used to plan goals and the instructions provide a "sketch plan" of how to achieve those goals. Technically this is still goal-directed behavior, and thus it is still easy to specify, but the added predefined heuristic control information has the potential to significantly speed up execution times. The approach even lends itself to an incremental style of development in which a prototype, which mainly uses goal-directed behavior, can be gradually refined (by reducing the nondeterminism) to production code, which mainly uses predefined behavior.

In most cases, a single application will employ more than one approach to generating a character's behavior. This is because different approaches are more appropriate for different problems. In particular, it often makes sense to implement simple "low-level" behaviors as predefined deterministic behaviors, reserving goal-directed specifications for "high-level" behavior. When we want real-time or more robust controllers it can make sense to introduce a third predefined level above the other two that can act as an "arbitrator" between the goal-directed behavior and the pre-defined behavior. In Chapter 7, we explain how to interface all the components together so that they can function as a unified whole.

1.4 Knowledge Acquisition

The simplest kind of knowledge a character can acquire for itself is the current state of its world. We refer to this kind of knowledge acquisition as *sensing*. The need for sensing in a virtual world is probably one of the largest potential stumbling blocks in the reader's understanding of this book. We therefore devote the entire next section to the issue.

The other kind of knowledge a character may need is domain knowledge about its world's dynamics. For the most part we will assume this knowledge is provided in advance, and we look extensively at how this knowledge can be specified using the intuitive notions of actions, their preconditions and their effects. Nevertheless, having a character acquire this knowledge automatically is a fascinating subject in its own right. It is, however, an extremely sophisticated kind of knowledge acquisition that would typically involve trying to spot repeated patterns in a large volume of observations on the effects of various actions. This kind of knowledge acquisition is called *learning*. We can even imagine a character that tries to learn not only about how its world behaves, but also about how other characters behave within its world. These other characters can be human avatars or the character could even try some kind of self-improvement by learning about its own behavior.

1.5 Phenomenology

Phenomenology is the philosophical term used to describe what the mind notices. For the case of a computer character's mind, it will notice whatever we choose for it to notice. In particular, it cannot notice aspects of its world that are not even represented within its cognitive model. It will also usually be the case that a cognitive character represents aspects of its world differently to the way they are represented in the rest of the computer program.

1.5.1 Robots

If this book were written exclusively for people building robots, we would have immediately added an extra caveat to the definition of a cognitive model. In particular, we would have claimed that a cognitive model is a robot's internal *simplified* model of its world. That is because the real world is such a complicated place that, even if we wanted to, we couldn't give the robot a perfect model of how it works because (despite what some people might claim) we simply don't have one. Of course, we have some very good ones, such as the ones you might learn about in advanced physics courses, but none of these is so perfect that it can always, under all circumstances, precisely predict the future. Besides, even if we could come up with some grand theory of how the universe works, it is unlikely that we want to have our robot encumbered with theories of quantum mechanics and special relativity as it, say, tries to avoid bumping into obstacles. We do not wish to wallow in esoteric points of philosophy any longer so we will assume the reader is convinced by now that a robot will have to make do with a simplified model of its world.

What about a computer character situated in some virtual world? Can we give a computer character a perfect model of its world? As we shall explain, the answer is that sometimes we can, and sometimes we can't, but we almost certainly would never want to.

1.5.2 The "True" World Model

Somewhere in the computer program that implements the virtual world there has to be a computational model of the virtual world. This computational model consists of a set of rules and equations that are applied to the current state of the world in order to obtain the new state. By repeating this process over and over again, starting from some given starting conditions, we can create a *forward simulation* of the virtual world. Moreover, if we rerun a simulation with exactly the same starting conditions, we expect to obtain exactly the same sequence of events as the last time we ran it. The computational model of the virtual world can range from something extremely simple that is just mixed in with the rest of the program, to, say, a totally separate dedicated module that implements a full physical simulator. The point is that there has to be some sort of computational model that is the "real" model of the virtual world and, for lack of a better name, we will refer to this model as the *true world model.* Therefore, if we want a computer character to have a perfect model of its world we can just give it the true world model. There are several good reasons why we usually don't want to do this.

Difficulty Depending on how the program is organized, making sure the character is using the true world model can be difficult and time consuming.

Efficiency Normally a character would like to consider a number of alternative courses of action. If considering each action sequence requires a complicated forward simulation then the character's decision-making process can be incredibly slow. For example, suppose a character considers all possible sequences of 5 actions chosen from a set of 4 available actions. That gives a total of $4^5 = 1024$ possible action sequences. If each forward simulation using the true world model takes just a $\frac{1}{32}$th of a second, then that still takes over half a minute to run through all the possible sequences. If the character can simulate the world using its simplified cognitive model of the world just 8 times faster, then the total time is reduced to just 4 seconds.[2]

Unrealistic behavior Characters with access to the true world model are, in effect, clairvoyant, and this ability to see into the future of their worlds can result in extremely unnatural looking behavior. For example, imagine such a character pushing over a tower of bricks. It would possess the ability to pre-compute the trajectories of all the blocks and use this information to pick a safe place to stand. Imagine how unrealistic and bizarre this character's behavior will look as it quietly stands there with a blasé air of sang-froid while large heavy blocks rain down around it. Of course, usually what we want is not a superhuman character, but one that uses a cognitive model to encode some common sense knowledge about being a safe distance from falling heavy objects. This character would push the blocks and then run frantically out of harm's way, just as we would expect it to.

Other characters Normally, there will be more than one character in the world. Even if all the characters represent the same type of things, what each of them actually "knows" about the world may be quite different. That is to say, each character will be *autonomous*. By making them independent, self-contained entities, we replicate the situation

---

[2]Note that, in a typical computer game only 10% of the CPU is available each frame for decision making. Of course, the character does not have to make a new decision each frame so the cost of decision making can be amortized over many frames, but even so, efficiency is extremely important.

in the real world and thus ensure a level of realism normally required in animations and games. We also simplify the task of instructing them since we need only concern ourselves with them one at a time. However, if any one of the characters now wants to predict the future precisely, it has to factor in the actions and reactions of all the other characters. This can evolve into a kind of arms race as each character tries to outsmart the others. That is, if character A considers an action, then it has to think what character B's response would be. Now suppose it knows that character B has its own model of character A inside its head. Then, to be sure about the future, character A must think about what character B will think about what it will do. Clearly, this can get very complicated very quickly. In particular, the only way to avoid this complexity would be to have a hierarchy of characters, with one omniscient character at the apex. Characters higher up in the hierarchy would have privileged access to the true world model containing models of all the other character's behavior lower down in the hierarchy. At possibly considerable computational expense, omniscient characters would be essentially free to manipulate the other characters to do most anything they wanted them to do.

The last reason listed above gives a big hint as to the reason why there are cases when, no matter how much we'd like to, we can't give a character the true world model. In particular, this happens when some of the other characters in the virtual world are controlled by an entity beyond the program's control. For example, suppose one of the characters is controlled by another remote computer running over a network, or (as in a computer game) by a human, or for that matter, a trained monkey. How could we hope to write down some rules that describe, with complete certainty, how the human controlled character will react to each of the computer character's actions? If we could then, we should think about switching careers, to psychology perhaps!

Therefore, we must conclude that, even in a virtual world, a cognitive model is, in general, a character's internal *simplified* model of its world. Moreover, it is highly unlikely that the representation we use for simulating the character's world will be appropriate for the character's internal representation of that world used for deciding how to behave. It is worth pointing out that there should be nothing shocking about having a different representation for simulating the character's world versus the character's internal representation of that world used for deciding how to behave. Having multiple representations for the same object is commonplace in computer graphics. For example, consider the process of rendering a geometric model.

For building the model we may choose to represent the model as a parametric surface. To take advantage of commonly available graphics hardware accelerators, we may then move to a representation in terms of strips of triangles in three dimensions. At the final stage of rendering, the objects will be represented as rows of pixels of differing intensities. The point is that at each stage a different representation of the same thing is appropriate.

1.5.3 Discretization

One common simplification, that we will see used repeatedly throughout this book, is for a character's cognitive model to represent discretized versions of continuous phenomena. A simple good example, is an object's position. Typically, an object's position within the virtual world varies smoothly over time, but within the character's cognitive model we might choose to represent the position on a discrete grid. In particular, we say that the grid cell that contains the object gives the position of the object. As long as the object moves around in a single cell no change in position is registered at the cognitive level. Only when the object's position has moved far enough to place it in a different cell do we say that it has moved. A big advantage of this is that it makes it particularly straightforward to leverage traditional automated reasoning techniques to implement goal-directed behaviors.

This kind of discretization raises many difficult problems. In particular, if the cells are too big an object can move around a lot without the fact registering at the cognitive level. This can lead to behavior that makes the character look dull-witted, jerky, and constantly surprised by events that it should have seen coming. At the other extreme, if the cells are small enough, then there is no way to tell that the character is not responding to continuous change in a smooth, natural, and continuous fashion. The disadvantage of small cells is that they can lead to a combinatorial explosion in the number of cells. This can bring some kinds of path planning activity to a grinding halt. Therefore, choosing the correct fidelity for the underlying discretization can require some trial and error. More usually it requires a more elaborate discretization scheme involving some kind of hierarchical adaptive grid.

Suppose we have overcome any technical difficulties and the character now thinks of object positions (including itself) in terms of grid cell locations. It uses this representation to decide that it wants to go to some adjoining cell. For example, it might decide it wants to move one cell west, say. Usually it is not acceptable for the character to simply teleport to the new location. Instead, it must move there gradually. That means we need to go from the character's discrete representation of its world back into the continuous one of the true world model. There is nothing to stop us doing this conversion at the cognitive level, but we usually prefer to leave out such messy details and introduce a low-level predefined behavior level. The key observation here is that, at the cognitive level, we often want to deal with a character's *intentions*. The low-level predefined level takes the character's high-level intentions and translates them into low-level motion commands. By way of analogy, if a person wants to reason about going to a particular location, the planning activity takes place at a fairly high-level. It is not normal to precisely fix a path, taking into account wind speed, blood sugar levels, etc. Unfortunately, the low-level predefined behavior level can usually not be one hundred percent guaranteed to fulfill those intentions. Thus, the character only possesses a simplified model of the results of its own actions.

1.5.4   Uncertainty

The most important result of the character only possessing a simplified model of its world is that, from its point of view, the world is now, to some extent, *unpredictable*. Obviously, if the cognitive model is an over simplification, then the character's world will appear so unpredictable that it is unlikely to be able to use its cognitive model to much advantage at all. Normally, however, it will be the case that the cognitive model is a reasonable approximation, but the longer the action sequence the character is contemplating, the more its anticipated effects will have drifted away from the true world model. This uncertainty about the ultimate effects of actions introduces a whole set of problems. In particular, the question arises about what the cognitive model represents. For example, a character's representation of an object's position could legitimately refer to the object's position in the true world model, or the position the character "thinks" it is in.

Of course, people and robots that live in the real world have to deal with this kind of uncertainty all the time. That is, when a person has to take some course of action, and they are not quite sure how it will turn out, they perform the action and then check to see what happened. If things didn't quite go as planned then they might have to take some corrective action. Therefore, to maintain the correlation to the true world model, the cognitive model needs to be updated regularly with information from the true world model. This is the process we refer to as *sensing*.

One of the biggest shortcomings of the early approaches to Artificial Intelligence (AI) was that it almost completely ignored the importance of this sensory feedback. In some circles, there has been such a strong backlash against this "traditional" AI that it has become unfashionable to suggest that a character or robot should make any sort of extensive deliberations before it acts. In this book, we take the view that sensory feedback is vitally important, but that if there is time, a character should use its cognitive model to do the best it can to think about what might happen before it commits to any particular course of action.

1.6 Implementation

Throughout this book we will be extremely careful to avoid tying anything that we say to any particular implementation or computer language. The reason for this is that we think it is best to leave it up to game designers, or animators, to decide how they would like to implement any of the ideas we will be expounding. Of course, certain computer languages have some built-in features that make it easier to develop certain kinds of algorithms. For example, it is particularly straightforward to develop goal-directed behavior in so called "logic programming" languages, but it is certainly not required. This is obvious if we consider that most logic programming languages are themselves, implemented in regular imperative programming languages. If you are a real masochist there is nothing to stop you using machine code, but we certainly wouldn't advise it.

In order to be implementation agnostic we place heavy emphasis on mathematical notation. Mathematics can be intimidating to some, so we are also careful to accompany all the mathematical definitions with explanations in plain English. In addition, throughout the book, there are lots of examples to help convey the intuition behind the mathematics. Nevertheless, mathematics is incredibly useful for expressing ideas as clearly as possible. This is because unlike natural language, there is much more widespread agreement about what the terms in the language mean among those who understand it. Computer languages also have the property that they are ostensibly devoid of ambiguity, but usually they are not a very convenient way for us to express ourselves.

1.6.1 Cognitive Modeling Language

The case studies at the end of the book are reasonably self-contained and are relatively light on mathematical content. In particular, we make extensive use of an alternative notation called CML (Cognitive Modeling Language). CML has a clear mapping to the underlying mathematics, but also has the nice property that it looks like a mixture of English and a regular imperative

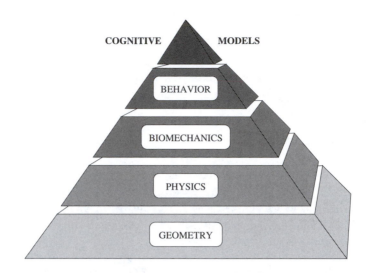

Figure 1.3. Hierarchy of models used in computer games and animation.

programming language like C. We introduce CML in Chapter 8 and we hope that readers find it intuitive.

1.7   Other Models

As depicted in Figure 1.3, cognitive models are only the tip of the iceberg of all the models that can be used to create compelling virtual worlds. Even if we are only interested in the top of the pyramid, we still need a basic appreciation of all the lower levels because these lower levels can have an impact on designs at the higher levels. For example, if we want to build a cognitive model for a character that we know will be situated in a physics-based world then we had better also think about designing a low-level behavior model to act as a buffer between the cognitive model and the physical model. Therefore, in the next chapter we give a brief introduction to some other models that are commonplace in computer games and animation.

Background

Before describing cognitive modeling in detail, it is helpful to provide some additional context. This will take the form of more detailed information on the other computational models that are important in games and animation. Aside from providing a stepping stone from older, more familiar ideas to new ones, this chapter will clarify many of the terms and definitions we will be using throughout the remainder of the book. Although it will not attempt a comprehensive survey, this chapter shall endeavor to provide enough details to make the book reasonably self-contained. Note that, since this chapter is essentially all background and further reading information, it has a slightly different format than the remaining chapters. In particular, all references are included in the text.

The first computational models used by animators and game designers were *geometric models*. Forward and inverse kinematics are now widely used tools in animation packages and computer games. The computer maintains a representation of how parts of the model are linked together and these constraints are enforced as the object is pulled around. This frees the animator or programmer from having to move every part of an articulated figure individually.

Similarly, using the laws of physics can free the animator or programmer from implicitly trying to emulate them when they generate motion. *Physical models* are now being incorporated into animation packages and game application programming interfaces. One reasonable way to do this is to build a computer model that explicitly represents intuitive physical concepts, such as mass, gravity, moments of inertia, etc.

Physical models have allowed the automation of animating passive objects, such as falling chains, and colliding objects. For animate objects, an active area of research is how to build *biomechanical models*. So far, it has been possible to use simplified biomechanical models to automate the process of locomotion learning in a variety of virtual creatures, such as fish, snakes, and some articulated figures.

Cognitive modeling comes out of the attempt to further automate the process of generating behavior by building *behavior models*. Thus, cognitive models are the next logical step in the hierarchy of models that have been used for computer games and animation. By introducing such models we make it easier to produce behavior by raising the level of abstraction at which the user can direct animated characters. This level of functionality is obtained by creating an explicit representation of the virtual world from the character's point of view that enables the characters themselves to do more of the work.

2.1 Geometric Models

Geometric models capture the form and appearance of a computer character. Many characters in animations and games can be quite effectively controlled even at this low-level and familiar tools for generating motion include key-framing and motion capture. Due to the predictable nature of motion, building cognitive models for characters that are controlled at the geometric level is generally much simpler.

2.1.1 Basics

In the most general case, the location and the shape of an object can change with time. A general scheme for describing the shape and location of an object was given in [134]. In particular, let each point in some object Ω (without loss of generality $\Omega = [0, 1]^n$) be named by its *material* (or *intrinsic*) coordinates $\mathbf{u}$. Then for some given $\mathbf{u} \in \Omega$ and time $t \in \mathfrak{T}$, the corresponding position in $\mathbb{R}^3$ can be given by specifying the function $\mathbf{q} : \Omega \times \mathfrak{T} \to \mathbb{R}^3$.

Intuitively, $\mathbf{q}(\mathbf{u}, t)$ describes the position of each point in the object as a function of time. Thus, the object is free to change position and shape without constraint.

2.1.2 Geometric Constraints

A geometric constraint is a method of stating that there are forces present
that cannot be specified directly but are known solely in terms of their effect
on the motion of the system. Such constraints pose two problems:

1. The coordinates are no longer independent;

2. The forces required to realize a constraint are not furnished *a priori*;
   they are among the unknowns that must be calculated or eliminated.

If a (possibly time-dependent) constraint can be written in the form
$f(\mathbf{q}_1, \mathbf{q}_2, \dots) = 0$, where $\mathbf{q}_i = \mathbf{q}_i(\mathbf{u}_i, t)$, then the constraint is said to be
holonomic. Otherwise it is said to be *nonholonomic*. Other constraints
will be considered as they arise, but first consider one of the most common
examples of a (holonomic) constraint—that of rigid body motion. It can be
expressed by equations that state that the distance between any two points
in the body remains constant over time: $\forall t_0, t_1 \in \mathfrak{T}; \mathbf{a}, \mathbf{b} \in \Omega$ $(|\mathbf{q}(\mathbf{a}, t_0) - \mathbf{q}(\mathbf{b}, t_0)| - |\mathbf{q}(\mathbf{a}, t_1) - \mathbf{q}(\mathbf{b}, t_1)| = 0)$.

2.1.3 Rigid Body Motion

The problem of working out the effects of the rigid body constraints on the
allowable motion is resolved (it turns out that the internal forces of constraint cancel each other out) by Chasles' theorem which states that the
most general displacement of a body satisfying the rigid body constraints
is a translation plus a rotation.[1] This produces a simple and convenient
way of representing rigid body motion in terms of homogeneous transformations (if required, see [44] for a definition of homogeneous coordinates and
transformations).

A rigid body can be located in space (see [55] for a detailed discussion)
by fixing, relative to the coordinate axes of some external coordinate system
$\mathcal{C}_0$, a local coordinate system $\mathcal{C}_1$ inside the rigid body. Let $\mathbf{S}_0^1(t)$ be the
homogeneous transformation matrix that maps $\mathcal{C}_0$ at time 0 into $\mathcal{C}_1$ at time
t, so that $\mathbf{S}_0^1(0) = \mathbf{I}$, where $\mathbf{I}$ is the identity matrix. A user can now specify
the amount the object should be rotated or translated within some time Δt
and the rigid body can be moved by automatically forming the corresponding
homogeneous transformation $\mathbf{C}$ and premultiplying it by $\mathbf{S}_0^1(t)$ to give the

---

[1]It is possible to pick the body-set of coordinates to give a rotation about the direction
of translation. This *screw* motion is much used in robotics.

new homogeneous transformation $\mathbf{S}_0^1(t+\Delta t) = \mathbf{C}\,\mathbf{S}_0^1(t)$. So, assuming $\mathbf{q}(\mathbf{u}, 0)$ is given, $\mathbf{q}(\mathbf{u}, t) = \mathbf{S}_0^1(t)\mathbf{q}(\mathbf{u}, 0)$.

2.1.4 Separating Out Rigid Body Motion

In [133] the above ideas on rigid body location were incorporated into the more general formulation that allows for deformation of shape. The basic idea was to produce a hybrid model with explicit deformable and rigid components. Thus, the body has its own coordinate frame $\mathcal{C}_1$ whose origin coincides with the body's center of mass $\mathbf{c}(t)$. The movement of $\mathcal{C}_1$ (represented by the transformation matrix $\mathbf{S}_0^1$) accounts for the rigid body motion, while the component due to shape deformation is represented with respect to $\mathcal{C}_1$ by a reference component $\mathbf{r}$ and a displacement component $\mathbf{e}$: $\mathbf{q}(\mathbf{u}, t) = \mathbf{S}_0^1(\mathbf{r}(\mathbf{u}, t) + \mathbf{e}(\mathbf{u}, t))$ (see Figure 2.1). Note that many instances of $\mathbf{S}_0^1$ and $\mathbf{e}$ exist that account for the same shape.

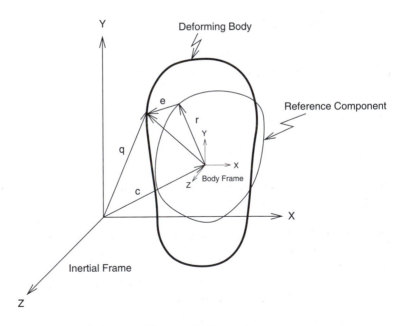

Figure 2.1. Kinematics.

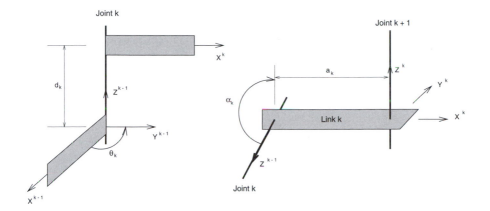

Figure 2.2. Joint and link parameters.

2.1.5 Articulated Figures

By generalizing the ideas in Section 2.1.3, it is possible to describe *articulated figures*. Many things, such as the human skeleton, can be modeled as an articulated figure. An articulated figure consists of a number of objects, known as *links*, connected by constraints, known as *joints*. In general, it is possible to have nonholonomic joint constraints but here it will be sufficient to consider holonomic joint constraints. A holonomic joint corresponds to the removal of one or more "degrees of freedom" from the object's allowable range of motion. Such a joint can be decomposed, without loss of generality, into a set of prismatic joints and a disjoint set of revolute joints. As the name suggests, prismatic joints move by translating in a plane, while revolute joints move by rotating about an axis.

Consider the case of an articulated figure that consists of a chain of links each connected by a joint. For an n-axis articulated figure, there are $n + 1$ links (link 0 is the *base* and link n is the *end-effector*) connected by n joints. Each joint has a set of *joint parameters* associated with it and each link has a corresponding set of *link parameters* (see Figure 2.2).

Let joint k connect link $k - 1$ to link k, and define the kth *joint variable* as a function of time t: $l_k(t) = \xi_k \theta_k(t) + (1 - \xi_k) d_k(t)$, where $\theta_k(t)$ is the angle of joint k at time t, $d_k(t)$ is the linear displacement of joint k at time t, and ξ_k is a function such that

$$\xi_k = \begin{cases} 1 & \text{if joint } k \text{ revolute,} \\ 0 & \text{if joint } k \text{ prismatic.} \end{cases}$$

Using the Denavit-Hartenberg notation [37], say, assign, for $0 \leqslant k \leqslant n$, a link coordinate frame $\mathcal{L}_k$ to the distal end of each link ($\mathcal{L}_n$ ends up at the tip).

Let $\mathbf{T}_{k-1}^k$ be a function of $l_k(t)$; that is, if the user specifies the amount a link should be rotated or translated within some time Δt, then $\mathbf{T}_{k-1}^k(l_k(t + \Delta t))$ represents the corresponding homogeneous transformation that gives the position of points in the kth link in terms of $\mathcal{L}_{k-1}$.

Using the notation of Section 2.1.3, let $\mathcal{L}_0 = \mathcal{C}_1$ and let $\mathbf{S}_0^1(t)$ represent the rigid body motion of the whole articulated figure. Then, given a complete vector of joint variables $\mathbf{l}(t) = (l_0(t), \ldots, l_n(t))$, it is possible to calculate the position of the end-effector at time t in terms of $\mathcal{C}_0$: $\mathbf{S}_0^n(\mathbf{l}) = \mathbf{S}_0^1 \, \mathbf{T}_0^1(l_1) \cdots \mathbf{T}_{n-1}^n(l_n)$. Problems arise with articulated figures containing closed loops (see [43]), but with suitable relabeling all of the above extends to articulated figures with more general topologies.

Thus, since link k's coordinate frame is defined in terms of link $k - 1$'s coordinate frame, rotating or translating link $k - 1$ causes all the $j \geqslant k$ links to move by the same amount. This makes direct manipulation of articulated figures easier.

Forward Kinematics

Let the *joint space* $\mathfrak{L} \subset \mathbb{R}^n$ of an articulated figure be the set of all possible joint vectors, and let the *configuration space* $\mathfrak{Z} \subset \mathbb{R}^6$ be the set of all possible configurations (position plus orientation) of the end-effector. Then the *forward kinematics* problem is to determine the function $\mathbf{w} : \mathfrak{L} \to \mathfrak{Z}$ that maps joint vectors to configuration vectors.

The means to calculate a solution to the forward kinematics problem have already been outlined in Section 2.1.5. Such a solution can be conveniently expressed in the form

$$\mathbf{S}_0^n(\mathbf{l}) = \begin{pmatrix} \mathbf{R} & \mathbf{p} \\ \mathbf{0} & 1 \end{pmatrix}$$

where $\mathbf{R}$ and $\mathbf{p}$ represent, respectively, the orientation and position of l_n in $\mathcal{C}_0$ at time t.

Inverse Kinematics

Many problems in animation and games (as well as robotics) are naturally phrased as constraining the end-effector to be in some configuration. The *inverse kinematics* problem is to determine the function $\mathbf{w}^{-1} : \mathfrak{Z} \to \mathfrak{L}$ that maps configuration vectors to joint vectors.

It is possible to cast this problem as an optimization problem and, in the graphics literature [6, 7], describe a numerical technique in which the user is given interactive control over how much time the algorithm spends on trying to compute a solution. For a specific geometric model it may also be possible to obtain a closed-form solution. Unfortunately no general technique exists for doing this and, even when such a solution does exist, it is usually difficult to derive.

An alternative approach is to examine the differential relationship (with respect to time) between $\mathbf{l}(t) \in \mathfrak{L}$ and $\mathbf{z}(t) \in \mathfrak{Z}$: $\dot{\mathbf{z}} = \mathbf{J}(\mathbf{l})\dot{\mathbf{l}}$, where $\mathbf{J}(\mathbf{l})$ is known as the *Jacobian matrix* of the end-effector:

$$J_{kj} = \frac{\partial w_k(\mathbf{l})}{\partial l_j} \quad 1 \leqslant k \leqslant 6, \ 1 \leqslant j \leqslant n.$$

This matrix effects a linear transformation that maps instantaneous joint space velocities into instantaneous configuration space velocities. This differential relationship can be used as the basis for numerical methods that can solve for a joint space *trajectory* in terms of a given configuration space trajectory. These techniques can also be extended to handle over-constrained and under-constrained problems (see [119]). How a trajectory, in any space, might be computed to start with is discussed from Section 2.2 onwards.

2.2   Kinematic Control

2.2.1   Key-framing

Suppose a motion sequence consists of k frames, each of which depicts the position and shape of some object at times $t_i \in \{t_0, \dots, t_{k-1}\} \subset \mathfrak{T}$. Let $\mathbf{q} : \Omega \times \mathfrak{T} \to \mathbb{R}^3$ be a user-defined partial function that specifies the position of any point on the object at the given times. Then, for each t_i, the set of values $\{\mathbf{q}(\mathbf{u}, t_i) | \mathbf{u} \in \Omega\}$ is known as a *key-frame*.

The function $\mathbf{q}$ need not be specified directly but can be calculated (using the techniques outlined previously) from, say, a trajectory through joint space. At the practical level, users usually define key-frames using interactive shape manipulation (assuming there is no rigid body motion constraint), forward and, if available, inverse kinematics procedures. Once the scene is in the desired configuration it is recorded and the process repeated until as many scenes as required are defined.

A widely used interactive direct manipulation technique is to have an actor kitted out with some motion detectors and have the movements of the actor mapped, in some useful way, to a corresponding object in the scene. While this ensures very realistic looking motion, it says nothing about the underlying mechanisms, it is hard to apply to figures with a different topology to the one used for the motion detection, and it is hard to modify in a realistic way. There has even been some work [30] on trying to adapt dance notations (for example, Labanotation) to develop a language for describing these motions. Unfortunately, while these "languages of movement" may have some merit as regards description, they have little use as a motion synthesis tool. It is simply too complicated and counterintuitive for a non-expert to script or alter motions using the low-level constructs available in these languages.

The transition from a discrete set of samples through the space in question to a smooth path is achieved by interpolation. In the above example, for some given $\mathbf{u}$, $\mathbf{q}$ is made a total function by using the set of values $\{\mathbf{q}(\mathbf{u}, t) | t \in t_0, \dots, t_{k-1}\}$ as control points for a space-time spline [127] (Most modern day systems use interpolating Catmull-Rom splines.) In conventional animation, this process of interpolation is commonly known as *in-betweening* and was quickly adopted by computer animation systems by making the computer responsible for producing the in-between frames [31]. Naively applying the same strategy to object orientations can lead to non-smooth rotations and so [122, 17] gave methods for using interpolation of quaternions that produces the desired smooth rotations.

Key-framing is a very flexible approach but a major drawback is that the length and realism of the motion is usually proportional to the amount of effort expended by the animator or programmer. However, it remains the most commonly used approach in commercial animation and game production today ([73] gives some helpful guidelines to would-be computer animators) and can easily be used to produce popular effects such as shape "morphing."

2.2.2 Procedural Control

There are many other ways to noninteractively define a trajectory through some space using principally kinematic methods. In particular, [20, 114] showed how a general purpose programming language (with some extensions for game and animation purposes) could be used to define arbitrarily complicated trajectories. Indeed the literature abounds with such definitions, usually they have been hand-crafted to solve some particular problem and sometimes they contain elements that are useful in a wider context. To name but a few: [6] used a network of special purpose processors to produce motion of a human-like figure; [149] created a hierarchical system that used finite state machines to generate walking and jumping motions; [53] used a mixture of inverse kinematics, simple rules, and some simple dynamics to create some very realistic motion of human walking; [76] gave an account of the robot motion planning problem and expounded a solution using commonly available graphics techniques; [116] used a combination of rules and inverse kinematics to calculate realistic grasps (this has also been the subject of much research in robotics); [106] described how multiple kinematic constraints can be applied to a three-dimensional human body model, so that it can be interactively manipulated with much more ease than would otherwise be possible; [71] described a manipulation motion planning system inspired by robotics research; and [7] discussed human modeling using mainly kinematic methods.

2.3 Physical Models

Physical models capture additional aspects of the world such as an object's mass, inertia, and how it responds to forces such as gravity. The use of physical models allows many motions to be created automatically and with unparalleled realism. Unfortunately, the cost of simulating the equations of motion make it less straightforward to build cognitive models for characters that inhabit such realistic worlds.

Some [106, 71] have pointed out that for low-speed motion, the probability of producing physically implausible looking motion is low and they even suggest using simple qualitative physics notions to improve the look of faster motion. However, all kinematic approaches to producing motion underconstrain the allowable motion so objects may be allowed to move in a completely unrealistic way.

The laws of classical physics constitute a precise statement of people's preconceptions about how everyday objects are expected to move. Some physics that is relevant to computer games and animation is described in Section 2.4.2. What follows describes the physics that is applicable to generating motion in general and discusses some of the implementation issues that arise.

2.3.1 Physics for Deformable Bodies

The physically realistic simulation of deformable bodies for animation and games was first addressed in [134]. The equations of motion can be written in Lagrange's form as

$$\frac{\partial}{\partial t}(\mu \frac{\partial \mathbf{q}}{\partial t}) + \gamma \frac{\partial \mathbf{q}}{\partial t} + \frac{\delta \varepsilon(\mathbf{q})}{\delta \mathbf{q}} = \mathbf{f}(\mathbf{q}, t),$$

where $\mathbf{q}(\mathbf{u}, t)$ is the position of point $\mathbf{u}$ at time t, $\mu(\mathbf{u})$ is the mass density, $\gamma(\mathbf{u})$ is the damping factor, $\mathbf{f}(\mathbf{q}, t)$ is the net externally-applied force and $\varepsilon(\mathbf{q})$ is a functional that measures the net instantaneous potential energy of the body. $\delta \varepsilon(\mathbf{q})/\delta \mathbf{q}$ is the variational derivative that measures the rate of change of the potential energy with respect to the deformation.

In [133] the corresponding equations for the hybrid model of Section 2.1.4 were given (the different representations give different practical benefits at the extremes of deformable behavior). The definition of $\varepsilon(\mathbf{q})$, based on the theory of elasticity, allows for objects to display elastic and inelastic motion. Through a discretization, based on the finite elements method, and the application of numerical integration techniques to the solution of the equations of motion, a computer implementation was possible. The discretization is equivalent to a model consisting of a number of point masses connected by springs. Such a model has been successful in modeling certain classes of animals such as snakes [94] and fish [137]. To produce more efficient implementations the allowable deformations can be restricted as in [103, 147, 42, 150]. It is also possible to have articulated bodies with deformable links [93].

2.3.2   Physics for Articulated Rigid Bodies

There are two commonly used approaches to deriving the equations of motion for a rigid articulated body: the Lagrange–Euler formulation and the Newton–Euler formulation. Both result in the same motion (indeed one may be derived from the other [55]) but they have different computational properties.

Lagrange's Equation

The Lagrange–Euler formulation is based on the concepts of generalized coordinates, energy, and generalized force (see [55] for an explanation). The approach makes the forces that maintain geometric constraints implicit, thus resulting in a reduced set of coordinates. This has the advantage that complex dynamic systems can sometimes be modeled in a simple, elegant fashion with a minimal set of coordinates. In addition, the terms in the final closed-form equations often have simple physical interpretations.

For an n-link articulated figure an appropriate set of generalized coordinates is the vector of joint variables. The generalized coordinates are chosen so that they are, at least for the case of holonomic constraints, independent. In particular, for articulated figures with no loops there are well known $O(n)$ methods for computing the accelerations of the joints [43]. For figures containing loops, and other nonholonomic constraints, it is not necessarily possible to derive a suitable set of generalized coordinates. Even if a set of coordinates can be found, computing the accelerations has worst case complexity of $O(n^3)$.

Newton–Euler Formulation

Unlike the Lagrange formulation, the Newton–Euler approach does not use the notion of generalized coordinates. This results in a full set of coordinates that are no longer necessarily independent and for which the (explicit) forces of constraint must be determined. For a rigid body whose center of mass is given by $c(t)$, the basic Newton–Euler equations of motion are

$$\sum \mathbf{f} = \mathbf{m}\ddot{\mathbf{c}} \quad \text{and} \quad \sum \boldsymbol{\tau} = \mathbf{I}\dot{\boldsymbol{\omega}} + \boldsymbol{\omega} \times \mathbf{I}\boldsymbol{\omega},$$

where $\mathbf{f}$ is the external force, $\mathbf{m}$ is the mass, $\ddot{\mathbf{c}}$ is the acceleration, $\boldsymbol{\tau}$ is the external torque, $\mathbf{I}$ is the inertia tensor, $\boldsymbol{\omega}$ is the orientation, and $\dot{\boldsymbol{\omega}}$ is the angular velocity.

The main contribution of study in the dynamics of articulated rigid bodies has been to come up with fast $O(n)$ recursive solutions based on the Newton–Euler formulation [43]. The recursive formulation exploits the chainlike structure of articulated figures, with the motion of each link represented with respect to its neighboring link. Given a joint-space trajectory, the velocities and accelerations of each link are computed recursively, starting at the base and propagating forward to the tip. This produces the *forward equations*, which are then used to compute the forces and torques acting on each link, starting at the tip and working backwards to the base (the *backward equations*).

Recently, [14] described a direct (i.e., nonrecursive, noniterative) technique based on Lagrange multipliers. The Lagrange multipliers are the unknown constraint forces. Since internal forces do no net work, we want to find the solution such that the internal forces of constraint disappear. This amounts to solving a large sparse matrix, which by exploiting its structure, can always be done in linear time. The approach handles arbitrary constraints, is conducive to good software design, and is simple to understand and implement. When there are no cycles the method has worst case complexity of $O(n)$.

2.3.3 Forward Dynamics

The forward dynamics problem is that of computing positions and velocities from given forces and torques. The unknowns in the equations of motion of the previous sections are the forces, torques, and accelerations. So the first part of the problem is to solve the equations of motion for the accelerations, in terms of the forces and torques.

In general, this gives a set of coupled second order nonlinear differential equations. Any set of nth order differential equations can be reduced to an equivalent first-order one of the form: $\dot{\mathbf{x}} = \mathbf{k}(\mathbf{x}(t), \mathbf{v}(t))$, where $\mathbf{v}(t)$ supplies values for all the unknown forces and torques. With suitable initial (or boundary) values $\mathbf{x}(t_0) = \mathbf{x}_0$, this system of equations can be numerically integrated over some interval $[t_0, t_1]$ to give positions and velocities $\mathbf{x}(t)$. A survey of numerical integration techniques for computer animation and games is given in [56].

Much early work in animation and games (as well as robotics) was concerned with producing programs that embodied the equations of motion for rigid body articulated figures [145, 4]. Software now exists that can take a physical description of some articulated figure and produce the corresponding equations of motion (for example, the "dynamics compiler" in [140]). Such software is now available in robust and efficient commercial *simulators* such as [131]. Thus, for inanimate objects it is possible to create realistic motion in a completely automatic way by using *simulation*. All the animator or programmer need do is define the physical object descriptions, set the initial conditions, and watch the motion unfold.

The situation is slightly complicated by the possibility that objects may collide. If a nonanalytic collision resolution algorithm is used, the springs and dampers can either be incorporated when a collision is detected (see Section 2.4.1) or, if all the points of possible contact can be surmised in advance, they can be included *a priori* in the equations of motion. If an analytic method is used in which a discontinuous change of velocity occurs, then when the simulator detects a collision it suspends the simulation, resolves the collision (see Section 2.4.2), and then restarts the simulation with the new initial conditions.

2.3.4 Inverse Dynamics

It is also possible to solve the equations of motion for the forces and torques in terms of the accelerations. Then given some desired motion it is possible (by differentiating twice) to calculate these accelerations to, in turn, calculate the forces and torques that would be required to produce such a motion.

In robotics the inverse dynamics formulation can be useful for calculating the torques necessary to move a robot along some specific path. In animation and games the goal is determining the motion, so if this is already known, there is not much need to calculate the forces and torques that will produce it. Exceptions to this are when the forces and torques are used to evaluate the feasibility of some defined motion, say for ergonomics [7]; or when a mixture of kinematic and dynamics is used in one application (see Section 2.3.5).

2.3.5 Additional Geometric Constraints

Several authors have considered the problem of adding other types of constraints to a physical simulation: [18] presented a menagerie of possible constraints for rigid bodies; [109] considered the application of constraints to deformable models.

The point of the constraint-based approach is to ease the problem of controlling a dynamic simulation. That is, part of the simulation can be controlled kinematically (for example, the endpoint of an articulated figure can be constrained to follow some path) and the rest of the simulation will move in accordance with the laws of physics. By using inverse dynamics to calculate the forces needed to enforce the constraint, the effects of these forces can be incorporated into the physics-based part of the simulation. This approach to creating motion is suggested by [68] in the context of articulated figures.

2.4 Noninterpenetration

A noninterpenetration constraint states that the intersection of two bodies can never include more than their boundaries. That is, for some object A, define F_A such that at any time $t \in \mathfrak{T}$ and for any given point $\mathbf{q} \in \mathbb{R}^3$,

$$F_A(\mathbf{q}, t) \begin{cases} > 0 & \text{if } \mathbf{q} \text{ is outside } A, \\ = 0 & \text{if } \mathbf{q} \text{ is on the boundary of } A, \\ < 0 & \text{if } \mathbf{q} \text{ is inside } A. \end{cases}$$

For any two bodies A and B whose positions are, respectively, specified by functions $\mathbf{q}_A$ and $\mathbf{q}_B$ a *noninterpenetration* is maintained by satisfying the nonholonomic constraint:

$$\forall t \in \mathfrak{T}; \mathbf{u}_A \in \Omega_A; \mathbf{u}_B \in \Omega_B \ (F_A(\mathbf{q}_B(\mathbf{u}_B, t), t) \geqslant 0 \ \wedge \ F_B(\mathbf{q}_A(\mathbf{u}_A, t), t) \geqslant 0)).$$

The first part of the problem, known as the *collision detection problem*, is to determine the time at which any two bodies first collide. That is, we seek a time t for which equality in the above expression is reached. The problem of determining the subsequent motion is known as the *collision resolution* and *resting contact* problem.

2.4.1   Collision Detection

Collision detection is a geometry problem and has been extensively studied in robotics and computer-aided design as part of the *collision avoidance* problem. The different demands of a collision detection algorithm for computer games and animation led [96] to study the problem in the context of virtual worlds. In particular an algorithm is given that uses point sampling at a given time to find a set of interpenetrating points for time dependent parametric surfaces and convex polyhedra.[2] A similar approach is used in [61] but the algorithm also searches for the time that the first collision occurred. In [10, 11], for bodies composed of both polyhedra and convex closed curved surfaces, temporal coherence is exploited to achieve faster average running times.

With the above approaches, if an object goes right through another object, between the times for which collisions are checked, then the algorithm will fail. As argued in [96], this can be made unlikely by checking regularly but this may be inefficient, especially if there is only a small number of collisions. So for time-dependent parametric surfaces, [143] uses the idea of a (user-definable) near-miss and analysis of derivatives for each surface type to avoid missing collisions. An approach based on interval analysis is presented in [124, 125]. The algorithm is reported to be robust, efficient, accurate to within a user-specified tolerance, and applicable to a wide range of time-dependent parametric and implicit surfaces. One of the most comprehensive treatments of collision detection can be found in [84].

2.4.2   Collision Resolution and Resting Contact

When two rigid bodies first come into contact, they exert a large force on each other for an infinitesimally small amount of time. This collision force, known as an *impulse*, results in a discontinuous change of velocity. The bodies may then remain in resting contact where *resting contact forces* prevent

---

[2]Concave polyhedra may be decomposed into a set of convex polyhedra.

subsequent interpenetrating. In [96], the nondeterministic problem of multiple simultaneous collisions is dealt with by a propagation method while [10] uses a simultaneous approach that is more efficient.

In [96], an analytic method that uses the principle of conservation of momentum to calculate the effects of impulsive forces on rigid bodies (including articulated figures) is given. In addition, for rigid and deformable bodies, a nonanalytic *penalty method*, equivalent to inserting a spring and damper between any two contact points, is described. Resting contact is modeled as a sequence of collisions. For deformable bodies [109, 133] introduce arbitrary penalty forces between colliding bodies to separate them.

Preventing interpenetration with penalty methods is slow and not necessarily physically correct, so a series of papers [10, 11, 12, 13, 15] sought to further investigate the use of analytic methods. The first step was to reformulate the noninterpenetration constraint for curved surfaces in a form that was specific enough to be differentiable. Then (in [10, 11, 12]), the problem of computing contact forces between a pair of bodies that contact at a point without friction was considered. Next, systems of bodies that behave according to the classical Coulomb model of friction were discussed. This leads to systems in which there are no solutions to the classical constraint force equations, as well as systems that admit multiple solutions for the constraint force equations and whose subsequent behavior is thus indeterminate. Both computational and practical complexity results for simulating such systems were given. In [13] an alternative iterative approach was presented that is claimed to be faster, more reliable, applicable to the case of dynamic and static friction, and simple enough to be implemented by a non-expert in numerical algorithms.

In [15], the analytic approach to noninterpenetration is applied to flexible bodies that are restricted to only undergo shape deformations that can be expressed as a global deformation. There is a problem with exactly determining the contact surface, which [50] solves by using a purely kinematic step in an implicit formulation of the notion of a deformable body.

2.5 Biomechanical Models

Real animals have muscles that they use to exert forces and torques on their own bodies in order to locomote. If we have already implemented physical models in a virtual world then in theory we can give the characters physically realistic bodies. The characters could then use their virtual muscles to move themselves around. We refer to the character's ability to exert some control over their motions as *actuated* (or animate) objects. Up until now the only approach that has been mentioned for producing movement of actuated objects has been simply to state their positions at given times. The point is that in the real world an animal cannot produce arbitrary forces and torques (as in the inverse dynamics approach) to enable it to follow any given path in space as it is constrained to move using the finite resources available in its muscles. Therefore realistic motion of actuated figures can only be achieved by either placing complete reliance on the skill of the animator or programmer to correctly interpret this limitation or by adopting this requirement and solving an associated control problem. This section will explore the second alternative for which some notions and nomenclature from control theory will be required. If further explanation is required, the reader should consult any introductory textbook on control theory (for example, see [39, 36]).

2.5.1   State Space

In computer games and animation the state vector is the vector that must contain all the quantities that are required to completely specify the position and velocities of all the points of all the objects in the scene. The system state equations are precisely the ones discussed in Section 2.3.3 that are required to compute the forward dynamics solution.

2.5.2   Output Vector

The output vector supplies the controller with all the information with which it must decide which action to perform. The controllers used in [146, 34, 85, 141] are all functions of time (open-loop controllers), while in [28, 140] functions of state (closed-loop controllers) are used. In [140], making the controller a function of the state is problematic as the state space grows exponentially as the objects become more complex. So in [139, 102, 123], closed-loop control functions of simple input sensors are used. Closed-loop controllers are more flexible in that their output is not fixed by the current time (as in an open-loop controller) but is a function of the current situation. An open-loop controller must be generated for each new scenario. Thus, where the cost of synthesizing a controller is prohibitive, a closed-loop controller represents a much more sensible approach.

2.5.3 Input Vector

The actions the controller chooses to perform are represented by input vectors. As stated in Section 2.3.3, in order to compute the forward dynamics solution (assuming the initial conditions are fixed), values must be supplied for all the unknown forces and torques. Therefore the input vector must supply these values.

Supplying actual torques and forces is counterintuitive so usually a simple muscle model is used. In general, no attempt has been made to realistically model the intricate complexity of muscles and tendons (see [32, 101] for more biomechanically based muscle models). Instead the effects are often approximated with a *spring and damper* which acts as a proportional-derivative controller that will tend (over time) to bring a joint, say, to some desired length (angle). As pointed out in [110], the spring and damper model emulates the ability of real animals to make their motion a lot more efficient (especially at high speeds) by using the springiness of their muscles and tendons to store energy from one movement to the next. Also as the spring extends further from its rest length, the restoring force becomes larger, thus automatically enforcing joint limits. A nonlinear spring is even more effective for enforcing joint limits but can give rise to stiff differential equations.

For a deformable model made up of point masses and springs, muscles can be modeled by designating some of the springs as actuated. This means that the input vector, as determined by some control function, is a reference setting for the equilibrium point of each actuated spring. Or, put more simply, the rest lengths of the springs are allowed to be changed by the control

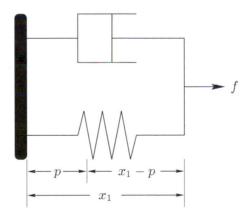

Figure 2.3. "Muscle" represented as a spring and damper.

function. For an articulated figure an analogous (and common) technique is
to insert a (possibly rotary) spring and damper at each joint. If the joint
is designated as actuated then the rest length (angle) of the spring is again
made the input value from some control function. By way of a concrete
example, consider the case of a single "muscle and tendon" represented by a
linear spring and damper (see Figure 2.3). Let the input v (as determined by
some control function p) represent the spring's rest length. Then, assuming
the output vector is just the system state, the force exerted by the spring is
$f = k_s(p(\mathbf{x}) - x_1) + k_d x_2$, where k_s is the spring stiffness, k_d is the damping
factor, and $\mathbf{x} = (x_1, x_2)$ is the state vector (the spring length x_1 and velocity
$x_2 = \dot{x}_1$). Incorporating this equation in the system state equations means
that control can be exerted over the system by varying the rest length p.

2.5.4   Control Function

The control function calculates values for the input vector from the given
output vectors.

Hand-crafted Controllers

One solution to producing a suitable control function to solve some control
problem is simply to leave it up to some human to define. A typical example
of a difficult control specification that can be *hand-crafted* in this way is one
of requiring a controller to make an object move like some particular animal.

For deformable models, [94, 137] presented hand-crafted controllers (for
snakes and fish, respectively) that consist of parameterized sinusoidal con-
tractions of spring rest lengths. There has been some success in hand-crafting
controllers for articulated figures: [29] generated parameterized human walks
that used a mixture of kinematics,[3] dynamics, and rules about gaits; [91]
produced a dynamic simulation of a walking statically stable cockroach controlled by sets of coupled oscillators; [27] achieved similar results for a real-
world six-legged creature; [110] showed how useful parameterized controllers
of hoppers, kangaroos, bipeds, and quadrupeds can be achieved by decom-
posing the problem into a set of simpler control problems; [128] created a
dynamic simulation of a biped walking by defining a finite-state machine
that adds and removes constraint equations. A good survey of these kinds
of approaches can be found in [9].

Many of these approaches produce very useful parameterized controllers.
The big drawback with handcrafted solutions, other than that they can be

---

[3]The kinematics is only used after the fact to improve the look of the motion.

extremely difficult to derive (especially for a complex articulated figure), is that they are not necessarily applicable to other systems. However, for obvious reasons, humanoid figures are often the subject of computer games and animations and so handcrafting a collection of useful controllers for a human like object is bound to be useful. It may even be possible to justify such an approach for other common animals.

Control through Optimization

The optimal control approach uses optimization to try and produce an *optimal controller*. In producing motion for games and animation the evaluation criterion is largely an aesthetic one, which in most cases only induces a partial order on the state space trajectories. Therefore the choice of a performance index is largely subjective. For some problems a natural performance index exists. For instance, if a motion sequence is required of a creature doing a high jump then it is natural to choose a performance index that will prefer higher jumps over lower ones. In many situations it seems natural to assume that a solution that uses less energy and less time should be preferred. In practice, a user-definable weighted combination of various criteria can be used to form a suitable performance index. By changing the weights the user can try and exert some rather indirect control over the look of the motion.

By using simple performance indices that reward low energy expenditure and distance traveled in a fixed time interval [139, 102, 123, 135, 141], motions have been produced that bear a distinct qualitative resemblance to the way that animals with comparable morphologies perform analogous (usually periodic) locomotion tasks. However, it is not clear that suitable performance indices could be formulated *a priori* that could be predicted to produce something like, say, a "happy walk." Also, the approach can not deal with really dynamic factors.

Objective-based Control

It has already been seen in Section 2.2 that a common way to specify the desired motion in computer games and animation is by using key-frames. It was only natural therefore that some of the earliest approaches to realistic control in games and animation should look at ways of producing physically plausible motions that "interpolated" given key-frames [146]. Given that the motion starts in one key-frame, the other key-frames define a goal that must be achieved. In addition, it is also necessary to concurrently satisfy the goal that the motion be in accordance with the laws of physics and that it be produced using the finite resources available in the creatures "muscles."

One approach that has been taken to solving these problems [146, 34, 85] has been to define a performance index and treat the problem as a constrained optimization problem. The idea is that an open-loop controller is synthesized by searching for values of the state space trajectory and the forces and torques that satisfy the goal and are minimal with respect to the performance index. This is achieved by numerical methods that iteratively refine a user-supplied initial guess. Giving the constrained optimization algorithm responsibility for arbitrating between the constraints (or goals) obviates the problem of dealing with over-constrained motion. Unfortunately, this means that for over-constrained problems compromise solutions can be produced that are not necessarily what the user wants. Even if the motion is not technically over-constrained, the numerical algorithm may still not be able to find a solution that completely satisfies the constraints.

Often what the user wants is that no compromise should be made with the laws of physics. If this is so then a method must be chosen in which the laws of physics are incorporated in some inviolable way. A common way to do this [140, 139, 102, 123, 141] is to simply reformulate the problem as an *unconstrained* optimization problem (as in Section 2.5.4). This means that the constraints are no longer hard and fast but rather the performance index is modified to reward motions the closer they come to satisfying the constraints.

2.5.5 Synthesizing a Control Function

There are some additional issues that arise in the process of synthesizing a control function:

Collisions and friction. Collisions and friction can have a detrimental effect on the numerical optimization algorithms that require access to derivatives [146, 34, 85]. This means that it is often necessary to formulate the problem so that arbitrary control, or no feedback control, is exerted during periods of time in which collisions occur. In contrast, the stochastic optimization techniques used in [139, 102, 123, 141] often produce trajectories that can be seen to take advantage of collisions and friction.

Generality. One of the first attempts to synthesize a controller for animation and game purposes was given in [28]. The paper employed techniques from optimal control theory for linear systems to create optimal controllers. Where motion of a linear system is required this approach is ideal. However, control problems are made much harder by nonlinearities and, unfortunately, most interesting motions are highly nonlinear.

Local minima. In practice, all numerical methods suffer from the problem of becoming trapped in local minima and thus it can not be guaranteed that the best solution has been attained. "Global" (stochastic) optimization algorithms can help in this regard [139, 102, 123]. Convergence to the global solution is guaranteed but the price paid is slow convergence. They are generally computationally intensive. Indeed, [102, 123] avail themselves of a massively parallel computer to achieve faster results and [102] circumvents an aspect of the problem by controlling the limb placement kinematically. In [34] it is recognized that for applications in animation (as opposed to games and robotics, say) user interaction is allowed, even at the level of helping the optimization process out of local minima.

Post-processing. In [139], a stochastic generate-and-test procedure is used to learn the weights for a network of connections between binary sensors and actuators. These weights are then refined by a modify-and-test procedure that searches for better solutions in the immediate vicinity. For deformable models, [59] uses a post-processing step to transform learned low-level control functions into a Fourier basis. It is then possible to abstract (by ignoring components with coefficients below a certain level) the control functions to yield a compact representation that is suitable for parameterization. The low-level control functions are open-loop controllers but they are incorporated into a high-level controller that is a function of the system state. This is done by simulating the effects of each possible low-level controller over some time interval and then picking the one that, in terms of the current goal, worked best. If simulation is computationally expensive and there are many low-level controllers, then this is inefficient. It is interesting to note that for nonstatically stable motions this approach cannot generally be used in a real-world controller. This is because in the real world we can not run time backward to "undo" our mistakes.

Representation. In practice, the control function and the state space trajectory are represented by a discrete set of basis functions over some finite interval of their domain. In [146] they are discretized as a finite set of samples. This can lead to problems of unwieldy dimensionality, so [34] split motions into different space-time windows and constrained the motion to be representable by a spline basis function. The dimensionality of the problem is further and drastically reduced in [85] by using techniques from compiler optimization to factor out common subexpressions and by using a hierarchical wavelet basis function to represent the motion. This purportedly leads to smaller control problems, better numerical conditioning and faster convergence. For highly nonlinear problems, however, difficulties may still remain in the numerical solution. The control function in [141] is a step function (called a "pose control graph") that can be viewed as a (cyclic) finite state machine with timed transitions between states.

Usability. The approach in [140] produces a family of optimal control solutions that can be reused and conveniently sequenced to produce complicated motion sequences. In [139, 102] the user is only required to supply a physical description of the object (including its sensors and actuators) and the algorithm will attempt to calculate "useful" modes of locomotion. In [123] even the creature morphology is generated automatically. While this may contain a degree of novelty, it is hard to imagine a wide range of situations in which it would be useful to allow a creature's appearance to be chosen at random.

2.6   Behavior and Cognitive Models

We refer to anything above simple locomotion as a character's *behavior*. The remaining chapters of this book are devoted to looking at how we can use behavioral and cognitive models to make it easier to generate various types of behavior. In this section, therefore, it is not necessary to go into extensive details on the subject. However, the work we will be describing in later chapters did not just spring out of nowhere. It was, instead, born of a research tradition that stretches back to the early days of computer graphics research. Much of this work is ongoing research and some of it takes a quite different, and legitimate, approach to the one described in this book. We encourage the reader who seeks an in-depth knowledge of the field to follow up on as many of the references as possible.

The seminal paper in behavior modeling for autonomous characters was Reynolds [115], in which behaviors, such as flocking behavior, were synthesized. Tu and Terzopoulos [137] have taken impressive strides towards creating realistic, self-animating autonomous characters through biomechanical modeling and established principles of behavioral animation. A criticism sometimes leveled at behavioral animation methods is that, robustness and efficiency notwithstanding, the behavior controllers are hard-wired into the code. Blumberg and Galyean [24] begin to address such concerns by introducing mechanisms that give greater control over behavior, and Blumberg's superb thesis considers interesting issues such as behavior learning [23]. In a similar vein, Perlin [104] describes fascinating work aimed at providing animators and programmers with useful behavior modeling tools. There is also an extensive and important body of relevant work in the intelligent autonomous agents literature [63, 19, 144, 148]. While we share similar motivations to previous researchers, this book takes a slightly different route. In particular, we place heavy emphasis on investigating important higher-level cognitive abilities such as knowledge representation and nondeterminism.

Previous work in the logic programming community (see [2] for many classic papers on logic programming) has also looked extensively at the use of nondeterminism to afford a more intuitive, and declarative approach to specifying character behavior. For example, Badler [7] and the Thalmanns [86] have applied AI techniques to produce inspiring results with animated humans. The work described in this book has been particularly motivated by work that has applied AI techniques to computer animation [49, 8, 87]. Unfortunately, none of this previous work takes a serious look at knowledge representation issues. The resulting lack of an explicit cognitive modeling framework means that many important topics, such as sensing, get neglected or completely ignored.

One of the key enabling technologies that will allow us to develop a coherent story on many important foundational issues is a rigorous and general first-order theory of action based on a version of the situation calculus [89]. The situation calculus is well-known, simple, and intuitive to understand. The version we use is inspired by new work in cognitive robotics that solves the frame problem [111], incorporates knowledge-producing actions (like sensing) [118], and allows advice to be conveniently given as a "sketch plan" [80]. A noteworthy point of departure from existing work in cognitive robotics is that we render the situation calculus amenable to use within highly dynamic virtual worlds by introducing interval valued epistemic fluents [47] to deal with sensing.

2.7 Notes

In this book we don't consider lighting models at all, since the lowest level of detail we mention is geometric models. That is, we do not discuss how to render those models at all. In most of our case studies we happen to use OpenGL®, but any other graphics API (Application Programmer's Interface) would suffice. For information about lighting models, the standard introduction to computer graphics is [44]. There are a huge number of books on computer games, but most of them are very basic "how to" programming guides and they do not treat the interesting intellectual problems that come up with any rigor. As far as we aware, this book is pretty much the first to cover the use of "intelligent" characters in computer games and animation from a serious scientific perspective. In other fields, however, there is a wealth of literature available on intelligent agents. In particular, the approach we describe in this book grew out of closely related work in *cognitive robotics* [58].

There are a number of good introductions to AI, for example [117] is probably one of most comprehensive recent publications. It also contains some information and references about the debate between different AI camps. Note that though we refer to the entities in computer animation and games as "characters," the phrase "autonomous agents" (or agents for short) is more commonplace in the AI literature.

Domain Knowledge

In this chapter we will look at how a character can effectively represent background knowledge about the dynamics of some particular domain within its world. The representation we describe is based on intuitive notions like actions, preconditions, and effects.

For characters that do not think for themselves, the representation is not particularly important because the programmer implicitly deals with most of the problems that come up. However, for characters that use their cognitive models to think for themselves, the representation can determine whether or not the character will have some basic common sense as it reasons about the effects of actions on its world. Some of the issues that come up are so much a part of our own notions of common sense that, at first, it can be difficult to even see why there is a problem.

3.1   Mathematical Logic

To express our ideas clearly and unambiguously we cannot rely solely on natural language; instead we must complement our explanations with precise mathematical definitions. When discussing cognitive models the branch of mathematics that turns out to be most useful for describing what is going on is mathematical logic. For most of this chapter no in-depth knowledge of mathematical logic is required. In particular, the notation and concepts found in the opening sections of any good introductory textbook on mathematical logic should be sufficient.

3.1.1   Notation

We will be using standard sorted first-order logic with equality. A general introduction to mathematical logic is beyond the scope of this book and so we will assume that the reader is either familiar with the basic ideas, or (if required) can consult a suitable reference. Nevertheless, there is some variation in the literature over symbols used and so we briefly clarify our own choices. In particular, we will use the following standard logical symbols: $\neg$ (not), $\wedge$ (conjunction, i.e., "and"), $\vee$ (disjunction, i.e., "or"), $\Rightarrow$ (implication), $\Leftrightarrow$ (equivalence/bi-implication), and $=$ (equality). Variables appear in italics e.g., x, y, z, a, ... and parenthesis will be used to resolve any ambiguity as to the order of application of any symbols. For any given interpretation we will use the following standard symbols for the parameters: $\forall$ (universal quantifier), $\exists$ (existential quantifier), and a (possible empty) set of n-ary function symbols (0-ary function symbols are called *constants*). Throughout the book, all unbound variables are implicitly assumed to be universally quantified.

3.1.2   Sorts

Sorts in mathematical logic are analogous to the notion of types in a regular programming language. Unless otherwise stated, all objects are of sort OBJECT. We shall also make use of the following standard number system sorts:[1]

$$\mathbb{B} \triangleq \text{Boolean numbers,}$$
$$\mathbb{N} \triangleq \text{Natural numbers,}$$
$$\mathbb{Z} \triangleq \text{Integer numbers,}$$
$$\mathbb{Q} \triangleq \text{Rational numbers,}$$
$$\mathbb{R} \triangleq \text{Real numbers.}$$

---

[1]Functions and other compound terms are assigned sorts based on their components in the usual way.

To avoid misunderstanding, we briefly clarify $\mathbb{B}$. In particular, there are two constants of sort $\mathbb{B}$, namely 0 and 1. There is one unary function: $\neg$ (negation); and two binary functions: $\wedge$ (and), $\vee$ (or).

In the next chapter, we shall want to ensure that all our number systems have maximal and minimal elements. We shall indicate these augmented number systems with a $\star$, for example the extended real numbers: $\mathbb{R}^\star = \mathbb{R} \cup \{-\infty, \infty\}$. We shall also denote subsets of our number systems with appropriate designators, for example the nonnegative reals $\mathbb{R}^+$.

3.2 Situation Calculus

The *situation calculus* is a way of describing changing worlds in sorted first-order mathematical logic. Since changing worlds are exactly what we want our intelligent characters to be thinking about, the situation calculus turns out to be perfectly suited to the task of describing many of the subtleties and problems that arise in knowledge representation. The situation calculus will form the theoretical underpinnings of the rest of the book. In particular, the *situation calculus* will provide the underlying semantics for the character's internal representation of its virtual world.

A *situation*, of sort SITUATION, is a "snapshot" of the state of the world. A domain-independent constant s_0, of sort SITUATION, denotes the initial situation. Actions, of sort ACTION, are the fundamental instruments of change in our ontology. The situation s', resulting from doing action a in situation s, is given by the distinguished function do : ACTION $\times$ SITUATION $\rightarrow$ SITUATION, such that $s' = do(a, s)$.

We shall use the following simple example to illustrate various points about knowledge representation for computer characters:

> Suppose we have two characters, call them Dognap and Jack, situated in some virtual world. The virtual world may be part of some computer game or perhaps the basis for some "virtual movie director" software. Regardless, let us suppose that Dognap is armed with a gun, and that Dognap wants to kill Jack. Let us further suppose that Jack is initially alive and that the gun is initially empty.

3.2.1 Fluents

Any property of the world that can change over time is known as a fluent. A *fluent* is a function, with a situation term as (by convention) its last argument. We shall restrict fluents to taking on values in one of the number system sorts. For any functional fluents that take on values in $\mathbb{B}$, we shall adopt the standard abbreviation that $\mathsf{Foo}(s)$ is just shorthand for $\mathsf{foo}(s) = 1$. We may refer to such fluents as *relational fluents*.

Let us now introduce some fluents to capture the salient details of our example. This will enable us to formalize the scenario within the situation calculus.

$\mathsf{Alive}(s)$	$-$	Jack is alive in state s.
$\mathsf{Aimed}(s)$	$-$	The gun is aimed at Jack in state s.
$\mathsf{Loaded}(s)$	$-$	The gun is loaded in state s.

Now, let's introduce the following actions:

load	$-$	Load the gun.
aim	$-$	Aim the gun at Jack.
shoot	$-$	Shoot the gun.

The possibility of performing action a in situation s is denoted by a distinguished predicate *Poss* : ACTION × SITUATION. Sentences that specify what the state of the world must be before performing some action are known as *precondition axioms*. We can give such axioms for the actions in our example:

Poss $(load, s)$	$-$	The gun can always be loaded.
Poss (aim, s)	$-$	The gun can always be aimed at Jack.
Poss $(shoot, s) \Rightarrow \mathsf{Loaded}(s)$	$-$	The gun can only be shot if it's loaded.

3.2.2   The Qualification Problem

The *qualification problem* is that of trying to infer when an action is possible. In our example, we only wrote down certain necessary conditions, we did not enumerate all the things that may prevent us from shooting the gun. For instance, we cannot shoot if the trigger is too stiff, or if the gun is encased in concrete, etc. By employing a *closed-world assumption*, we may obviate this problem and assume that our set of necessary conditions is also a sufficient set. For instance, under this assumption our precondition axiom for *shoot* now becomes:

$$Poss\,(shoot, s) \Leftrightarrow \mathsf{Loaded}(s).$$

In general, we have the following definition:

Definition 3.2.1 (Action Precondition Axioms). *Action precondition axioms give necessary and sufficient conditions* $\pi_a(\vec{x}, s)$ *for when an action* $a(\vec{x})$ *is possible. They are of the form*

$$\textit{Poss}\,(a(\vec{x}), s) \Leftrightarrow \pi_a(\vec{x}, s).$$

3.2.3 Effect Axioms

Effect axioms give necessary conditions for a fluent to take on a given value after performing an action. We can use effect axioms to state the effects of the actions on the fluents in our example:

$\textsf{Loaded}(do(\textit{load}, s))$	$-$	The gun is loaded after loading it.
$\textsf{Aimed}(do(\textit{aim}, s))$	$-$	The gun is aimed at Jack after aiming it.
$\textit{Poss}\,(\textit{shoot}, s) \wedge \textsf{Aimed}(s)$	$\Rightarrow$	$\neg\textsf{Alive}(do(\textit{shoot}, s))$
	$-$	If the gun is aimed at Jack and it can be shot then he is dead after shooting it.

All that now remains to complete our first pass at formalizing our example is to specify the initial situation:

$\textsf{Alive}(s_0)$	$-$	Initially Jack is alive.
$\neg\textsf{Aimed}(s_0)$	$-$	Initially the gun is not aimed at Jack.
$\neg\textsf{Loaded}(s_0)$	$-$	Initially the gun is not loaded.

3.2.4 The Frame Problem

On the surface, the *frame problem* seems trivial and yet it plagued artificial intelligence research for years. Simply stated it is the problem of stating what remains unchanged when we do something. When we start trying to make more intelligent characters for computer games and animation we run into the same problem. Therefore, it is important to have an understanding of the problem and some of the proposed remedies.

At first, it can be hard to appreciate why there is a problem at all because, in English, when we say that something happens if we do a particular action, we implicitly assume that this is all that happens. In our example, we only wrote down what changed after an action; we did not write down all the things that stayed the same. For instance, the gun stayed loaded after aiming it, and the gun did not turn into a horse after loading it, etc. The question is, if we don't tell it, how can a computer character know that nothing else happens?

For a dumb character, one that just blindly follows rules without thinking, there is no problem. By definition, however, we want an intelligent character to be constantly thinking for itself and considering all sorts of possibilities—even things we never thought of in advance. The problem is that we do not want it to consider possibilities that are ridiculous. There are so many ridiculous possibilities that it is hopeless to expect the programmer to have to start listing them out as things not to consider. In particular, if we have $\mathcal{A}$ actions and $\mathcal{F}$ fluents, then we must write down a set of $\mathcal{A} \times \mathcal{F}$ "frame" axioms that state what stays the same. Even worse, the character would react too slowly if, every time it thought about doing something, it had to look through an extremely long list of things that are not going to happen. Therefore, in common sense reasoning about actions, it seems essential to assume that, unless explicitly told otherwise, things stay the same. We will state this "law of inertia" formally in this section.

A solution to the frame problem, that avoids having to list all the frame axioms, turns out to be fairly straightforward. The idea is to assume that our effect axioms enumerate all the possible ways that the world can change. This closed world assumption provides the justification for replacing the effect axioms with *successor state* axioms. For instance, the successor state axiom for $\mathsf{Alive}(s)$ states that Jack is alive, if and only if, he was alive in the previous state and he was not just shot:

$$\mathit{Poss}(a, s) \Rightarrow [\mathsf{Alive}(do(a, s)) \Leftrightarrow \mathsf{Alive}(s) \wedge \neg(a = \mathit{shoot} \wedge \mathsf{Aimed}(s))]. \quad (3.1)$$

In general, we have the following definition:

Definition 3.2.2 (Successor State Axioms). *Suppose $\gamma_f(\vec{y}, z, a, s)$ is a first-order formula whose free variables are among $\vec{y}, z, a, s$. Assume it states all the necessary conditions under which action a, if performed in s, results in $f(\vec{y}, s)$ becoming equal to z. Then, the corresponding successor state axiom, that assumes the given conditions are also sufficient ones, is of the form*

$$\mathit{Poss}(a, s) \Rightarrow$$
$$[(f(\vec{y}, do(a, s)) = z) \Leftrightarrow (\gamma_f(\vec{y}, z, a, s)) \vee (f(\vec{y}, s) = z \wedge \neg \exists z' \; \gamma_f(\vec{y}, z', a, s))].$$
$$(3.2)$$

It is instructive to consider what this definition means for a relational fluent F. Let $\gamma_F^+(\vec{y}, a, s)$ be a disjunction of all the positive effects of the action a, and $\gamma_F^-(\vec{y}, a, s)$ be a disjunction of all the negative effects. Then the successor state axiom for F is

$$Poss(a, s) \Rightarrow [F(\vec{y}, do(a, s)) \Leftrightarrow (\gamma_F^+(\vec{y}, a, s) \vee (F(\vec{y}, s) \wedge \neg\gamma_F^-(\vec{y}, a, s)))].$$

Note that successor-state axioms can be generated automatically from the relevant effect axioms by simple syntactic manipulation. Therefore, for most of the examples in this book we will only provide effect axioms. That is, we implicitly assume that the effect axioms will be converted to successor-state axioms before they are used to do any common sense reasoning.

3.2.5 The Ramification Problem

The ramification problem is closely related to the frame problem. In particular, it considers the problem of trying to predict what will change and what will stay the same when we have fixed relationships between aspects of the world, i.e., *state constraints*.

Suppose we add to our example the fluents

NearBomb(s) — Jack is near the position of the bomb in state s;
Fire(s) — There is a fire in state s;

the action

detonate — The bomb is detonated;

the effect axiom (assuming it is always possible to detonate the bomb):

Fire($do(detonate, s)$) — There is a fire after detonation;

and the state constraint

Fire(s) $\wedge$ NearBomb(s) $\Rightarrow$ $\neg$Alive(s)
— If Jack is near a fire, then he is dead.

Then, detonating the bomb when Jack is next to it, has the implicit side-effect of killing Jack. Such side-effects are known as ramifications. So the *ramification problem* is that of trying to determine all the implicit side-effects of actions caused by the presence of state constraints. In general, state constraints may give rise to intractable problems. However, in some cases, we can deal with the ramification problem by making all the side effects explicit. This can be done automatically by "compiling" the state

constraint into the successor state axioms. For example, we can modify the
successor state axiom for Alive(s) as follows:

$$Poss\,(a, s) \Rightarrow [\text{Alive}(do(a, s)) \quad \Leftrightarrow \quad \text{Alive}(s) \wedge \neg(a = shoot \wedge \text{Aimed}(s)) \wedge$$
$$\neg(a = detonate \wedge \text{NearBomb}(s))].$$

The reader who has ever programmed using pointers will be only too familiar with the ramification problem. In particular, pointers introduce state
constraints between variables so that modifying the data pointed to by one
variable can have the side-effect of implicitly modify the data pointed to by
another variable. If the programmer is not exceptionally careful unexpected
changes can occur. These "unexpected changes" are a good example of what
we are calling the ramification problem.

3.2.6 Defined Fluents

A *defined* fluent is a fluent defined (possibly recursively) in terms of other
fluents. Therefore, its value changes implicitly as the other fluents change.
Thus defined fluents can be used to express state-constraints. After reading
the last section we know we have to worry about the ramification problem.
However, defined fluents can be used safely within an application provided
we place our defined fluents in a strict hierarchy (i.e., no circular definitions),
and no actions mentioned explicitly are in any of the definitions.
For example, we can add the fluent Frightened that is defined to be true if
Jack has a loaded gun aimed at him.

$$\text{Frightened}(s) \Leftrightarrow \text{Loaded}(s) \wedge \text{Aimed}(s)$$

3.2.7 Exogenous Actions

As we explained in Chapter 1, Section 5, there will often be aspects of
a character's domain that we cannot, or do not want to, formalize. For
example, suppose a character is interested in the position of a ball floating
in an ocean. It is ridiculous to give a character a detailed understanding of
the motion of the waves, wind, etc. This will often be the case for phenomena
that are outside the character's ability to control. We should like to simply
define an action like *moveBall(x)* and say that it is caused by mysterious
external forces. Such actions are referred to as *exogenous* actions. While the
cause of an exogenous action is difficult to state, its effect need not be. For
example, the *moveBall(x)* simply moves the ball to the position x. Later
on, in Chapter 7, Section 2.1, we explain how these exogenous actions can
be generated by the true world model.

3.3 Discussion

For the technically-minded reader, the material described in this chapter is fertile ground for advanced research in knowledge representation. Any results obtained have applications in computer animation, games, robotics, web-based agents, and anywhere else autonomous agents are used. Some of the open research areas are listed below.

Continuous Processes In [108], the situation calculus was first extended to provide a representation for continuous processes. In particular, a time-line is defined that corresponds to a sequence, beginning with s_0, of situations. The sequence of situations, called *actual situations*, is totally ordered, and the actions which lead to different actual situations are said to have *occurred*. In [112], a related approach is introduced which uses the idea of *natural actions*. In many ways, interval arithmetic is a more natural way to model continuous processes on a computer and such an approach has been successfully used in work not based on the situation calculus. There has also been an initial attempt to apply such an approach to the situation calculus [132]. An interesting project, would be to look at the possibility of using some kind of time interval semantics to model continuous phenomena within the situation calculus.

Concurrency The notion of concurrent actions was introduced into the situation calculus in [77]. Concurrency is handled by interleaving. For example, we say that the concurrent execution of *load* and *aim* occurs between two states if, and only if, both *load* and *aim* occur, interleaved in some fashion, between the two states.

In all our case studies containing multiple characters, each character is autonomous. Thus, we have emergent concurrent behavior. The point is that we do not explicitly *specify* the concurrent behavior anywhere. Emergent behavior is a powerful, albeit clumsy, tool that is widely hailed as a feature in other works in behavior animation. Regardless, it would be an interesting project to apply some of the work on concurrency to the realm of computer games and animation.

Mental States In the next chapter we discuss the problem of representing a character's knowledge. There remains, however, a wealth of additional difficult concepts to consider, such as goals and intentions [38, 121], hysteresis, memory [82], etc. Once again, it is not the case that our characters do not have intentions, goals, etc. It is just that we view only certain fluents as representing a character's goals and intentions at the meta-level. That is, there is no way, within our language, of determining that a fluent pertains to the world, or to the character's mental state. Put more bluntly, we simply consider a character's brain to be part of the world. The price we pay for this simplification is that a character can not reason about its own goals and intentions in the same manner as a human might. The ultimate goal of a lot of work that seeks to add such functionality to cognitive characters is to create *rational characters*. To create rational characters for games and animation would also be a worthy project. It would be particularly interesting to decide what the correct definition of rational was in this case. For example, we would not necessarily want a non-player character in a computer game that decided the rational thing to do was to always run away and hide from player characters.

3.4 Notes

There are many excellent introductions to mathematical logic, for example see [41]. The situation calculus was first introduced by John McCarthy in [89]. The version we are using in this chapter is derived from [111]. The running example was adapted from the well known "Yale shooting problem" [62]. The qualification problem was introduced in [88]. In [52, 83], some additional subtleties, including those that arise when we allow state constraints, are discussed. The frame problem was introduced in [89], its solution, over twenty years later, was given in [111]. The corresponding approach to the ramification problem is discussed in detail in [83]. The simple solution of using defined fluents in strict hierarchies is introduced in [90].

People with computer science backgrounds generally have a great appreciation for elegant data-structures and clear type hierarchies. This has allowed them to see through some of the historical baggage that mathematical logic inherited from its philosophical roots. For example, our characterization of "relations" simply as Boolean-valued functions was taken from [65].

Sensing

This chapter deals with how we can represent a character's uncertainty about its world. This is vitally important if we want to be able to describe the effects of sensing actions. Once again, unless we are careful we can run into serious problems. In particular, if we use previous approaches to the problem, we would end up with an elegant theory, but nothing that could be implemented on a computer.

This chapter is by far the most mathematically challenging in the book. The reason for this is that we are describing a relatively new approach to sensing and some readers will not be convinced unless they see all the mathematical details that justify it formally. However, if the reader is happy to take our word for it that the new approach works, and simply wants to know how to use it, then the sections marked with a † can be skipped without loss of continuity.

4.1 Knowledge Producing Actions

Up until now we have thought of actions as having effects on the world. We can, however, imagine actions whose only effect is to change what the character knows about its world. For example, imagine a character that lives in a fiery dungeon. Before it opens a dungeon door, it should check to see if it's safe to enter by feeling how hot the door is. The action of testing the door's temperature has no effect on the world, but it does change the character's knowledge about its world. Sensing actions are therefore referred to as *knowledge producing actions*. An everyday example of a knowledge producing action is the act of looking up a person's phone number before placing a telephone call.

We can imagine writing precondition axioms for a character based on the state of its knowledge about its world. For example, the following precondition axiom states that it is only possible for a character to open a door x, if it knows the door is not too hot (less than 400 degrees Kelvin, say) and it has the key.

$$\textit{Poss}\,(\textit{openDoor}(x), s) \Leftrightarrow \textit{Knows}\,(\text{temp}(x) < 400, s) \wedge \text{HaveKey}(s)$$

The new part of this axiom is the $\textit{Knows}\,(\text{temp}(x) < 400, s)$ part, and that is what we will explain in what follows.

As we explained back in Chapter 1, Section 5, sensing is a vitally important topic. It is, however, a topic that is either ignored or "glossed over" in AI textbooks. One of the major reasons for this is that finding a principled way to integrate sensing into a framework in which characters can think for themselves can be difficult.

Figure 4.1. Before sensing, worlds where the light is on, or off, are possible.

Figure 4.2. After sensing, only worlds where the light is on are possible.

Historically, the way to incorporate knowledge producing actions into the situation calculus is to define an epistemic fluent to keep track of all the worlds a character thinks it might possibly be in. In Figure 4.1, we depict a character unable to decide which world it was in. That is, whether in its world, the light is on or off. Figure 4.2 shows the character turning around to see that the light is in fact turned on. The result of this sensing action is shown in the figure as the character discarding some of the worlds that it previously thought were possible. In particular, since it now knows that the light is on in its world, it must throw out all the worlds in which it thought the light was turned off. In this section, we give the mathematical details of how this notion is modeled in the situation calculus.

4.1.1 An Epistemic Fluent

The way a character keeps track of the possible worlds or, as the case may be, possible situations, is to define an epistemic fluent K. The fluent keeps track of all the K-related worlds. These K-related worlds are precisely the ones in the bubbles above the character's head in the figures mentioned previously. They are the situations that the character thinks might be its current situation. So we write $K(s', s)$ to mean that in situation s, as far as the character can tell, it might be in the alternative situation s'. That is, the character's knowledge is such that s and s' are indistinguishable. It can only find out if it is or not by sensing the value of certain terms, for example terms such as $\mathsf{light}(s)$.

When we say a character *knows* that the value of a term τ, in a situation s, is some constant c, we mean that τ has the value c in all the K-related worlds. For convenience, we introduce the following abbreviation,

$$\mathit{Knows}\,(\tau = c, s) \triangleq \forall s'\ \mathsf{K}(s', s) \Rightarrow \tau[s'] = c, \tag{4.1}$$

where $\tau[s']$ is the term τ with the situation arguments inserted. For example, if $\tau = \mathsf{phoneNo}(\mathsf{Jack})$ then $\tau[s] = \mathsf{phoneNo}(\mathsf{Jack}, s)$. Note that for simplicity we are considering the case where we have only one character. For more than one character we simply need to make it clear which character knows what. For example, $\mathit{Knows}\,(\mathsf{Dognap}, \tau = c, s)$ indicates that Dognap knows the value of τ.

When a character knows the value of a term, but we do not necessarily know the value of the term, we use the notation $\mathit{Kref}(\tau, s)$ to say that the character *knows the referent* of τ:

$$\mathit{Kref}(\tau, s) \triangleq \exists z\ \mathit{Knows}\,(\tau = z, s). \tag{4.2}$$

We now introduce some special notation for the case when τ takes on values in $\mathbb{B}$. In particular, since there are only two possibilities for the referent, we say we *know whether* τ is true or not:

$$\mathit{Kwhether}\,(\tau, s) \triangleq \mathit{Knows}\,(\tau = 1, s) \lor \mathit{Knows}\,(\tau = 0, s). \tag{4.3}$$

4.1.2 Sensing

Without loss of generality, we can now make the simplifying assumption that for each term τ, whose value we are interested in sensing, we have a corresponding knowledge-producing action sense_τ. In general, if there are n knowledge-producing actions, sense_{τ_i}, $i = 0, \ldots, n - 1$, then we shall assume there are n associated situation-dependent terms, $\tau_0, \ldots, \tau_{n-1}$. The corresponding successor state axiom for K is then

$$Poss\,(a,s) \Rightarrow [\mathsf{K}(s'', do(a,s)) \Leftrightarrow$$
$$\exists s'\ (\mathsf{K}(s',s) \wedge (s'' = do(a,s'))) \wedge$$
$$((a \neq sense_{\tau_0} \wedge \cdots \wedge a \neq sense_{\tau_{n-1}})$$
$$\vee\, (a = sense_{\tau_0} \wedge \tau_0(s') = \tau_0(s))$$
$$\vdots$$
$$\vee\, (a = sense_{\tau_{n-1}} \wedge \tau_{n-1}(s') = \tau_{n-1}(s)))]. \quad (4.4)$$

The above successor state axiom captures the required notion of sensing and solves the frame problem for knowledge producing actions. We shall explain how it works through a simple example. In particular, let us return to the problem of sensing the current temperature.[1] Firstly, we introduce a fluent temp : SITUATION $\rightarrow \mathbb{R}^+$, that corresponds to the temperature (in Kelvin) in the current situation. For now, let us assume that the temperature remains constant:

$$Poss\,(a,s) \Rightarrow \mathsf{temp}(do(a,s)) = \mathsf{temp}(s). \quad (4.5)$$

We will have a single knowledge-producing action *senseTemp*. This gives us the following successor state axiom for K:

$$Poss\,(a,s) \Rightarrow [\mathsf{K}(s'', do(a,s)) \Leftrightarrow \exists s'\ (\mathsf{K}(s',s) \wedge (s'' = do(a,s'))) \wedge$$
$$((a \neq sense\,Temp) \vee (a = sense\,Temp \wedge \mathsf{temp}(s') = \mathsf{temp}(s)))]. \quad (4.6)$$

The above axiom states that for any action other than *senseTemp* the set of K-related worlds is the set of images of the previous set of K-related worlds. That is, if s' was K-related to s, then the image $s'' = do(a, s')$, of s' after performing the action a, is K-related to $do(a, s)$. Moreover, when the character performs a *senseTemp* action, in some situation s, the effect is to restrict the set of K-related worlds to those in which the temperature agrees with the temperature in the situation s. In other words, *senseTemp* is the only knowledge-producing action, and its effect is to make the temperature denotation known: $Kref(\mathsf{temp}, do(sense\,Temp, s))$.

4.1.3 Discussion

The formalization of knowledge within the situation calculus using the epistemic fluent K makes for an elegant mathematical specification language. It

---

[1]We choose to use a scalar-valued quantity because it simplifies the notation. In general, a character will need to sense vector-valued quantities and, of course, it is trivial to extend the notation.

is also powerful. For example, suppose we have an effect axiom that states that if a gun is loaded then the character is dead after shooting the gun:

$$\text{Loaded}(s) \Rightarrow \text{Dead}(do(shoot, s)).$$

Furthermore, suppose we know the gun is initially loaded $Knows\,(\text{Loaded}, s_0)$, then we can infer that we know the character is dead after shooting the gun $Knows\,(\text{Dead}(do(shoot, s_0)))$.

Unfortunately, there are some problems. One set of problems is associated with implementation; the second applies to reasoning about real numbers, both in theory and in practice.

Implementation

The implementation problems revolve around how to specify the initial situation. In particular, specifying the initial situation may involve having to list an exponential number of possible worlds. For example, if we do not know initially if the gun is loaded, then we might consider listing explicitly the two possible worlds s_a and s_b, such that:

$$\text{K}(s_a, s_0) \wedge \text{K}(s_b, s_0) \wedge \text{Loaded}(s_a) \wedge \neg\text{Loaded}(s_b)$$

As we add more relational fluents, the situation gets worse. In general, if we have n such fluents, there will be 2^n initial possible worlds that we have to list. Once we start using functional fluents, however, things get even worse: we cannot, by definition, list the uncountably many possible worlds associated with not knowing the value of a fluent that takes on values in $\mathbb{R}$.

Intuitively, we need to be able to specify rules that characterize, without having to list them all, the set of initial possible worlds. It may be possible to somehow coerce a logic programming language like Prolog into such an achievement. Perhaps, more reasonably, we could consider using a modal logic theorem prover. However, such theorem provers are often inefficient and experimental. In addition, in the introduction we advanced the idea of a rapid prototyping approach in which we could gradually remove the nondeterminism from our specifications. In this way, we might hope to eventually refine a specification so that it can be run without the need for an underlying theorem prover. This idea must, sadly, be forsaken if we are to ingrain the need for a theorem prover into our approach to sensing.

Ignoring all the above concerns, let us assume that we can specify rules that characterize the set of initial possible worlds. For example, suppose that initially, we know the temperature is between 10 and 50 Kelvin. We might express this using inequalities:

$$\forall s'\ \text{K}(s', s_0) \Rightarrow 10 \leqslant \text{temp}(s') \leqslant 50.$$

This, however, brings us to our second set of problems related to reasoning about real numbers.

Real Numbers

We just wrote down the formula that corresponds to

$$\textit{Knows}\,(10 \leqslant \text{temp} \leqslant 50, s_0). \tag{4.7}$$

Suppose we are now interested in what this tells us about what we know about the value of the temperature squared. In general, if we know a term τ lies in the range $[u, v]$, we would like to be able to answer questions about what we know about some arbitrary function f of τ. Such questions take us into a mathematical minefield of reasoning about inequalities. Fortunately, the field of interval arithmetic has already charted a path through this minefield.

4.2 Interval Arithmetic

To address the issues we raised in Section 4.1.3, we turn our attention to interval arithmetic. Some of the immediate advantages interval arithmetic affords us are listed below:

- Interval arithmetic enables us to move all the details of reasoning about inequalities into the rules for combining intervals under various mathematical operations.

- Interval arithmetic provides a finite (and succinct) way to represent uncertainty about a large, possibly uncountable, set of alternatives. Moreover, the representation remains finite after performing a series of operations of the intervals.

- Writing a sound procedure for evaluating ground expressions involving interval arithmetic is a trivial task. Moreover, we can evaluate expressions in time that is linear in the length of the query. Returning valid and optimal intervals is more challenging (see Section 4.7).

- There is no discrepancy between the underlying theory of interval arithmetic, and the corresponding implementation.

We construct interval arithmetics from our previously available number systems as follows:

- For each number system $\mathbb{X}$, we add a new number system sort $\mathcal{I}_{\mathbb{X}}$. The constants of $\mathcal{I}_{\mathbb{X}}$ are the set of pairs $\langle u, v \rangle$ such that $u, v \in \mathbb{X}$ and $u \leqslant v$. There are functions and predicates corresponding to all the functions and predicates of $\mathbb{X}$.

- For an interval $\boldsymbol{x} = \langle u, v \rangle$, we use the notation $\underline{\boldsymbol{x}} = u$ for the lower bound, and $\overline{\boldsymbol{x}} = v$ for the upper bound.

- The function width, returns the width of an interval $\boldsymbol{x}$, i.e., $\mathsf{width}(\boldsymbol{x}) = \overline{\boldsymbol{x}} - \underline{\boldsymbol{x}}$.

- When we have a number x and an interval $\boldsymbol{x} = \langle u, v \rangle$, such that $u \leqslant x \leqslant v$, we say that $\boldsymbol{x}$ contains x and we write $x \in \boldsymbol{x}$. Similarly for two intervals $\boldsymbol{x}$, $\boldsymbol{y}$ such that $\underline{\boldsymbol{y}} \leqslant \underline{\boldsymbol{x}}$ and $\overline{\boldsymbol{x}} \leqslant \overline{\boldsymbol{y}}$, we say that $\boldsymbol{y}$ contains $\boldsymbol{x}$ and we write $\boldsymbol{x} \subseteq \boldsymbol{y}$.

- For two intervals $\boldsymbol{x}_0$, $\boldsymbol{x}_1$, we say that $\boldsymbol{x}_0 \leq \boldsymbol{x}_1$ if, and only if, $\overline{\boldsymbol{x}}_0 \leqslant \underline{\boldsymbol{x}}_1$.

- When we do not want to specify which particular number system we are using, we will use $\perp$ and $\top$ to represent, respectively, the minimum and maximum elements. For example, in $\mathbb{R}^{\star}$, $\langle \perp, \top \rangle = \langle -\infty, \infty \rangle$.

As an example, consider the case of the number system $\mathcal{I}_{\mathbb{B}}$. There are three numbers in this number system: $\langle 0, 0 \rangle$, $\langle 0, 1 \rangle$ and $\langle 1, 1 \rangle$. Note that we have $\langle 0, 0 \rangle \leqslant \langle 0, 1 \rangle \leqslant \langle 1, 1 \rangle$, $\langle 0, 0 \rangle \subset \langle 0, 1 \rangle$, and $\langle 1, 1 \rangle \subset \langle 0, 1 \rangle$. In $\mathbb{B}$, 1 and 0 can be used to represent, respectively, "true" and "false". Similarly, $\langle 1, 1 \rangle$, $\langle 0, 1 \rangle$ and $\langle 0, 0 \rangle$ in $\mathcal{I}_{\mathbb{B}}$ can be used to represent, respectively, "known to be true," "unknown," and "known to be false." We thus get what amounts to a *three-valued logic* which, by way of example, we develop further in Section 4.3.

Complex numbers are also made up of a pair of (real) numbers, and operations on them are defined in terms of operations on the reals. However, it would lead to confusion if, when reading a text on complex analysis, we could not comprehend complex numbers as a separate entity, distinct from pairs of real numbers. We therefore forewarn the reader against making the same mistake for intervals. That is, although numbers in $\mathcal{I}_{\mathbb{X}}$ are made up of a pair of numbers from $\mathbb{X}$ it is important to treat them as "first-class" numbers in their own right.

4.3   Interval-valued Epistemic Fluents

The epistemic K-fluent that we discussed previously allowed us to express
a character's uncertainty about the value of a fluent in its world. Unfortunately, in Section 4.1.3, we saw there were implementation problems associated with trying to represent a character's knowledge of the initial situation.
Fortunately, in the previous section we saw that intervals also allow us to
express uncertainty about a quantity. Moreover, they allow us to do so in
a way that circumvents the problem of how to represent infinite quantities
with a finite number of bits. It is, therefore, natural to ask whether we can
also use intervals to replace the troublesome epistemic K-fluent.

The answer, as we shall seek to demonstrate in the remainder of this
chapter, is a resounding "yes." In particular, we shall introduce new epistemic fluents that will be interval-valued. They will be used to represent a
character's uncertainty about the value of certain nonepistemic fluents.

We have previously used functional fluents that take on values in any
of the number systems: $\mathbb{B}$, $\mathbb{R}$, etc. There is nothing noteworthy about now
allowing fluents that take on values in any of the interval numbers systems:
$\mathcal{I}_{\mathbb{B}}$, $\mathcal{I}_{\mathbb{R}}$. Firstly, let us distinguish those regular fluents whose value may be
learned through a knowledge-producing action. We term such fluents *sensory
fluents*. Now, for each sensory fluent f, we introduce a new corresponding
interval-valued epistemic (IVE) fluent $\mathcal{I}_f$.

For example, we can introduce an IVE fluent $\mathcal{I}_{\text{temp}} : \text{SITUATION} \rightarrow \mathcal{I}_{\mathbb{R}^{*+}}$.
We can now use the interval $\mathcal{I}_{\text{temp}}(s_0) = \langle 10, 50 \rangle$ to state that the temperature is initially known to be between 10 and 50 Kelvin. Similarly,
we can even specify that the temperature is initially completely unknown:
$\mathcal{I}_{\text{temp}}(s_0) = \langle 0, \infty \rangle$.

We can now define successor-state axioms for IVE fluents. This is done
in much the same way as it was for regular fluents. For example, suppose we
have a perfect sensor, then the following successor-state axiom states that
after sensing, we "know" the temperature in the resulting situation,

$$Poss(a, s) \Rightarrow [\mathcal{I}_{\text{temp}}(do(a, s)) = \boldsymbol{y} \Leftrightarrow$$
$$(a = senseTemp \land \overline{\boldsymbol{y}} = \underline{\boldsymbol{y}} = \text{temp}(s)) \lor (a \neq senseTemp \land \mathcal{I}_{\text{temp}}(s) = \boldsymbol{y})].$$
$$(4.8)$$

Seeking to make IVE fluent ubiquitous necessitates an alternative definition for *Knows* that does not mention the K-fluent. To this end, we introduce
a new abbreviation, $\mathcal{I}_{Knows}$ such that for any term τ, $\mathcal{I}_{Knows}(\tau, s) = \langle u, v \rangle$
means that τ's *interval value* is $\langle u, v \rangle$. By "interval value" we mean the
value we get by evaluating the expression according the set of rules that we

shall discuss in Section 4.8. For now, let us just consider the case when τ is some fluent f. When f is a sensory fluent then $\mathcal{I}_{Knows}$ is the value of the corresponding IVE fluent, otherwise it is completely unknown:

$$\mathcal{I}_{Knows}(f, s) = \begin{cases} \mathcal{I}_f(s) & \text{if } f \text{ is a sensory fluent,} \\ \langle \bot, \top \rangle & \text{otherwise.} \end{cases} \tag{4.9}$$

We now take the important step of redefining *Knows* to be the special case when $\mathcal{I}_{Knows}(\tau, s)$ has collapsed to a thin interval:

$$\textit{Knows}'\,(\tau = c, s) \Leftrightarrow \mathcal{I}_{Knows}(\tau, s) = \langle c, c \rangle. \tag{4.10}$$

The definitions of *Kref*, and *Kwhether* are now in terms of the new definition for *Knows'* . As required, this new definition does not involve the problematic epistemic K-fluent.

4.4 Inaccurate Sensors

By slightly modifying the definition of *Knows'*, we can also extend it easily to model inaccurate (noisy) sensors. In particular, we can say that we know a fluent's value to within some Δ, if the width of the interval is less than twice Δ:

$$\textit{Knows}'(\Delta, f = z, s) \triangleq \mathcal{I}_f(s) \subseteq \langle z - \Delta, z + \Delta \rangle. \tag{4.11}$$

If we have a bound of $\pm\Delta$ on the greatest possible error for the sensor that recorded the temperature, then we can state that the value sensed for the temperature is within $\pm\Delta$ of the actual value:

$$Poss\,(a, s) \Rightarrow$$
$$[\mathcal{I}_{\text{temp}}(do(a, s)) = \langle u, v \rangle \Leftrightarrow$$
$$(a = \textit{senseTemp} \wedge u = \max(\underline{\mathcal{I}_{\text{temp}}(s)}, \text{temp}(s) - \Delta) \wedge$$
$$v = \min(\text{temp}(s) + \Delta, \overline{\mathcal{I}_{\text{temp}}(s)})) \vee$$
$$(a \neq \textit{senseTemp} \wedge \mathcal{I}_{\text{temp}}(s) = \langle u, v \rangle)]. \tag{4.12}$$

4.5 Sensing Changing Values

Until now, we only considered sensing fluents whose values remain constant. That is, once a fluent becomes known then it stays known. If the value of a known fluent changes then the character will automatically know the fluent's new value. In many cases this is somewhat counterintuitive. For example, if one has checked the temperature once, then it is quite natural to assume that after a certain period of time the information may be out of date. That is, we would expect to have to sense the temperature periodically.

Using the epistemic K-fluent to model information becoming out of date corresponds to adding possible worlds back in. Unfortunately, the K-fluent keeps track of a character's knowledge of all the sensory fluents all at once. It can therefore be hard to specify exactly which worlds the character should be adding back into its consideration. In contrast, with intervals, there is nothing noteworthy about allowing the particular relevant interval to expand. We must simply ensure that our axioms maintain the state constraint that the interval bounds the actual value of the fluent.

At the extreme, we can have fluents that are constantly changing in unpredictable ways. We can model this with exogenous actions. We assume that the current temperature changes in a completely erratic and unpredictable way, according to some exogenous action *setTemp*. Then, we can write a successor-state axiom for temp that simply states that the temperature is whatever it was set to:

$$Poss\,(a, s) \Rightarrow \text{temp}(do(a, s)) = z \Leftrightarrow$$
$$[(a = setTemp(z)) \vee (a \neq setTemp \wedge \text{temp}(s) = z)].$$

We can, also, write a successor state axiom for $\mathcal{I}_{\text{temp}}$. In particular, if we again assume accurate sensors, we can state that the temperature is known after sensing it, otherwise, it is completely unknown:

$$Poss\,(a, s) \Rightarrow [\mathcal{I}_{\text{temp}}(do(a, s)) = \langle u, v \rangle \Leftrightarrow$$
$$(a = senseTemp \wedge u = v = \text{temp}(s)) \vee (a \neq senseTemp \wedge u = 0 \wedge v = \infty)].$$
$$(4.13)$$

Note that this definition works because, by definition, $\forall s\ \text{temp}(s) \in \langle 0, \infty \rangle$. At first glance it may appear strange that we have, for example,

$$\mathcal{I}_{\text{temp}}(do(setTemp(2), s)) = \langle 0, \infty \rangle.$$

Upon reflection, however, the reader will hopefully recall that our intention is to use the IVE fluents to model a character's knowledge of its world. There-

fore, until sensing, the character rightly remains oblivious as to the effect of
the exogenous action *setTemp*. For the fluent that keeps track of the temperature in the virtual world, we of course get that $\text{temp}(do(setTemp(2), s))$
$= 2$.

If we have a bound on the maximum rate of temperature change, per
unit time (Δtemp, say), and we add the ability to track the time to our
axiomatization, then can do a lot better. Suppose we have an action *tick*
that occurs once per unit of time. Moreover, we limit exogenous actions to
only occurring directly before a tick action. Then we can have a successor-
state axiom that states the temperature is known after sensing; or after a
period of time it is known to have changed by less than some maximum
amount; otherwise it is unchanged:

$$Poss(a, s) \Rightarrow [\mathcal{I}_{\text{temp}}(do(a, s)) = \langle u, v \rangle \Leftrightarrow$$
$$(a = senseTemp \land u = v = \text{temp}(s)) \lor$$
$$(a = tick \land \exists u_p, v_p \; \mathcal{I}_{\text{temp}}(s) = \langle u_p, v_p \rangle \land$$
$$u = \max(0, u_p - \Delta\text{temp}) \land v = v_p + \Delta\text{temp}) \lor$$
$$(a \neq senseTemp \land a \neq tick \land \mathcal{I}_{\text{temp}}(s) = \langle u, v \rangle]. \quad (4.14)$$

This type of axiom can be used to "plan to re-plan." That is, the degra-
dation in the character's knowledge level is predictable and can be used as
the basis for a re-planning action.

4.6 Correctness[†]

Our ultimate aim is, that in an implementation, we can use IVE fluents
to completely replace the troublesome K-fluent. Nevertheless, within our
mathematical theory, there is nothing to prevent our IVE fluents co-existing
with our previous sole epistemic K-fluent. Indeed, if we define everything
correctly then there are many important relationships that should hold between the two. These relationships take the form of state constraints and, as
we shall show, can be used to express the notion of validity and optimality of
our IVE fluents. If these state constraints are maintained as actions are performed, then the IVE fluents completely subsume the troublesome K-fluent.
This will turn out to be true until we consider knowledge of general terms,
in which case we can maintain validity but may have to sacrifice our original
notion of optimality (see Section 4.8).

4.6.1 Validity and Optimality

First let's define what it means for an IVE fluent to be valid.

Definition 4.6.1 (Validity). *For every sensory fluent f, we say that the corresponding IVE fluent $\mathcal{I}_f$ is a* valid *interval if f's value in all of the K-related situations is contained within it:*

$$\forall s, s' \; \mathsf{K}(s', s) \Rightarrow f(s') \in \mathcal{I}_f(s).$$

Note that, since we have a logic of knowledge (as opposed to belief), we have that every situation is K-related to itself: $\forall s \; \mathsf{K}(s, s)$. Thus, as an immediate consequence of Definition 4.6.1, we have that if an IVE fluent $\mathcal{I}_f$ is valid, then it contains the value of f: $\forall s \; f(s) \in \mathcal{I}_f(s)$.

The validity criterion is a state constraint that ensures the interval value of the IVE fluents is wide enough to contain all the possible values of the sensory fluents. It does not, however, prevent intervals from being excessively wide. For example, the interval $\langle -\infty, \infty \rangle$ is a valid interval for any IVE fluent that takes on values in $\mathcal{I}_{\mathbb{R}^\star}$. The notion of narrow intervals is captured in the definition of optimality.

Definition 4.6.2 (Optimality). *A valid IVE fluent $\mathcal{I}_f$ is also* optimal *if it is the smallest valid interval:*

$$\forall \; \boldsymbol{y}, s, s' \; \mathsf{K}(s', s) \Rightarrow (f(s') \in \boldsymbol{y} \Rightarrow \mathcal{I}_f(s) \subseteq \boldsymbol{y}).$$

4.6.2 Equivalences

We shall now consider some of the consequences and applications of interval-valued fluents to formalizing sensing under various different assumptions. Our goal will be to show that we can maintain valid and optimal intervals as we perform actions. This leads to the soundness and completeness result given at the end of the section.

Firstly, we note that there is always an initial valid IVE fluent.

Lemma 4.6.1. *For any initial situation s_0 and sensory fluent f, we have $\mathcal{I}_f = \langle \bot, \top \rangle$ is a valid interval.*

Proof. The proof of the theorem is immediate from the fact that, by definition, $\langle \bot, \top \rangle$ bounds any possible value for f. So, in particular, it bounds all the values f can take in all the initial K-related situations. $\square$

It is also reasonable to assume that there will also be an initial optimal interval. If there is no such initial optimal interval, then all the correctness results in this section still hold, but the completeness results won't hold until after the first sensing action.

Lemma 4.6.2. *If the initial set of* K-*related situations is either completely unspecified, or specified with inequalities that are as tight as possible (i.e., maximally restrictive), then we can find an initial optimal IVE fluent for each of the sensory fluents.*

Proof. **Case (i)** The initial set of K-related situations is completely unspecified. That is, initially we are completely ignorant of a sensory fluent f's value. Then, the maximal interval is also clearly optimal. That is, $\langle \bot, \top \rangle$ is the *only* interval that bounds all possible values for f in the initial K-related situations. Since it is the unique valid interval it must, by definition, be an optimal interval.

Case (ii) We have a specification such as

$$(\forall s' \ \mathsf{K}(s', \mathsf{S}_0) \Rightarrow u \leqslant f(s') \leqslant v) \wedge$$
$$\neg \exists \ u', v' \ [u < u' \wedge v' < v \wedge (\forall s' \ \mathsf{K}(s', \mathsf{S}_0) \Rightarrow u' \leqslant f(s') \leqslant v')].$$

Then, consider $\mathcal{I}_f(\mathsf{S}_0) = \langle u, v \rangle$. As required, this is clearly the smallest valid interval.

$\square$

In what follows, we make the three following assumptions about all sensory fluents f:

1. The value of $\mathcal{I}_f$, in the initial situation, is optimal and valid. This assumption is justified by Lemma 4.6.1 and Lemma 4.6.2.

2. The successor-state axiom for f is such that f remains constant:

$$\mathit{Poss}(a, s) \Rightarrow [f(\mathit{do}(a, s)) = f(s)]. \tag{4.15}$$

3. The successor-state axioms for each of the corresponding IVE fluents $\mathcal{I}_f$ are of the following form:

$$\mathit{Poss}(a, s) \Rightarrow [\mathcal{I}_f(\mathit{do}(a, s)) = \boldsymbol{y} \Leftrightarrow$$
$$(a = \mathit{sense}_f \wedge \overline{\boldsymbol{y}} = \underline{\boldsymbol{y}} = \mathsf{f}(s)) \vee (a \neq \mathit{sense}_f \wedge \mathcal{I}_f(s) = \boldsymbol{y})]. \tag{4.16}$$

In Sections 4.4 and 4.5, we discussed how to relax some of these constraints. For now, let us state our main correctness result.

Theorem 4.6.1. *With the above assumptions, for all situations s, and sensory fluents f, every IVE fluent $\mathcal{I}_f$ is valid and optimal.*

Proof. We shall prove the result by induction on s. We note that the base case follows by Assumption 1. Therefore, we need only consider the case when $s^* = do(a, s)$.

By induction, we may assume that

$$\forall s' \; \mathsf{K}(s', s) \Rightarrow f(s') \in \mathcal{I}_f(s),$$

and that $\mathcal{I}_f(s)$ is optimal. We seek to prove that

$$\forall s'' \; \mathsf{K}(s'', s^*) \Rightarrow f(s'') \in \mathcal{I}_f(s^*), \tag{4.17}$$

and that $\mathcal{I}_f(s^*)$ is optimal.

Case (i) Consider the case when $a \neq sense_f$. Let us fix an s'' such that $\mathsf{K}(s'', s^*)$. Note that since K is reflexive we can be sure that such an s'' exists. Therefore, by the successor-state axiom for K (Equation 4.4) there is an s' such that

$$s'' = do(a, s') \wedge \mathsf{K}(s', s).$$

By induction we can thus infer that

$$f(s') \in \mathcal{I}_f(s).$$

Now by the successor-state axiom for f (Equation 4.15), we have that $f(s'') = f(s')$, which gives us

$$f(s'') \in \mathcal{I}_f(s).$$

Then, by the successor-state axiom for $\mathcal{I}_f$ (Equation 4.16), $\mathcal{I}_f(s^*) = \mathcal{I}_f(s)$, and

$$f(s'') \in \mathcal{I}_f(s^*),$$

as required for validity. This also shows that, to be a valid interval for $\mathcal{I}_f(s^*)$, the interval must also be a valid interval for $\mathcal{I}_f(s)$. Now, by the assumption of optimality, any interval narrower than $\mathcal{I}_f(s)$ would not be valid. Therefore, $\mathcal{I}_f(s)$ is also the narrowest valid interval for $\mathcal{I}_f(s^*)$.

Case (ii) Similarly, when $a = sense_f$, then by the successor-state axiom for
K (Equation 4.4), there is an s' such that

$$s'' = do(a, s') \wedge \mathsf{K}(s', s) \wedge f(s') = f(s).$$

Therefore,

$$f(s') \in \langle f(s), f(s) \rangle.$$

Now by the successor-state axiom for f (Equation 4.15), we have
$f(s'') = f(s')$, which gives us

$$f(s'') \in \langle f(s), f(s) \rangle.$$

Then, by the successor-state axiom for $\mathcal{I}_f$ (Equation 4.16), $\mathcal{I}_f(s^\star) = \langle f(s), f(s) \rangle$, and

$$f(s'') \in \mathcal{I}_f(s^\star).$$

as required for validity. To show optimality, consider that the width
of $\langle f(s), f(s) \rangle$ is 0. Therefore, there can be no narrower interval and
so the interval must also be optimal.

$\square$

As a corollary we have that the definition of *Knows* given in Equation 4.1
is equivalent to the one given in Equation 4.10.

Corollary 4.6.1. *For any sensory fluent f,*

$$Knows\,(f = c, s) \Leftrightarrow Knows'\,(f = c, s).$$

Proof. Let us assume *Knows* $(f = c, s)$. By Equation 4.1 this is equivalent to

$$\forall s'\; \mathsf{K}(s', s) \Rightarrow f(s') = c.$$

Now by Theorem 4.6.1, $\mathcal{I}_f$ is valid and optimal, therefore $\mathcal{I}_f(s) = \langle c, c \rangle$,
which by Equation 4.10 is the definition of *Knows'* $(f = c, s)$.

Now let us assume *Knows'* $(f = c, s)$, then by Equation 4.10, we have that
$\mathcal{I}_f(s) = \langle c, c \rangle$. Once again by applying Theorem 4.6.1, we must have that

$$\forall s'\; \mathsf{K}(s', s) \Rightarrow f(s') \in \langle c, c \rangle.$$

Since $\langle c, c \rangle$ has width 0, we can re-write this as

$$\forall s'\; \mathsf{K}(s', s) \Rightarrow f(s') = c,$$

which by Equation 4.1 is the definition of *Knows* $(f = c, s)$, as required. $\square$

The above theorem means that any correctness results proved for *Knows*, carry over to *Knows'*. In particular, in [118] the authors prove the following correctness results for *Knows*:

- Knowledge-producing actions do not change the state of the world.

- If an action a does not affect a fluent P, and does not provide any information about anything related to P, then nothing is learned about a fluent P by doing an action a.

- A character never forgets.[2]

4.7 Operators for Interval Arithmetic[†]

Back in Section 4.1.3, one of our original motivations for introducing intervals was the promise of being able to conveniently calculate what we know about a term from our knowledge of its subcomponents. For example, suppose in a situation s we know the value of a fluent $f(s)$, what do we know about $(f(s))^2$?

The answer to this question leads us to the large and active research area of interval arithmetic. The fundamental principle used is that interval versions of a given function should be guaranteed to bound all possible values of the noninterval version. For example, let us consider a function $\phi : \mathbb{R} \to \mathbb{R}$. The interval version of this function is $\mathcal{I}_\phi : \mathcal{I}_\mathbb{R} \to \mathcal{I}_\mathbb{R}$. The result of applying $\mathcal{I}_\phi$ to some interval $\boldsymbol{x}$ is another interval $\boldsymbol{y} = \mathcal{I}_\phi(\boldsymbol{x})$. We say that the $\boldsymbol{y}$ is a *valid* interval if, for every point $x \in \boldsymbol{x}$, we have that $\phi(x) \in \boldsymbol{y}$. Note also that for any valid interval $\boldsymbol{y}$, if $\boldsymbol{y} \subseteq \boldsymbol{y}'$, then $\boldsymbol{y}'$ is also a valid interval. If, for every interval $\boldsymbol{x}$, $\mathcal{I}_\phi(\boldsymbol{x})$ gives a valid interval then we say that $\mathcal{I}_\phi$ is a *sound interval version* of ϕ.

As we might expect from our previous discussions, defining a sound interval version of any function is trivial. In particular, we just let the interval version return the maximal interval of the relevant number system. For example, the function that, for any argument, returns $\langle -\infty, \infty \rangle$ is a sound interval version of any function $\phi : \mathbb{R} \to \mathbb{R}$.

Hence, we see that once again we also need to be concerned about returning intervals that are as narrow as possible. The *optimal interval version* of a function ϕ is thus defined to be the *sound interval version* that, for every argument, returns the smallest valid interval. Unfortunately, for most

---

[2]In Section 4.5 we relaxed this assumption.

interesting functions, no such interval versions are known to exist. There are three basic approaches that have been found to address this shortcoming:

Subdivision The standard tool in the interval arithmetic arsenal is subdivision. Suppose we have an interval x and we evaluate $\mathcal{I}_\phi(x)$ to give us an interval that is too wide. Then we subdivide x into x_l and x_r such that $x = x_l \cup x_r$. We then evaluate each half separately in the hope that $\mathcal{I}_\phi(x_l) \cup \mathcal{I}_\phi(x_r) \subset \mathcal{I}_\phi(x)$. In practice, this usually works well although it can result in a combinatorial explosion in the number of intervals.

Special forms Consider the expression $t + (50 - t)$. If we evaluate this expression naïvely for the interval $\langle 0, 50 \rangle$, we get back the interval $\langle 0, 100 \rangle$. It is clear, however, that the expression simplifies to 50 and the optimal interval is thus $\langle 50, 50 \rangle$. Therefore, researchers have looked at various standard forms for expressions in an attempt to give better results when evaluating the expression using intervals. For example, the so called "centered forms" give rise to quadratic (as opposed to linear) convergence to the exact answer when subdividing.

Generalized interval arithmetic The final approach we mention is an approach that was only recently discovered by Jeffrey Tupper [138]. The idea is that instead of using constants to bound an interval we use linear functions. Thus, for linear expressions such as $t + (50 - t)$, we can define operators that are guaranteed to return optimal intervals. Of course, we can then recreate similar problems by considering quadratic expressions but we can also generalize interval arithmetic all the way up to intervals that use general Turing machines as bounds!

4.8   Knowledge of Terms[†]

Back in Section 4.3 we introduced the abbreviation $\mathcal{I}_{Knows}$. In Equation 4.9 we defined $\mathcal{I}_{Knows}$ for fluents and in what follows we shall show how to define $\mathcal{I}_{Knows}$ for general terms. We begin by stating what it means for our definitions to be valid.

Definition 4.8.1 (Validity for terms). *For every term τ, we say that the corresponding interval value of the term given by $\mathcal{I}_{Knows}(\tau, s)$ is a valid interval if τ's value in all of the K-related situations is contained within it:*

$$\forall s, s' \; \mathsf{K}(s', s) \Rightarrow \tau[s'] \in \mathcal{I}_{Knows}(\tau, s).$$

Fortunately, the general notion of soundness for interval arithmetic carries over into our notion of validity for $\mathcal{I}_{Knows}$.

Theorem 4.8.1. *Suppose $\mathcal{I}_\phi$ is a sound interval version of an n-ary function $\phi : \mathbb{X}^n \to \mathbb{X}$. Furthermore, let $\boldsymbol{x}_0, \ldots, \boldsymbol{x}_{n-1} \in \mathcal{I}_\mathbb{X}$ be, respectively, valid intervals for $\mathcal{I}_{Knows}(\tau_0, s), \ldots, \mathcal{I}_{Knows}(\tau_{n-1}, s)$. Then, $\mathcal{I}_\phi(\boldsymbol{x}_0, \ldots, \boldsymbol{x}_{n-1})$ is a valid interval for $\mathcal{I}_{Knows}(\phi(\tau_0, \ldots, \tau_{n-1}), s)$.*

Proof. Suppose the theorem is false. Then $\mathcal{I}_\phi(\boldsymbol{x}_0, \ldots, \boldsymbol{x}_{n-1})$ is not a valid interval for $\mathcal{I}_{Knows}(\phi(\tau_0, \ldots, \tau_{n-1}), s)$. That is,

$$\forall s' \ \mathsf{K}(s', s) \Rightarrow \phi(\tau_0[s'], \ldots, \tau_{n-1}[s']) \in \mathcal{I}_\phi(\boldsymbol{x}_0, \ldots, \boldsymbol{x}_{n-1})$$

is false. That is, for some K-related situation s' we have that

$$\phi(\tau_0[s'], \ldots, \tau_{n-1}[s']) \notin \mathcal{I}_\phi(\boldsymbol{x}_0, \ldots, \boldsymbol{x}_{n-1}).$$

This, however, violates the assumption that $\mathcal{I}_\phi$ is a sound interval version of ϕ. □

The important consequence of this theorem is that our definition of $\mathcal{I}_{Knows}$ for terms can stand upon the shoulders of previous work in interval arithmetic. That is, we can define $\mathcal{I}_{Knows}$ recursively in terms of sound interval versions of functions. Assuming the same assumptions as in Theorem 4.8.1, we have that

$$\mathcal{I}_{Knows}(\phi(\tau_0, \ldots, \tau_{n-1}), s) = \mathcal{I}_\phi(\boldsymbol{x}_0, \ldots, \boldsymbol{x}_{n-1}).$$

Note that some of our functions may be written using *infix* notation, in which case we may refer to them as *operators*. The important aspect of this definition is that we do not have to redesign a plethora of operators for interval arithmetic and prove each of them sound. In the previous section we noted the difficulties associated with defining optimal versions of operators. We also noted that there are a number of ways to deal with the problem. Each of the methods we outline maintains validity and is thus appropriate for us to use. The particular method we choose to narrow our intervals can be thought of as an implementation detail.

4.9 Usefulness†

For $\mathcal{I}_\mathbb{R}$, the standard set of useful interval arithmetic operators is listed below. Elsewhere in the text we rely on context to imply the intended meaning, but here interval versions of operators, and relations, are given in bold.[3]

---

[3] For additional useful operators, the reader should consult the references on interval arithmetic (see Section 4.10). The references also describe how to remove the assumptions

Definition 4.9.1 (Operators for $\mathcal{I}_\mathbb{R}$).

$$
\begin{aligned}
x + y &= \langle \underline{x} + \underline{y}, \overline{x} + \overline{y} \rangle \\
x - y &= \langle \underline{x} - \overline{y}, \overline{x} - \underline{y} \rangle \\
x \times y &= \langle \min\{\underline{x}\underline{y}, \underline{x}\overline{y}, \overline{x}\underline{y}, \overline{x}\overline{y}\}, \max\{\underline{x}\underline{y}, \underline{x}\overline{y}, \overline{x}\underline{y}, \overline{x}\overline{y}\} \rangle \\
\frac{1}{x} &= \langle \frac{1}{\overline{x}}, \frac{1}{\underline{x}} \rangle, \qquad \text{provided } 0 \notin x \\
x \div y &= x \times \frac{1}{y}
\end{aligned}
$$

The above definitions enable us to evaluate $\mathcal{I}_{Knows}$ for terms taking on values in $\mathbb{R}$. Note that, in the above definitions we do not use the equality symbol in the set theoretic sense. That is, the right hand side is the interval defined by the interval operator on the left. As we explained in section 4.7, the intervals obtained will be sound, but not necessarily optimal. Let us now let us look at some useful operators for $\mathcal{I}_\mathbb{B}$.

Definition 4.9.2 (Operators for $\mathcal{I}_\mathbb{B}$).

$$
\begin{aligned}
\tau = \langle u, v \rangle &\Leftrightarrow \quad \neg\tau = \langle \neg v, \neg u \rangle \\
\tau_0 = \langle u_0, v_0 \rangle \wedge \tau_1 = \langle u_1, v_1 \rangle &\Rightarrow \quad \tau_0 \wedge \tau_1 \subseteq \langle u_0 \wedge u_1, v_0 \wedge v_1 \rangle \\
\tau_0 \wedge \tau_1 = \langle u, v \rangle &\Rightarrow \quad \tau_0 \subseteq \langle u, 1 \rangle \\
\tau_0 = \langle u_0, v_0 \rangle \wedge \tau_1 = \langle u_1, v_1 \rangle &\Rightarrow \quad \tau_0 \vee \tau_1 \subseteq \langle u_0 \vee u_1, v_0 \vee v_1 \rangle \\
\tau_0 \vee \tau_1 = \langle u, v \rangle &\Rightarrow \quad \tau_0 \subseteq \langle 0, v \rangle \\
[\exists x \ \tau(x)] = \langle u, v \rangle &\Rightarrow \quad \tau(c) \subseteq \langle 0, v \rangle, \quad \text{for any constant } c \\
\text{For some constant } c, \quad \tau(c) = \langle u, v \rangle &\Rightarrow \quad [\exists x \ \tau(x)] \subseteq \langle u, 1 \rangle \\
[\forall x \ \tau(x)] = \langle u, v \rangle &\Rightarrow \quad \tau(c) \subseteq \langle u, 1 \rangle, \quad \text{for any constant } c \\
\text{For some constant } c, \quad \tau(c) = \langle u, v \rangle &\Rightarrow \quad [\forall x \ \tau(x)] \subseteq \langle 0, v \rangle
\end{aligned}
$$

These definitions enable us to evaluate $\mathcal{I}_{Knows}$ for terms taking on values in $\mathbb{B}$. In contrast to the definitions for $\mathbb{R}$, this time the defintions are explicitly in terms of $\subseteq$. Either form of definition is acceptable, but it is good to be clear on the reason for the two different styles.

For interval arithmetic over $\mathbb{B}$ we can, once again, only guarantee valid results, not optimal ones. For example, if we assume $\tau = \langle 0, 1 \rangle$, then we get that $\tau \vee \neg\tau \subseteq \langle 0, 1 \rangle$. While this is valid, it is clearly not optimal. Since

---

on the reciprocal operator, how to implement the operators efficiently on a computer, and how to define operators for generalized interval arithmetics.

there are only two numbers in $\mathbb{B}$, we can subdivide to perform an exhaustive search for the optimal value. That is, let $\tau = \tau_0 \cup \tau_1$, where $\tau_0 = \langle 0, 0 \rangle$, and $\tau_1 = \langle 1, 1 \rangle$. Now we get that $\tau_0 \vee \neg\tau_0 = \langle 1, 1 \rangle$, and $\tau_1 \vee \neg\tau_1 = \langle 1, 1 \rangle$. With more variables, the exhaustive search approach has worst case exponential complexity. In general, it may be observed that if each variable occurs only once in an expression, then evaluating it will yield an optimal result. Also, if we start with thin intervals then we will also get an optimal result. Finally, for a propositional formula in Blake canonical form, evaluation with intervals *always* yields an optimal result. Moreover, all propositional formulas can be converted to this form. Thus we can evaluate propositional formulas in linear time and get optimal results. The catch is that converting propositional formulas to Blake canonical form is NP–hard.

When we consider quantifiers, the above rules would not form the basis of a particularly useful procedure for evaluating expressions. We recall that the simplest correct procedure would be the one that always just returns the interval $\langle 0, 1 \rangle$. For queries containing quantifiers, the procedure that follows from the above rules is almost as useless, except that it works adequately when we tell it about a specific instance.

As we should expect, intervals do not provide us with a means to magically circumvent complexity problems. What they do provide, however, is the ability to track our progress in solving a problem. For the majority of real world problems, where exact knowledge is not imperative, this will often allow us to stop early once we have a "narrow enough" interval. At the very least, we can give up early if convergence is too slow. This should be contrasted to other methods of evaluating expressions where we can never be sure whether the method is completely stuck, or is just about to return the solution.

4.9.1 Examples

Let us now consider some more examples in which our interval arithmetic approach can be shown to be useful and correct. Since *Knows'* is correct with respect to *Knows*, we know that we can not derive any false relationships using *Knows'*. The important point is that, as we shall now proceed to demonstrate, many true and useful relationships hold.

Suppose we have two relational fluents P and Q, and that we know P is true or we know Q is true. Then

$$\textit{Knows}\,(P, s) \vee \textit{Knows}\,(Q, s).$$

Using the K-fluent it is not hard to see that this implies that we know P or Q:

$$Knows\,(P \vee Q, s).$$

Proof. The proof involves expanding out the definition of *Knows*.

$$Knows\,(P, s) \vee Knows\,(Q, s) \triangleq (\forall s'\ \mathsf{K}(s', s) \Rightarrow P(s')) \vee (\forall s''\ \mathsf{K}(s'', s) \Rightarrow Q(s'')),$$

and then proceeding by case analysis. First consider the case when

$$\forall s'\ \mathsf{K}(s', s) \Rightarrow P(s').$$

Then we can weaken the postcondition to give

$$\forall s'\ \mathsf{K}(s', s) \Rightarrow P(s') \vee Q(s').$$

The other case is symmetrical, and the result follows from the definition of *Knows* given in Equation 4.1.   □

It is also not hard to see that the implication does *not* hold the other way around. As a counterexample, consider the case when we have exactly two K-related situations: s_a and s_b, such that $P(s_a)$, $\neg Q(s_a)$, $\neg P(s_b)$ and $Q(s_b)$.

Now consider the same example using interval-fluents. Once again we can easily prove that

$$Knows'\,(P, s) \vee Knows'\,(Q, s) \Rightarrow Knows'\,(P \vee Q, s).$$

Proof. We begin by expanding the definitions:

$$\mathcal{I}_{Knows}\,(P, s) = \langle 1, 1 \rangle \vee \mathcal{I}_{Knows}\,(Q, s) = \langle 1, 1 \rangle,$$

and proceed by case analysis. When

$$\mathcal{I}_{Knows}\,(P, s) = \langle 1, 1 \rangle,$$

from Definitions 4.9.2 we have that

$$\mathcal{I}_{Knows}\,(P \vee Q, s) = \langle 1, 1 \rangle.$$

The other case is symmetrical, and the result follows from the definition of *Knows'* given in Equation 4.10.   □

Conversely, if we start from the assumption

$$Knows'(P \lor Q, s) \triangleq \mathcal{I}_{Knows}(P \lor Q, s) = \langle 1, 1 \rangle,$$

then all that Definitions 4.9.2 allow us to conclude is tautologies, namely that $\mathcal{I}_{Knows}(P, s) \subseteq \langle 0, 1 \rangle$ and $\mathcal{I}_{Knows}(Q, s) \subseteq \langle 0, 1 \rangle$. That is, we can say nothing about our knowledge of P or our knowledge of Q. So, as we should hope, the implication does *not* hold the other way around.

Let us now consider some more examples. Consider knowing P to be false: $Knows(\neg P, s)$ versus not knowing P: $\neg Knows(P, s)$. Firstly, if we assume that K is reflexive, then we have that

$$Knows(\neg P, s) \Rightarrow \neg Knows(P, s).$$

Proof. The proof is straightforward. We don't know P if, in at least one of the K-related worlds, P is false. So, if P is false in all the K-related worlds the result follows. We just have to be careful that there are any K-related worlds at all. This can be inferred from the fact that K is reflexive, so $\mathsf{K}(s, s)$. □

The implication clearly does not hold in the other direction. Likewise, we have that

$$Knows'(\neg P, s) \Rightarrow \neg Knows'(P, s).$$

Proof.

$$Knows'(\neg P, s)$$
$$\triangleq \quad \mathcal{I}_{Knows}(\neg P, s) = \langle 1, 1 \rangle$$
$$\Rightarrow \quad \mathcal{I}_{Knows}(P, s) = \langle 0, 0 \rangle$$
$$\Rightarrow \quad \mathcal{I}_{Knows}(P, s) \neq \langle 1, 1 \rangle$$
$$\Rightarrow \quad \neg \mathcal{I}_{Knows}(P, s) = \langle 1, 1 \rangle.$$

□

Conversely

$$\neg Knows'(P, s)$$
$$\triangleq \quad \neg \mathcal{I}_{Knows}(P, s) = \langle 1, 1 \rangle$$
$$\Rightarrow \quad \mathcal{I}_{Knows}(P, s) = \langle 0, 0 \rangle \lor \mathcal{I}_{Knows}(P, s) = \langle 0, 1 \rangle.$$

Case (i)

$$\mathcal{I}_{Knows}(P, s) = \langle 0, 0 \rangle$$
$$\Rightarrow \quad \mathcal{I}_{Knows}(\neg P, s) = \langle 1, 1 \rangle,$$

but for Case (ii)

$$\mathcal{I}_{Knows}(P, s) = \langle 0, 1 \rangle$$
$$\Rightarrow \quad \mathcal{I}_{Knows}(\neg P, s) = \langle 0, 1 \rangle$$

so as we should hope, the implication does not hold the other way around.

Now, consider the example of $\exists x \ Knows(P(x), s)$, versus $Knows(\exists x \ P(x), s)$. Firstly we have that

$$\exists x \ Knows(P(x), s) \Rightarrow Knows(\exists x \ P(x), s).$$

Proof. $Knows(\exists x \ P(x), s)$ holds if in each K-related situation s' there is a constant $c_{s'}$ such that $P(c_{s'}, s')$ holds. Note, the constant $c_{s'}$ that makes $P(x, s)$ true can be a different constant in each s'. Our assumption, however, is that there is some constant c such that $P(c, s')$ holds in every K-related situation s'. Therefore, in each K-related situation s', we can simply set $c = c_{s'}$, and the result follows. $\qquad\square$

The implication clearly does not hold in the other direction.
Now consider the same example using intervals. We also have that

$$\exists x \ Knows'(P(x), s) \Rightarrow Knows'(\exists x \ P(x), s).$$

Proof.

$$\exists x \ Knows'(P(x), s)$$
$$\triangleq \exists x \ \mathcal{I}_{Knows}(P(x), s) = \langle 1, 1 \rangle.$$

Then, for some constant c, we have that

$$\mathcal{I}_{Knows}(P(c), s) = \langle 1, 1 \rangle$$
$$\Rightarrow \quad \mathcal{I}_{Knows}(\exists x \ P(x), s) \subseteq \langle 1, 1 \rangle$$
$$\Rightarrow \quad \mathcal{I}_{Knows}(\exists x \ P(x), s) = \langle 1, 1 \rangle.$$

$$\square$$

In the other direction we have that

$$Knows'\,(\exists x\ P(x),s)$$
$$\triangleq\ \mathcal{I}_{Knows}(\exists x\ P(x),s)=\langle 1,1\rangle$$
$$\Rightarrow\ \mathcal{I}_{Knows}(P(c),s)\subseteq\langle 0,1\rangle,$$

which is a tautology, from which we can (rightly) conclude nothing.

Finally, in Section 4.1.3, we saw that we could make deductions based on *modus ponens*. Fortunately, we can perform similar reasoning with intervals.

Theorem 4.9.1. *Let τ_0 and τ_1 be terms for that take on values in $\mathbb{B}$, such that $\langle u,v\rangle$ is a valid interval value for $\mathcal{I}_{Knows}(\tau_0,s)$, and $\tau_0[s]\Rightarrow\tau_1[s]$. Then, $\mathcal{I}_{Knows}(\tau_1,s)\subseteq\langle u,1\rangle$.*

Proof. Since $\langle u,v\rangle$ is a valid value for $\mathcal{I}_{Knows}(\tau_0,s)$, by Definition 4.8.1, we have that

$$\mathcal{I}_{Knows}(\tau_0,s)=\langle u,v\rangle\triangleq\forall s'\ \mathsf{K}(s',s)\Rightarrow\tau_0[s']\in\langle u,v\rangle.$$

In particular, $u\tau_0[s']$. Also, by the assumption that $\tau_0[s]\Rightarrow\tau_1[s]$, we have that $\tau_0[s']\leqslant\tau_1[s']$. Hence, $u\leqslant\tau_0[s']\tau_1[s']\leqslant 1$, to give us that

$$\forall s'\ \mathsf{K}(s',s)\Rightarrow\tau_1[s']\in\langle u,1\rangle.$$

Therefore, by Definition 4.8.1, $\langle u,1\rangle$ is a valid interval for $\mathcal{I}_{Knows}(\tau_1,s)$, as required. $\qquad\square$

4.10 Notes

The first approach to incorporating knowledge-producing actions into the situation calculus was described in [97]. In [118], the same approach was extended to include a solution to the frame problem. Our description (in Section 4.1.1) of the defining *Knows*, using the K-fluent, is taken from [118]. As we explained in the text, the approach is particularly important from a theoretical perspective. In particular, the correctness results for *Knows* (and hence by extension for *Knows'*) are proven. The approach described in [16] uses a different approach, but still suffers from the problem of how to represent the initial situation that we described in Section 4.1.3. In [5], an elaborate scheme is devised to extend the K-fluent approach to handle noisy sensors. Extending the approach to also handle sensing changing values is a work in progress. The latest results can usually be found at [58].

Unfortunately, most people who study theoretical problems in AI don't seem to be very concerned about implementation. By the same token, most practitioners are not very interested in theoretical issues and often come up with ad hoc solutions from which it can be hard to make any significant generalizations. Probably the most unfortunate side-effect of this polarization is that there are few researchers able to appreciate a principled solution that is also easy to implement. The approach we advocate in the text, that uses interval arithmetic, is our own. It was thought up in 1997, and was first published in [47, 45] and, as far as we are aware, remains the only proposal for incorporating sensing into a cognitive model in a way that can be easily implemented on a computer.

Traditionally, interval arithmetic was used to address the innumerable problems with the ability of floating point arithmetic to accurately represent real arithmetic. For example, consider the real number $\sqrt{2}$. This real number cannot be represented exactly by any finite decimal. However, it can be represented by the *exact* interval $\langle 1.41, 1.42 \rangle$. What this interval can be used to express is that $\sqrt{2}$ lies somewhere between 1.41 and 1.42. That is, it expresses our uncertainty about the exact value of $\sqrt{2}$ when expressed as a decimal. With modern computers our degree of uncertainty can be made miniscule and this is part of the appeal of interval arithmetic. Interval arithmetic was first proposed in [98, 99]. The centered forms are documented in [1]. Jeffrey Tupper's thesis on generalized interval arithmetic is undoubtedly a work of genius [138], but it is also "notationally dense." While we look forward to the publication of a simplified version, readers might like to experience some of the potential of interval arithmetic by downloading his remarkable reliable graphing program GRAFEQ[126]. In [105], interval arithmetic is compared to probability as a means of representing uncertainty. Blake canonical form is described in [21]. In [79], it is used in the way we describe in Section 4.9 to develop a three-valued logic for efficient run-time reasoning.

Note that IVE fluents represent *uncertainty intervals* about time-dependent variables. They do not represent and are unrelated to *time intervals* of the sort that have been used in the underlying semantics of various temporal logics (for example see [107]).

In the previous chapter, we first identified relations with Boolean-valued functions. In this chapter, this simplification avoids us having to treat relations as a special case when we produce interval versions of our number systems. The three-valued logic that arises naturally from the "intervalization" of the Booleans is further explicitly documented in [138]. It is also implicitly discussed in [79].

Character Instruction

In this chapter, we discuss the problem of instructing an autonomous character on how to behave. As we explained in Chapter 1, we assume that a character's behavior is completely determined by the sequence of actions that it executes. We distinguish two broad possibilities for instructing a character on how to behave: *predefined behavior* and *goal-directed behavior*. Of course, in some sense, all of a character's behavior is defined in advance by the animator/programmer. Therefore, to be more precise, the distinction between predefined and goal-directed behavior is based on whether the character can nondeterministically select actions or not.

What we mean by nondeterministic action selection is that whenever a character chooses an action it also remembers the other choices it could have made. If, after thinking about the choices it did make, the character realizes that the resulting sequence of actions will not result in a desirable outcome, then it can go back and consider any of the alternative sequence of actions that would have resulted from a different set of choices. It is free to do this until it either finds a suitable action sequence, or exhausts all the (possibly exponential number of) possibilities.

A character that can nondeterministically select actions is usually a lot easier to instruct, but has a slower response time. In particular, we can tell a cognitive character what constitutes a "desirable outcome" by giving it goals, and it can then use its background domain knowledge to figure out whether it believes a given action sequence will achieve those goals or not. Although we are using the word "nondeterministic" in a precise technical sense, the trade-off between execution speed and programming effort should already be a familiar and intuitive concept for many readers.

A third possibility we will consider is something of a compromise between the two extremes of predefined and goal-directed behavior. In particular, we introduce the notion of *complex actions* and explain how they can be used to provide goals, and a "sketch plan" for how to achieve those goals.

Before we continue, it is worth pointing out that sometimes people identify a particular class of programming languages with a particular kind of behavior. For example, logic programming languages are often associated with nondeterministic goal-directed behavior, and regular imperative languages with deterministic predefined behavior. While it is true that logic programming languages have built-in support for nondeterministic programming, there is nothing to stop us implementing either kind of behavior in any programming language we choose (assuming it is Turing complete). To avoid unnecessary confusion, we shall not tie the following discussion to any particular programming languages.

5.1   Predefined Behavior

There are many convenient techniques we can use to predefine a character's behavior. In this book, however, we are more interested in techniques for which the character's behavior is not completely determined in advance. Therefore, we shall not attempt a comprehensive survey of techniques for predefining behavior. Instead, we shall take a brief look at two particularly popular approaches: reactive behavior rules, and hierarchical finite-state machines (HFSM).

5.1.1   Reactive Behavior Rules

We will use the term *reactive behavior* when a character's behavior is based solely on its perception of the current situation. What we mean by this is that the character has no memory of previous situations it has encountered. In particular, there is no representation of its own internal state and so it will always react in the same way to the same input stimuli, regardless of the order in which the inputs are received. A simple way to encode reactive behavior is as a set of stimulus-response rules. This has a number of important advantages:

- Although the set of rules might be short, and each of the rules very simple, that doesn't necessarily mean the behavior that results from the character following the rules is simple at all. That is, we can often capture extremely sophisticated behavior with some simple rules.

- We can usually evaluate the rules extremely quickly so there should be no problem obtaining real-time response from our characters.

- There is no need to worry about all the knowledge representation issues we discussed in the last chapter. That is, the characters are not doing any thinking for themselves; we have done it all for them, in advance.

The use of reactive behavior rules was also one of the first approaches proposed for generating character behaviors, and it is still one of the most popular and commonplace techniques. Great success has been obtained in developing rule sets for various kinds of behavior, such as flocking and collision avoidance. As an example of a simple stimulus-response rule that can result in extremely sophisticated behavior, consider the following rule:

if blockedAhead **then** turnLeft **else** goStraight

Believe it or not, this simple "left-hand rule" will let a character find its way through a maze. It is an excellent example of how one simple little rule can be used to generate highly complex behavior. The character that follows this rule doesn't need to know it is in a maze, or that it is trying to get out. It blindly follows the rule and the maze-solving ability simply "emerges." Someone else did all the thinking about the problem in advance and managed to boil the solution down to one simple instruction that can be executed mindlessly. This example also shows how difficult thinking up these simple sets of reactive behavior rules can be. In particular, it is hard to imagine being the one who thought this rule up in the first place, and it even requires some effort to convince oneself that it works.

We can thus see that despite some of the advantages, there are also some serious drawbacks to using sets of reactive behavior rules:

- The biggest problem is thinking up the correct set of rules that leads to the behavior we want. It can require enormous ingenuity to think of the right set of rules and this can be followed by hours of tweaking parameters to get things exactly right.

- The difficult and laborious process of generating the rules will often have to be repeated, at least in part, every time we want to effect even a slight change in the resulting behavior.

- Since the behavior rules are deterministic, once an action is chosen, there is no way to reconsider the choice. There are many cases when a cognitive character could use its domain knowledge to quickly anticipate that an action choice is not appropriate. An autonomous character has no ability to make such judgements and, regardless of how appropriate it is, must blindly follow the predefined behavior rules that pertain to the current situation.

- When there are many rules it is quite likely their applicability will overlap and they could give conflicting suggestions on which action to choose. In such cases some *conflict resolution* strategy must be employed.

It is often easier to write a controller if we can maintain some simple internal state information for the character. One popular way to do this is with HFSM that we discuss in the next section.

5.1.2   Hierarchical Finite-state Machines (HFSM)

Finite-state machines (FSMs) consist of a set of states (including an initial state), a set of inputs, a set of outputs, and a state transition function. The state transition function takes the input and the current state and returns a *single* new state and a set of outputs. Since there is only one possible new state, FSMs are used to encode deterministic behavior. It is commonplace, and convenient, to represent FSMs with *state transition diagrams*. A state transition diagram uses circles to represent the states and arrows to represent

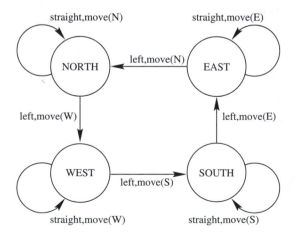

Figure 5.1. The WhichDir FSM.

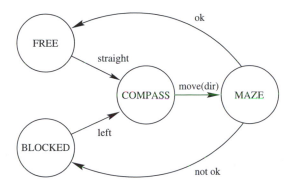

Figure 5.2. HFSM that uses the WhichDir FSM.

the transitions between states. Figure 5.1 depicts an FSM that keeps track of which compass direction a character is heading each time it turns "left:"

As the name implies, an HFSM is simply a hierarchy of FSMs. That is, each node of an HFSM may itself be an HFSM. Just like functions and procedures in a regular programming language, this provides a convenient way to make the design of an FSM more modular. For example, if a character is at coordinates (x, y), Figure 5.2 depicts an HFSM that uses the FSM in Figure 5.1 as a submodule to calculate the new cell after turning "left," or moving one cell ahead.

HFSMs are powerful tools for developing sophisticated behavior and it is easy to develop graphical user interfaces to assist in building them. This has made them a popular choice for animators and game developers alike.

HFSMs maintain much of the simplicity of sets of reactive-behavior rules but, by adding a notion of internal state, make it easier to develop more sophisticated behaviors. Unfortunately, they also have some of the same drawbacks. In particular, actions are chosen deterministically and there is no explicit separation of domain knowledge from control information. This can lead to a solution which is messy, hard to understand and all but impossible to maintain. In Section 9.1, we can see a comparison of a goal-directed behavior specification of a camera controller versus an HFSM one. Just like reactive-behavior rules, there can also be a large amount of work involved if we want to obtain even slightly different behavior from an HFSM.

5.2   Goal-directed Behavior

The first step in describing goal-directed behavior is to come up with a way to define a cognitive character's goals. As in previous chapters, the situation calculus provides a simple and intuitive theoretical framework to explain how this can be done. In particular, a character's goals can be expressed in terms of the desired value of various relevant fluents. A goal can therefore be expressed as a defined fluent, i.e., a fluent defined in terms of other fluents (see Chapter 3, Section 2.6). For instance, if we recall the running example from Chapter 3, we can state that Dognap's goal is to kill Jack:

$$\text{goal}(s') \Leftrightarrow \neg Alive(s').$$

Clearly, Dognap will have achieved this goal in any situation s' for which goal(s') is true. We recall that any situation is either the initial situation s_0, or of the form $s' = do(a_{n-1}, \cdots, do(a_0, s_0) \cdots)$. Therefore, if goal$(s_0)$ is not true, then Dognap must *search* for a sequence of n actions, $a_0, \ldots, a_{n-1}$, such that

$$\text{goal}(do(a_{n-1}, \cdots, do(a_0, s_0) \cdots)).$$

5.2.1   Situation Tree

To explain how characters can automatically search for sequences of actions that meet their goals, we will introduce the idea of a *situation tree*. In particular, we can think of the actions and effects as describing a tree of possible future situations. The root of the tree is the initial situation s_0, each branch of the tree is an action, and each node is a situation. Figure 5.3 shows an example of a tree with n actions, $a_0, a_1, \ldots, a_{n-1}$.

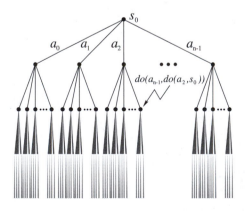

Figure 5.3. An abstract situation tree.

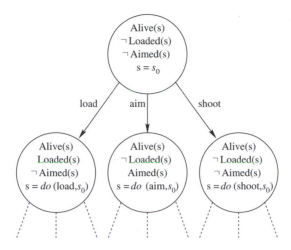

Figure 5.4. A concrete example of a situation tree.

The value of the fluents at each node (situation) is determined by the effect axioms. Figure 5.4 shows a simple concrete example using the Dognap and Jack example, and the corresponding effect axioms, that we described in Chapter 3.

A *goal situation* is a situation in which the goal fluent is true. For example, in Figure 5.4 we can see that if the goal is still to kill Jack then the situation

$$s' = do(\textbf{shoot}, do(\textbf{aim}, \text{s}_0))$$

is a goal situation. We can see that in this example there are many goal situations, for example

$$s' = do(\textbf{shoot}, do(\textbf{aim}, do(\textbf{aim}, \text{s}_0)))$$

is another goal situation. In general, however, there is no guarantee that a goal situation exists at all. If a goal situation does exist, then any action sequence that leads to one of the goal situations is called *a plan*.

Figure 5.5 shows a simple abstract situation tree with just three actions, and three goal situations. We will use this figure to illustrate how a character can search the tree to automatically find a plan (a path) that leads from the initial situation (the root) to a goal situation. Depending on how we choose to search the tree we will find different plans (paths). In particular, we can see some common search strategies being applied. We can see that a bounded

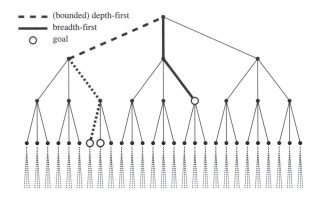

Figure 5.5. An abstract situation tree with just three actions.

depth-first search strategy finds the plan $[a_0, a_2, a_0]$, whereas a breadth first search finds $[a_1, a_2]$.

A breadth-first search tries exhaustively searching each layer of the tree before proceeding to the next layer. That is, it considers all plans of length 0, then all plans of length 1, etc. Thus, a breadth-first search is guaranteed to find a plan if there is one. Moreover it will find the shortest such plan. Unfortunately, a breadth-first search requires an exponential amount of memory as the character has to remember all the previous searches.

A depth-first search doesn't require an exponential amount of memory as there is no need to explicitly store large portions of the tree. That is, a depth-first search only needs to remember one branch of the tree at a time. It keeps looking down this one branch until it gets to a goal, or it reaches a leaf node. If it reaches a leaf-node, it backs up to the previous node and searches another branch. If there are no more branches, it backs up one step further and proceeds recursively until it has searched the entire tree. Unfortunately, even if there is a goal in the tree, depth-first search is not guaranteed to find it. In particular, it is quite likely that the tree will have branches that are infinite. That is, the character can just keep doing some sequence of actions over and over again, but it never leads to a goal. A depth-first search can get sidetracked by searching down one of these fruitless infinite branches. Because it never reaches a goal, or a leaf node, the algorithm never terminates. Another drawback of a depth-first search is that even if it does find *a plan*, this plan is not guaranteed to be the shortest possible plan. Depending on the application, this may or may not be important.

A bounded depth-first search attempts to resolve some of the limitations of a depth-first search by putting a bound on how deeply in the tree the search can proceed. Now the search backs up if it finds a leaf node, *or* if the maximum search depth is exceeded. It is even possible to iteratively search with a deeper and deeper bound. To avoid redoing the work of the previous search, the results of the last search can be stored so that we don't have to begin from scratch each time the depth bound is increased. Unfortunately, we are now back to remembering large portions of the tree and, just like a breadth-first search, this requires an exponential amount of memory.

In the worst case, the situation tree does not contain any goal situations. If this is the case, then any exhaustive search algorithm will take an exponential amount of time to respond that there is no plan available to achieve the goal. This is one of the major limitations of planning and is something we will look at in more detail in the next section. In the meantime, we mention that looking for different search algorithms is an important topic in AI research and the interested reader should consult the further reading section. One of the most interesting new developments is the use of stochastic search algorithms.

It should also now be apparent how choosing actions nondeterministically entails searching for appropriate action sequences in a search space that potentially grows exponentially. This corresponds to the usual computer science notion of computational complexity. Another interesting point to note is that CPU processing power is also growing exponentially. Therefore, according to Moore's law, our computer characters can be expected to be able to search one layer deeper in the situation tree every eighteen months or so.

5.3   The Middle Ground

As we explained, for predefined behaviors the character doesn't have to do any searching for actions that achieve its goals. It simply follows the instructions it was given and ends up at a goal situation. In effect, for a given set of inputs, the path through the tree of possible situations has been determined in advance. If the predefined behaviors were defined properly, then the path that they specify through the tree will lead to a goal situation.

In this section, the question we want to ask is whether there is some middle ground between asking the character to do all the work at run-time and asking the programmer to all the work at compile time. In particular, consider that on the one hand we have predefined behavior which corresponds to a single path through the situation tree, and on the other hand we have goal-directed behavior which corresponds to searching the whole tree. Clearly, the middle ground has to be searching some subset of the tree.

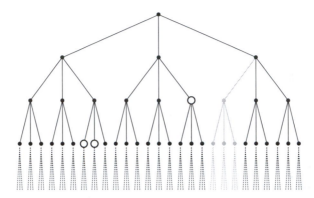

Figure 5.6. Preconditions preclude portions of the tree.

Note that this "middle ground" is still technically goal-directed behavior, but we now have control over how much nondeterminism is allowed in the behavior specification. Only in the limiting case, when we have removed all the nondeterminism, does the behavior reduce to deterministic predefined behavior.

5.3.1   Precondition Axioms

Although we might not have realized it, we have already seen one way to exclude parts of the situation tree from the search space. In particular, precondition axioms prune off whole chunks of the tree by stating that not all actions are possible in all situations. Figure 5.6 shows an example of an abstract tree in which it is not possible to do an action a_2 because an action a_1 changed something which made it impossible.

While preconditions are important for cordoning off parts of the situation tree, they are a clumsy way to try and coerce a character to search a particular portion of the tree. In particular, we need a way to give a character general purpose heuristics to help it find a goal faster. For example, we might want to give the character a heuristic that will cause it look at certain groups of actions first, but we do not want to absolutely exclude the other actions.

The hard part of exploiting the middle ground between predefined and goal-directed behavior is to think up a useful way to specify subsets of the tree. In the next section, we will introduce a convenient way to specify arbitrary subsets of the situation tree to search.

5.3.2 Complex Actions

We would like to provide a character with a "sketch plan" and have it responsible for filling in the remaining missing details. In this way, we salvage some of the convenience of the planning approach while regaining control over the complexity of the planning tasks we assign the character. We will show how we can use the idea of *complex actions* to write sketch plans.

The actions we discussed previously, defined by precondition and effect axioms, are referred to as a *primitive actions.*[1] Complex actions are abbreviations for terms in the situation calculus; they are built up from a set of recursively defined operators. Any primitive action is also a complex action. Other complex actions are composed using various operators and control structures, some of which are deliberately chosen to resemble a regular programming language. When we give a character a complex action α, there is a special macro *Do* that expands out α into terms in the situation calculus. Since complex actions expand out into regular situation calculus expressions, they inherit the solution to the frame problem for primitive actions.

Complex actions are defined by the macro $Do(\alpha, s, s')$, such that s' is a state that results from doing the complex action α in state s. The complete list of operators for the (recursive) definition of *Do* are given below. Together, the operators define an instruction language we can use to issue direction to characters. The mathematical definitions can be difficult to follow, but we will explain the basic ideas more clearly using numerous examples of complex actions throughout the remainder of this book.[2]

(Primitive Action) If α is a primitive action then, provided the precondition axiom states it is possible, do the action.

$$Do(\alpha, s, s') \triangleq Poss(\alpha, s) \wedge s' = do(\alpha, s).$$

(Sequence) $\alpha \, ; \, \beta$ means do action α, followed by action β.

$$Do((\alpha \, ; \, \beta), s, s') \triangleq \exists s^* \, (Do(\alpha, s, s^*) \wedge Do(\beta, s^*, s')).$$

(Test) p? succeeds if p is true, otherwise it fails.

$$Do(\phi?, s, s') \triangleq \phi[s] \wedge s = s',$$

where $\phi[s]$ is ϕ with situation arguments inserted, e.g., if $\phi = $ Alive then $\phi[s] = $ Alive(s)).

---

[1]The term "primitive action" is only meant to indicate an action is an atomic unit, and not a compound action. Unfortunately, the term can be misleading when the action actually refers to some sophisticated behavior, but we will stick with the term as it is widely used in the available literature.

[2]In Chapter 8, we mention two freely available implementations of complex actions that can be studied for a more practical insight into how the macro expansion works.

(Nondeterministic choice of actions) $\alpha \mid \beta$ means do action α or action β.

$$Do\left((\alpha|\beta), s, s'\right) \triangleq Do\left(\alpha, s, s'\right) \vee Do\left(\beta, s, s'\right)$$

(Conditionals) **if** p α **else** β **fi** is just shorthand for $p?\ \overset{\circ}{\circ}\ \alpha \mid (\neg p)?\ \overset{\circ}{\circ}\ \beta$.

(Non-deterministic iteration) $\alpha \star$ means do α zero or more times.

$$Do\left(\alpha^{\star}, s, s'\right) \triangleq$$
$$\forall P\ \{[\forall s_1\ P(s_1, s_1)] \wedge \forall s_1, s_2, s_3\ [P(s_1, s_2) \wedge Do\left(\alpha, s_2, s_3\right) \Rightarrow P(s_1, s_3)]\}$$
$$\Rightarrow P(s, s').$$

(Iteration) **while** p **do** α **od** is just shorthand for $(p?\ \overset{\circ}{\circ}\ \alpha)^{\star}|(\neg p?)$.

(Nondeterministic choice of arguments) $(\pi\ x)\ \alpha$ means pick some argument x and perform the action $\alpha(x)$.

$$Do\left((\pi x)\alpha(x), s, s'\right) \triangleq \exists x\ Do\left(\alpha(x), s, s'\right)$$

(Procedures) **proc** $P(x_1, \dots, x_n)$ α **end** declares a procedure. The mathematical definition is just the situation calculus version of standard Scott-Strackey's least fixed-point definition of (recursive) procedure execution.

$$Do\left((\mathbf{proc}\ P(x_1, \dots, x_n)\alpha\ \mathbf{end})\ \beta, s, s'\right) \triangleq$$
$$\forall P\ [\forall x_1, \dots, x_n, s_1, s_2\ Do\left(\alpha, s_1, s_2\right) \Rightarrow$$
$$Do\left(P(x_1, \dots, x_n), s_1, s_2\right)] \Rightarrow Do\left(\beta, s, s'\right).$$

The procedure can be called as $P(x_1, \dots, x_n)$.

$$Do\left(P(x_1, \dots x_n), s, s'\right) \triangleq P(x_1[s], \dots x_n[s], s, s').$$

The macro expansion $Do\left(\alpha, s, s'\right)$ specifies a relation between two situations s and s', such that s' is a situation that results from doing the complex action α in situation s. In general, there is not a unique s', so if we have some initial situation s_0, a complex action *program*, and a bunch of precondition and effect axioms, then $Do\left(program, s_0, s'\right)$ specifies a subset of the situation tree. Figure 5.7 shows a quick example of how a complex action can be used to limit the search space to some arbitrary subset of the situation tree. The other thing we can see from the figure is that the mathematical syntax can be rather cryptic. Therefore, in Chapter 8, we introduce some alternative syntax for defining complex actions that is more intuitive and easy to read.

On its own, just specifying subsets of the situation tree is not particularly useful. Therefore, we would normally explicitly mention the goal within the complex action. We shall see many examples of this in what follows. For now, suppose the complex action *program* is such a complex action. If we can find

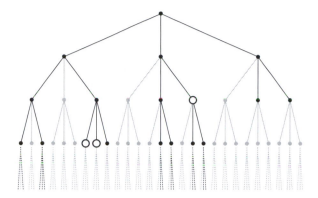

Figure 5.7. Effect of the complex action $(a_0\star; a_2; (a_0|a_1|a_2))|(a_1; (a_1|a_2)\star)$ on a situation tree.

any $s' = do(a_{n-1}, \cdots, do(a_0, s_0) \cdots)$ such that $Do(program, s_0, s')$, then the plan of length n, represented by the actions $a_0, \ldots, a_{n-1}$, is the behavior that the character believes will result in it obtaining its goals. Finding such an s' is just a matter of searching the (pruned) situation tree for a suitable goal situation. Since we still end up searching, research in planning algorithms is just as relevant to this section as to the straight goal-directed specification section.

5.3.3 Implementation

Note that we defined the notion of a situation tree to help us visualize some important ideas. We do not mean to suggest that in any corresponding implementation that there need be (although, of course, there may be) any data structure that explicitly represents this tree. In particular, if we explicitly represent the tree, then we need a potentially exponential amount of memory. Therefore, it makes more sense to simply build portions of the tree on demand, and delete them when they are no longer required. In theorem provers and logic programming languages (e.g., Prolog), this is exactly what happens continually behind the scenes.

Logic programming languages also make it straightforward to underspecify the domain knowledge. For example, it is perfectly acceptable to specify an initial state that contains a disjunction, e.g., OnTable(cup, s_0) $\vee$ OnFloor(cup, s_0). Later on, we can include information that precludes a previously possible disjunct, and the character will still make valid inferences without us having to go back and alter any of the previous information. If we do not need such a sophisticated notion of elaboration tolerance, then it might be simpler to build a situation tree explicitly. Moreover, if the tree is not too deep, or if it is heavily pruned, it needn't be excessively large and thus can be fast to search. Whether such a shallow, or sparse, tree is useful or not will depend on the particular application, but in computer games and animation there are countless examples where a character with even a moderate ability to plan ahead can be extremely useful.

5.4   A Simple Tutorial Example: Maze Solving

We already looked at some predefined behavior for solving a maze. Let's take a look at a goal-directed approach to the problem. Of course, since there are well-known predefined behaviors for maze solving, we would not suggest using a goal-directed approach in a real application. Therefore, this section is simply meant as a tutorial example to show how some of the pieces from this, and Chapter 3, fit together.

5.4.1   Domain Knowledge

Let us suppose we have a maze defined by a predicate $\mathsf{Free}(c)$, that holds when, and only when, the grid cell c is "free." That is, it is within range and is not occupied by an obstacle.

$$\mathsf{Free}(c) \Leftrightarrow \mathsf{InRange}(c) \wedge \neg\mathsf{Occupied}(c), \quad \text{where}$$
$$\mathsf{InRange}((x,y)) \Leftrightarrow 0 \leqslant x < \mathsf{size}_x \wedge 0 \leqslant y < \mathsf{size}_y$$

$\mathsf{Occupied}(c)$, size_x, and size_y each depend upon the maze in question. In addition, there are two maze dependent constants start and exit that specify the entry and exit points of a maze. Figure 5.8 shows a simple maze and the corresponding definition.

We also need to define some functions that describe a path within the maze. We say that the adjacent cell "North" of a given cell is the one directly above it, similarly for "South," "East," and "West."

$$\mathsf{adjacent}((x,y),d) = \begin{cases} (x+1,y) & \text{if } d = \text{north} \\ (x-1,y) & \text{if } d = \text{south} \\ (x,y+1) & \text{if } d = \text{east} \\ (x,y-1) & \text{if } d = \text{west} \end{cases}$$

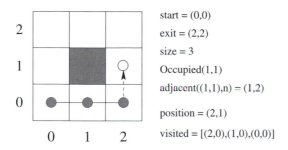

Figure 5.8. A simple maze.

There are two fluents; position denotes which cell contains the character in the current situation, and visited denotes the cells the character has previously visited.

The single action in this example is a *move* action that takes one of four compass directions as a parameter. It is possible to move in some direction d, provided the cell to which we are moving is free and has not been visited before.

$$Poss\,(move(d,s)) \Leftrightarrow \exists c\; c = \mathsf{adjacent}(\mathsf{position}(s),d) \wedge \mathsf{Free}(c) \wedge c \notin \mathsf{visited}(s)$$

Figure 5.9 shows the possible directions a character can move when in two different situations.

A fluent is completely specified by its initial value and its successor-state axiom. For example, the initial position is given as the start point of the maze and the effect of moving to a new cell is to update the position accordingly.

$$\mathsf{position}(s_0) = \mathsf{start}$$
$$Poss\,(a,s) \Rightarrow [\mathsf{position}(do(a,s)) = p' \Leftrightarrow (\exists d\; a = move(d) \wedge$$
$$p' = \mathsf{adjacent}(\mathsf{position}(s),d)) \vee (\neg\exists d\; a = move(d) \wedge p' = \mathsf{position}(s))]$$

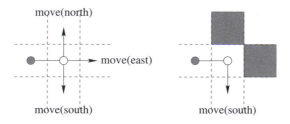

Figure 5.9. Possible directions to move.

So for example, in Figure 5.8, if the character has previously been to the locations marked with the filled dots, and in situation s the character moves north to the unfilled dot, then we have that $\mathsf{position}(s) = (2,0)$ and that $\mathsf{position}(do(move(\mathsf{north}), s)) = (2,1)$.

The list of cells visited so far is given by the defined fluent $\mathsf{visited}(s)$. It is defined recursively on the situation to be the list of all the positions in previous situations (we use standard Prolog list notation).

$$\mathsf{visited}(S_0) \triangleq []$$

$$\mathsf{visited}(do(a, s)) \triangleq \begin{cases} [\mathsf{position}(s)|\mathsf{visited}(s)] & \text{if } \exists d\ a = move(d) \\ \mathsf{visited}(s) & \text{otherwise} \end{cases}$$

For example, in Figure 5.8, when

$$s = do(move(\mathsf{east}), do(move(\mathsf{east}), do(move(\mathsf{north}), S_0))),$$

we have that $\mathsf{position}(s) = (2,1)$, and that $\mathsf{visited}(s) = [(2,0),(1,0),(0,0)]$.

5.4.2 Character Instruction

We have now completed telling the character everything it needs to know about the concept of a maze. Now we need to move on and use complex actions to tell it about its goal and any heuristics that might help it achieve those goals. As a first pass, let's not give it any heuristics, but simply provide a goal-directed specification of maze-solving behavior. Using complex actions we can express this behavior elegantly as follows:

$$\textbf{while } \mathsf{position} \neq \mathsf{exit } \textbf{ do}$$
$$(\pi\ d)\ move(d)$$
$$\textbf{od}$$

Just like a regular "while" loop, the above program expands out into a sequence of actions. Unlike a regular "while" loop, it expands out, not into one particular sequence of actions, but into *all possible* sequences of actions. The precondition axioms that we previously stated, and the exit condition of the loop, define a possible sequence of actions. Therefore, any free path through the maze, which does not backtrack and ends at the exit position, meets the behavior specification.

Note that the use of regular programming constructs may initially cause confusion to the reader of the above code. Most of the work is being done by the nondeterministic choice of arguments operator "π." The example makes it clear that by "nondeterministic" we do not mean that anything random is happening; we simply mean that we can specify a large number of possibilities all at once. In particular, the $(\pi\ d)$ construct should be read as "pick the *correct* direction d." For the mathematically inclined, perusing the definitions may serve to alleviate any sense of bewilderment. To make things even clearer we shall, however, consider the expansion of the complex actions in terms of their definitions. The expansion is based on the simple maze described previously in Figure 5.8.

In the initial situation we have

$$\text{position}(s_0) \neq \text{exit}.$$

Thus the guard of the "while" loop holds and we can try to expand

$$Do\left((\pi\ d)\ move(d), s_0, s\right).$$

Expanding this out into the full definition gives

$$(Poss\left(move(\text{north}), s_0\right) \wedge s = do(move(\text{north}), s_0)) \vee$$
$$(Poss\left(move(\text{south}), s_0\right) \wedge s = do(move(\text{south}), s_0)) \vee$$
$$(Poss\left(move(\text{east}), s_0\right) \wedge s = do(move(\text{east}), s_0)) \vee$$
$$(Poss\left(move(\text{west}), s_0\right) \wedge s = do(move(\text{west}), s_0)).$$

However, from the action preconditions for *Poss* and the definition of the maze we can see that:

$$Poss\left(move(\text{north})\right) \wedge \neg Poss\left(move(\text{south})\right) \wedge$$
$$Poss\left(move(\text{east})\right) \wedge \neg Poss\left(move(\text{west})\right)$$

This leaves us with

$$s = do(move(\text{north}), s_0) \vee s = do(move(\text{east}), s_0).$$

That is, there are two possible resulting situations. That is why we refer to this style of program as nondeterministic.

In contrast, in situation $s = do(move(\text{north}), s_0)$ there is only one possible resulting situation. We have that $Do\left((\pi\ d)\ move(d), s, s'\right)$ expands out into $s' = do(move(\text{north}), s)$.

If we expand out the macro

$$Do\left(\textbf{while } \text{position} \neq \text{exit } \textbf{do}(\pi\ d)\ move(d)\ \textbf{od}, s_0, s_f\right)$$

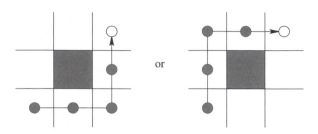

Figure 5.10. Valid behaviors.

from start to finish, we get

$$s_f = do(move(\text{east}),$$
$$do(move(\text{east}),$$
$$do(move(\text{north}),$$
$$do(move(\text{north}), s_0)))) \vee$$
$$s_f = do(move(\text{north}),$$
$$do(move(\text{north}),$$
$$do(move(\text{east}),$$
$$do(move(\text{east}), s_0)))).$$

So, as depicted in Figure 5.10, our "program" does indeed specify all paths through the maze.

Although we disallow backtracking in the final path through the maze, the character may use backtracking when it is reasoning about valid paths. In most of the mazes we tried, the character can reason using a depth-first search to find a path through a given maze quickly. For example, Figure 5.11 shows a path through a reasonably complicated maze that was found in a few seconds.

To speed things up, we can start to reduce some of the nondeterminism by giving the character some heuristic knowledge. For example, we can use complex actions to specify a "best-first" search strategy. In this approach, we will not leave it up to the character to decide how to search the possible paths, but constrain it to first investigate paths that head toward the exit. This requires extra lines of code, but could result in faster execution.

For example, suppose we add an action *goodMove*(d), such that it is possible to move in a direction d if it is possible to "*move*" to the cell in that direction and the cell is closer to the goal than we are now.

$$Poss\,(goodMove(d), s) \Leftrightarrow Poss\,(move(d), s) \wedge \text{Closer}(\text{exit}, d, \text{position}(s)).$$

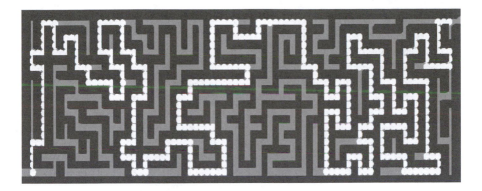

Figure 5.11. Maze solving in practice.

Now we can rewrite our high-level controller as one that prefers to move toward the exit position whenever possible.

$$\textbf{while } \text{position} \neq \text{exit } \textbf{do}$$
$$\textbf{if } \exists d \; Poss(goodMove(d)) \textbf{ then}$$
$$(\pi \; d) \; goodMove(d)$$
$$\textbf{else}$$
$$(\pi \; d) \; move(d)$$
$$\textbf{fi}$$
$$\textbf{od}$$

At the extreme, there is nothing to prevent us from coding in a simple deterministic strategy such as the "left-hand" rule. For example, if we introduce a defined fluent dir that keeps track of the direction the character is traveling, and a function ccw that returns the compass direction counterclockwise to its argument, then the following complex action implements the left-hand rule.

$$(move(\text{dir})\star; \; move(\text{ccw}(\text{dir})))\star$$

The important point is that using complex actions does not rule out any of the algorithms one might consider when writing the same program in a regular programming language. Rather, it opens up new possibilities for high-level specifications of behavior at a cognitive level of abstraction.

5.5 Discussion

Complex actions provide a convenient tool for giving a character "advice" in the form of heuristic rules that will help it solve problems faster. In general, the search space will still be exponential, but reducing the search space can make the difference between a character that can plan 5 steps ahead, say, and one that can plan 15 steps ahead. That is, we can get characters that appear a lot more intelligent

The possibility also exists for incremental refinement of a specification, perhaps, from a high-level specification to the point where it more closely resembles a controller written using a conventional imperative programming language. That is, we can quickly create a working prototype by relying heavily on goal-directed specification. If this prototype is too slow, we can use complex actions to remove more and more of the nondeterminism. If required, we can even do this to the point where the behavior is completely predefined.

To sum up, if we can think of, or look up, a simple predefined way to produce the behavior we are interested in, then it makes a lot of sense to use it. This is especially so if we don't think the behavior will need to be modified very often, or at least if the anticipated modifications are minor ones. It is not surprising, therefore, that a lot of simple reactive behavior is implemented using simple reactive behavior rules. For simple reactive behavior, like collision avoidance, it is not hard to think of a small set of reactive behavior rules that will do the job. Moreover, once we have this set of rules working, it is unlikely that we will need to modify it.

We have tried to make it clear that one type of behavior can be implemented using a variety of techniques. We have, therefore, chosen not to classify behavior according to what the character is trying to achieve, but rather on the basis of the technique used to implement it. The reader should note however that some others do try to insist that behavior in the real world is of a certain type, and its virtual world counterpart must therefore be implemented in a particular way. Unfortunately, this leads to lots of confusion and disagreement among different research camps. In particular, there are those who advocate using predefined behavior rules for implementing every kind of behavior, no matter how complex. In the sense that, given enough time and energy it can be done, they are correct. However, they are somewhat like the traditional animator who scoffs at the use of physical simulators to generate realistic-looking motion. That is, to the traditional animator a physical simulator is an anathema. She has an implicit physical model in her head and can use this to make realistic motion that looks just as good (if not better), and may only require the computer to do some simple "inbetweening." Compared to the motion that needs a physical simulator to execute, the key-framed approach is lightning fast. If we could all have the skill of a professional animator there would not be so much call for physical simulators. Unfortunately, most of us do not have the skill to draw physically-correct looking motion and are happy to receive all the help we can get from the latest technology. Even artists who can create the motion themselves might prefer to expend their energies elsewhere in the creative process.

In the same vein, many of us don't have any idea of how to come up with a simple set of stimulus-response rules that implement some complex behavior. Perhaps, we could eventually come up with something, but if we have something else we'd rather do with our time it makes sense to get the characters themselves to do some of the work for us. If we can tell them what we want them to achieve, and how their world changes, then perhaps they can figure it out for themselves.

We should also point out that there are those who advocate a cognitive modeling approach for every kind of behavior, even simple reactive ones. This view also seems too extreme as, to coin a phrase, there is no point "using a sledgehammer to crack a nut." If we have a simple reactive behavior to implement, then it makes sense to look for a simple set of predefined rules. Also, if lightning-fast performance is an absolute must, then we might be forced to use a predefined approach, no matter how tough it is to find the right set of rules.

Of course, there is a big gray area in which there is no clear answer as to whether we should just stick with predefined behavior rules or not. In such cases, the choice of how to proceed can depend on personal preference and the available tools and expertise. Obviously, this book is primarily aimed for those who decide to go the cognitive modeling route.

5.6 Notes

For some basic information on FSMs see [66]. For more in-depth information on predefined behavior techniques, consult [40, 9, 136]. There are even some commercial character development packages that use HFSMs to define character behavior. See [100] for a fascinating discussion on maze-solving techniques. Many of the classic papers on planning can be found in [2]. See [120] for some work on the use of stochastic techniques for planning. Prolog is the best known nondeterministic programming language and there are numerous references, for example see [25].

The complex action macro expansion is closely related to work done in proving properties of computer programs [54]. Our definitions are taken from those given in [80]. A more up-to-date version, that includes support for concurrency, appears in [78]. See [129] for the Scott-Strackey least fixed-point definition of (recursive) procedure execution.

Learning

When discussing cognitive characters that can learn, the relevant branch of computer science is *machine learning*. Machine learning is a broad and complex subject, so a complete survey is well beyond the scope of this book. In this chapter, our aim is simply to explain how learning fits in with cognitive modeling. In particular, we will discuss the possibility of characters learning effect axioms, and learning fast approximations to goal-directed behaviors.

Up until now we have been responsible for providing characters with domain knowledge about their world's dynamics. That is, we had to think up suitable precondition and effect axioms. Now we want to look at how a character can *acquire* that knowledge by itself through learning about its world. In many cases it would be too ambitious to expect a character to come up with a complete description of its world's dynamics all on its own, but it may still be helpful if it can learn just some single effect and precondition axioms.

In the last chapter, we also looked at how a character can use goal-directed behavior to automatically select a plan of action. Since this approach already has the character doing most of the work it seems that there is not much left to do. However, we also noted that, at run-time, planning can be expensive. In contrast, predefined behavior can usually be executed quickly, but requires us to do more work in advance. Therefore, in this chapter, we will also look at how we can learn some predefined behavior from an existing goal-directed behavior. If we can do this, then we have the best of both worlds. That is, it is not usually hard to think of a way to specify behavior in a goal-directed way, so once we have this we can then automatically "compile" the behavior into a predefined behavior so that it is also fast to execute. Once again, the ideal approach may be too ambitious and we will settle for being able to learn predefined behavior that provides a reasonable approximation to the goal-directed behavior.

6.1 Machine Learning

Almost all machine learning problems have some sort of *concept learning* at their heart. In order to learn a particular concept we give a character a *training set*. The training set contains *instances* that are labeled with values of the *target function* that the character is trying to learn. The character uses the training set to obtain a *learned function* that associates instances with labels. The idea is that the learned function, in some way, *generalizes* the training set examples. Thus, new instances will be classified in the same way as "similar" instances in the training set.

In this section, we will discuss the basic ideas from machine learning within the context of our previous theoretical framework. In particular, we will consider a character that knows something about its current situation s, and wants to learn to use that information to predict something about a future situation $do(a, s)$. Depending on what the character is trying to learn the action a will be given, or could be the thing the character is trying to learn.

6.1.1 Learning Effect Axioms

One of the things a character can try and learn is to predict the value of some fluent f_t in the given situation $do(a, s)$. So here, the target function is the value of $f_t(do(a, s))$. From previous chapters we know that, in general, the value of $f_t(do(a, s))$ will depend on the action a, on the value of f_t in the previous situation $f_t(s)$, and on any number of other fluents in the previous situation $f_0(s), \ldots, f_{n-1}(s)$. All these things on which the resulting value of f_t depends, are called *attributes*.[1] Note that, to be completely general, we should not discount the possibility of using, as attributes, the value of fluents in situations further back than the current situation. For the sake of

---

[1] Attributes are also sometimes referred to as *features*, or *variables*.

simplicity we ignore this possibility in what follows, but it is a trivial matter to extend the discussion to include attributes based on fluent values all the way back to the initial situation s_0.

The vector of the $n + 2$ attributes $(a, f_t(s), f_0(s), \ldots, f_{n-1}(s))$ is an instance. Each instance is labeled according to the value of $f(do(a, s))$. In the special case that f is Boolean valued, we call $f(do(a, s)) = 1$ a *positive instance*, and $f(do(a, s)) = 0$ a *negative instance*. The set of labeled instances is the training set.

6.1.2   Learning Precondition Axioms

Learning a precondition axiom is similar to learning an effect axiom because we want the character to learn to predict something about the effect of an action. In particular, we want it to predict whether an action is possible. Before we discuss learning precondition axioms, it is helpful to introduce a defined fluent Disaster. The definition of the fluent Disaster will depend on the application and is up to the user to define. For example, here is a possible definition based on the maze example of Chapter 5:

$$\mathsf{Disaster}(s) = \mathsf{pos}(\mathsf{character}) = p \wedge \neg \mathsf{Free}(p).$$

We can now define the target function f_t to be

$$f_t(do(a, s)) = \neg \mathsf{Disaster}(do(a, s)).$$

With this definition of f_t, positive instances occur if nothing disastrous happened. Note that, if you are reading this book to learn how to build real-world intelligent robots you probably don't want it to try and learn precondition axioms. That is because, unlike in a virtual world, we can't just reset the simulation. Therefore, in order to create the negative instances something disastrous might happen, which could destroy your expensive robot, or worse.

In the next chapter we discuss using a low-level fail-safe behavior system to sit underneath a high-level reasoning layer. Such a setup might also make it troublesome to learn precondition axioms as the low-level system might simply prevent disasters from occurring. That is, to the reasoning layer it would just seem as if nothing at all is happening rather than something potentially disastrous. Re-engineering the interface between the two layers to notify the higher-level that it was trying to do something dangerous might be more troublesome than simply writing the precondition axiom out by hand.

6.1.3 Learning Behavior

When we learn effect axioms, we want to predict the value of a fluent from, among other things, the action performed. To learn a behavior we need to go the other way. In particular, we are given the desired value of some "goal" fluent $f_g(do(a_t, s))$ as one of the attributes in the instance vector, and we want to learn to pick the action a_t that will produce that value. In machine learning terms, the target function is the action selection mechanism that picks the appropriate action a_t. Training instances will be labeled with the action selection mechanism's choices of a_t for the given instance vectors.

6.2 Creating a Training Set

Since the training set is used to generate a learned function, the learned function is going to be only as good as the training set from which it was derived. That is, the performance of the learned function is crucially dependent on how representative the training set is of the problems the character will actually encounter after it has finished learning. If the character sees an example unlike any in the training set there is little hope that the learned function will be useful. Therefore, we should expect that there would be some trial and error associated with getting a reasonable learned function. Thus, learning should be viewed as a tool to improve the quality of our computer characters' behavior and not just as a labor saving device for lazy programmers.

6.2.1 Manual Input

Machine learning techniques are especially useful when we have an existing solution to a problem, but find it hard to encode it with a simple set of rules. A typical scenario when this is the case is if the "existing solution" is a human expert who finds it difficult to articulate precisely how she makes her decisions. Machine learning techniques hold out the promise of a program being able to mimic the expert without us ever having to explicitly understand how the expert is making her decisions. Of course, if we can easily write down how the expert is making her decisions, then we don't really need machine learning techniques. In such cases it is simpler, faster, and more robust to just write down the rules (in some suitable computer language) and use them directly.

A highly pertinent example of creating a training set by having a human expert go through and label some instances arises in computer games. In particular, we can record a human game player's responses to different situations and use this to create a training set. In this way we can, potentially, create computer characters that can mimic the behavior of various human players. Clearly, being able to capture the behavior of legendary computer game players is incredibly useful.

6.2.2 Precondition and Effect Axioms

To automatically create a training set for learning effect axioms and precondition axioms the character can use its sensing abilities. In particular, the character needs to note the value of the attributes before it executes an action. After executing the action it can label the instance with the perceived value of the target function. [2]

6.2.3 Behavior

In the previous chapter we showed how a character can automatically plan actions to achieve its assigned goals. The major drawback with this approach is that it can be too slow for real-time performance. However, we could take this slow method and use it (offline) to generate a training set. The training set can then be the input to the process of creating a learned function. In general, the learned function is only an approximation of the original function, but it can be evaluated fast enough to yield real-time performance.

For example, suppose we have a complex action *select* that is designed to achieve some goal f_g. One of the attributes will be the value v of the goal f_g that the character is trying to achieve. Let the other attributes be the complete list of fluents that are mentioned in the complex action, $f_0, \ldots, f_{n-1}$. We can now create a training set of instances of the form $(v, f_0, \ldots, f_{n-1})$ for a range of possible values of all the attributes. Each of these instances is now labeled with the appropriate action (calculated with *select*) to take, given the value of the attributes. If *select* returns a whole sequence of actions then, since we are only trying to learn a rough approximation, we can just record the first one, say.

Note that, if we have some highly complicated complex action, with many levels of nested loops, we cannot even hope to learn a reasonable approximation. In particular, we suggested only using values for the attributes before

---

[2]In Chapter 7, Section 3, we call executing an action *committing* to the action and we discuss the topic in a more general setting.

the complex action was executed. Of course, the complex action would interweave actions with testing fluent values so our suggestion is an extremely crude one. Therefore, we should (at least to begin with) try and restrict our application of machine learning techniques to approximating simple, shorter pieces of code where we are more likely to be successful.

6.2.4 Size Does Matter

As we mentioned earlier, how well the learned function approximates the target function depends on how well the training set represents the target function. If the training set contains only one kind of example, then the learned function will exhibit only that one kind of behavior. Ideally there should be an example of every possible behavior in the training set, but for any nontrivial target function this would make the training set too large. Therefore, we have to strike a balance between the size of the training set versus the accuracy with which the learned function approximates the target.

Suppose we require that the learned function should always be within some given tolerance of the target function. We would like to be able to use this to calculate the required size of the training set. For any reasonable tolerance the training set will still be too large. Therefore, we shall require only that the learned function is within some tolerance δ with some probability p. If we make assumptions on the probability distribution for picking the training set instances, we can now, in theory, calculate upper and lower bounds for the size of the training set. This is what people study in *computational learning theory* but it turns out that it is hard to get useful bounds.

Because it is so hard to calculate how large the training set should be, people have adopted some simple heuristics that seem to work in practice. For example, in the neural network community, people sometimes choose the number of training instances to be approximately three times the number of free weights. Of course, care must still be taken to ensure that these examples are evenly distributed across the possible range of behaviors of the target function.

6.2.5 Discretization

In general, the attributes in a training set could be real-valued, and instances could be labeled with real-values, or multiple actions, or actions with real-valued parameters. Learning algorithms try to spot patterns in the training set data that they can use to classify the instances. If we have real-valued quantities, or even quantities that can take on a lot of values, some learning algorithms can have problems noticing the patterns that emerge in the data. The chances of patterns emerging are greatly increased if we can lump values together into a small number of categories (bins, ranges, intervals, or buckets). This process of lumping "similar" values together is called *discretization.*

For example, consider the following set of pairs of values. Imagine, the first value in each pair is the angle of a character's prey, and the second value is the action it chooses.

{ (45.7, E), (137.2, E), (159.8, S), (41.9, N), (48.4, N), (92.3, E), (203.7, S), (231.3, W), (345.8, N), (123.4, E), (192.1, S), (130.2, S), (303.8, W), (351.7, N), (133.2, E), (139.6, S), (134.2, S), (227.2, W), (35.3, N), (128.3, E), (152.1, S), (225.6, W), (40.9, N), (80.3, E), (43.7, E), (150.9, S), (260.4, W), (320.2, N), (50.8, E), (201.1, S), (226.3, S), (232.7, W), (328.7, N), (126.7, E), (39.6, E), (192.9, S), (229.8, W), (14.5, N), (73.5, E), (258.0, W), (320.3, W), (339.3, N), (67.6, E), (278.1, W), (18.7, N), (33.2,N) }

Without processing the data in some way, it is pretty hard to spot any patterns. Therefore, let's discretize the data into four categories:

angle	East?	South?	West?	North?
(45,135]	10	2	0	1
(135,225]	1	8	0	0
(225,315]	0	1	9	0
(315,45)	2	0	1	11

Now we can immediately see that there is an obvious correlation between the angle of the prey and the direction the character heads in. Learning algorithms are also extremely sensitive to how the training set data is discretized. The exact ranges we choose to discretize the values will depend on the training set. We will also need to decide whether to pick the values by hand, choose some uniform distribution, or even use some sophisticated discretization algorithm.

6.2.6 Picking Attributes

Clearly, the usefulness of the training set depends critically on choosing the right attributes to include. In many cases it is obvious what the attributes should be, but sometimes it is not. If it turns out that the learned function is not performing as hoped, it is worthwhile to go back and reexamine the

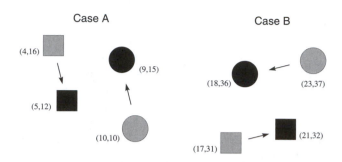

Figure 6.1. Two instances of identical behavior.

assumptions we made on the relevant attributes. Based on the results of this analysis, it may be necessary to generate a new training set that includes values for the missing attribute.

One solution is to initially assume all the fluents are relevant. Unfortunately, if the number of fluents is large, this could significantly increase the time it takes to learn. It also means that when the learned function is used it requires values for attributes that might not even contribute to the final output. This latter problem can be avoided by performing a post-processing step on the learned function. The precise method used to do this will depend of the representation of the learned function. For example, in a decision tree it should be straightforward as we can explicitly see which fluents are being used to classify the instances. For a neural network, the fluents that are not pertinent will have zero, or perhaps very low, weights associated with them on the input layer and can thus sometimes be removed.

It can also be the case that we picked the right attributes, but unwittingly represent them in such a way as to make the correlation between instances hard to discover. For example, look at Figure 6.1 which depicts two instances in some hypothetical training set. A naïve transcription of these two instances yields the following training data:

pos(circle)(s)	pos(square)(s)	pos(circle)($do(a, s)$)	pos(square)($do(a, s)$)
(10,10)	(4,16)	(9,15)	(5,12)
(23,38)	(17,31)	(18,37)	(21,33)

It is clear from the diagram, however, that the two training instances are actually examples of precisely the same relative behavior of the square and the circle. The second case is simply the first one, rotated ninety degrees and translated. Therefore, let's choose new attributes that express the circle's position relative to the cube. In particular, let's use the circle's distance from the cube, and its angle from the cube's direction of travel (assuming it remains constant). The new training set data now looks as follows:

dist(circle)(s)	ang(circle)(s)	dist(circle)$(do(a, s))$	ang(circle)$(do(a, s))$
$6\sqrt{2}$	$\arccos(\frac{5}{34}\sqrt{2}\sqrt{17})$	5	$\arccos(-\frac{8}{85}\sqrt{17})$
$6\sqrt{2}$	$\arccos(\frac{5}{34}\sqrt{2}\sqrt{17})$	5	$\arccos(-\frac{8}{85}\sqrt{17})$

Now it is obvious to us, and more importantly, to a learning algorithm, that these two instances are both examples of the same behavior. As we saw in the last section, the success of the learning algorithm depends critically on its ability to spot patterns in the training data. Simply by using relative coordinates we have doubled the number of training instances that clearly exhibit similar behavior and this greatly increases the chances of learning something useful.

6.3 Representation of the Learned Function

The next important question we must ask ourselves is how are we going to represent the learned function. Popular choices include, but are not limited to, artificial neural networks, decision trees, or artificial genotypes. Deciding which representation to use depends on the particular learning problem, but also on personal preferences, the available software and the available expertise. There is a well-known quote in the machine learning literature that says "neural networks are the second best way of doing just about anything, and genetic algorithms are the third." Of course, many people would disagree and some display an almost religious fervor about their particular favorite representation, so it is hard to make objective statements about which methods are best. Nevertheless, it is true that neural networks and genetic algorithms can be applied to a wide range of problems with relative ease. Of course, the resulting performance can vary widely but there is never any harm to try a quick implementation to see if it works. If it doesn't work then we can invest the extra time to come up with a different approach.

Even if the first method does work it is still wise to question whether the method being used is excessively complex. That is, we should attempt to use the simplest representation that we can. There is no point in using an elaborate neural network if we could have gotten by with learning a few coefficients of a polynomial, say. Otherwise, the final application will be more complicated and slower than is strictly necessary.

At the other extreme we cannot expect an overly simplistic representation to learn some deep and complicated concept. A good analogy here is choosing polynomials to interpolate a given set of points. That is, to interpolate $n+1$ points requires, in general, a polynomial of at least degree n. In the same vein we cannot expect a neural network with only a few free weights to be able to learn to play chess like a grand master.

Any kind of introduction to specific machine learning techniques is well beyond the scope of this book. Moreover, since there are so many existing books on the subject it would be a waste of time. We will however, try to explain how some of the more popular representations can be incorporated into cognitive models.

6.3.1   Incorporating Learned Functions

Representing cognitive models in terms of precondition axioms and effect axioms is extremely convenient when they are specified by hand. However, when cognitive models are acquired automatically the representation is likely to be quite different. For example, we could use a neural network to represent a cognitive model. A neural network can approximate all kinds of target functions, discrete, continuous and vector-valued. They are especially well suited to learning from noisy complex training sets that typically result from real-world experiments. However, the resulting learned function is usually represented as a collection of weight assignments to some network topology. Therefore, we need to be able to incorporate learned functions, regardless of their representation, into the character's knowledge base.

Effect Axioms

Integrating a learned function into an effect axiom is not particularly difficult. It will however, depend on what the original target function was. For example, if the target function was to learn the effect of a single action a_t on a single fluent f_t, then the learned function f_l can be incorporated into an effect axiom as follows:

$$f_t(s) = v \wedge f_0(s) = v_0 \wedge \cdots f_{n-1}(s) = v_{n-1} \Rightarrow$$
$$f_t(do(a_t, s)) = f_l(a_t, v, v_0, \ldots, v_{n-1}),$$

where the arguments to f_l are the attributes that made up the instances in the original training set. Note that there could also be other effect axioms that were specified manually. Assuming they are all consistent, the effect axioms can then be collected and incorporated into one successor-state axiom as described in Chapter 3, Section 2.4. The character can then reason about its world using all the effect axioms regardless of how they were obtained.

The only problem that might occur is that all the effect axioms might not be consistent. For example, we might end up with a positive effect axiom that says the fluent becomes true in a certain situation, and a negative effect axiom that says the fluent becomes false in the same situation. This can be caused by noise in the training data, some important attribute being missing from the training instances, or even human error. At run-time we can automatically spot if an inconsistency arose, but unfortunately there is provably no algorithm that, in general, is guaranteed to terminate when trying to determine *a priori* whether a given set of first-order sentences is inconsistent.

If the target function was something more like a successor-state axiom then integrating it will be slightly different. A successor-state axiom has the property that it gives the value of a fluent for *all* actions, even ones that we didn't think of in advance. This is part of what we referred to as elaboration tolerance in Chapter 5, Section 3.3. A learned successor-state axiom will generally not have this property because the list of attributes is finite and had to include all the actions that we wanted to learn about. That is, f_l will simply not be defined for actions that were not mentioned in the original training set. We will therefore refer to f_l as a pseudo successor-state axiom. It can easily be transformed into a proper successor-state axiom as follows:

$$Poss(a, s) \Rightarrow [f_t(do(a, s)) = z \Leftrightarrow$$
$$((a \in A \wedge f_t(s) = v \wedge f_0(s) = v_0 \wedge \cdots f_{n-1}(s) = v_{n-1} \wedge$$
$$f_l(a_0, \ldots, a_{m-1}, v, v_0, \ldots, v_{n-1}) = z) \vee (a \notin A \wedge f_t(s) = z),$$

where $A = \{a_0, \ldots, a_{m-1}\}$, the m actions that were in the attribute list. Note that, the above axiom assumes there are no other effect axioms lying around. If there are then these can easily be incorporated into the final successor-state axiom just as before.

There are other possible arrangements of learned and manually specified effect axioms and precondition axioms, but the reader should understand the basic approach for incorporating a learned function into the canonical representation of a cognitive model.

Behavior

In Section 6.1.3, we discussed the possibility of learning to approximate a goal-directed behavior. Just as before, we might want to incorporate the learned function into behavior that was specified manually using complex actions, say. This is very straightforward. In particular, let ϕ be the learned approximation of the complex action *select*. Furthermore, let the attributes that ϕ depends on be among the fluents $f_0, \ldots, f_{n-1}$. Then ϕ tries to pick an action a that will achieve the goal $f_g(s) = v$ (as in Section 6.1.3) and we

can just replace *select* with the new complex action that takes advantage of
the learned function:

$$(f_0 = y_0 \wedge \cdots \wedge f_{n-1} = y_{n-1})?\, {}^\circ_\circ\, \pi(a)\ \phi(v, y_0, \ldots, y_{n-1}, a).$$

This new complex action can obviously be treated just as any other complex
action. In particular, it can be a component of some larger complex action.

We might, at this point, be tempted to ask if we can expect our characters
to learn to create arbitrary complex actions of their own? To show how
difficult this would be, imagine we have a character in a computer game
that has a big pile of bullets of mixed calibers and it needs to sort them into
separate piles according to size. Can we expect the character to come up
with an efficient sorting algorithm? For example, can we expect it to invent
an algorithm like heap sort? The answer is that this sort of capability is way
beyond current machine learning techniques. The reason it is such a hard
problem is that it seems that inventing new algorithms is a task requiring the
full force of human ingenuity, creativity, and intelligence. Therefore, until
we have characters that can compare to humans in their intellectual abilities
they are not going to be able to do this kind of automatic programming.
Moreover, if we did have such intelligent computer characters then why not
just have them read this book and write computer games for us!

6.3.2 Decision Trees

When the target function is discrete (or can be discreteized in a meaningful
way), decision trees are a good way to represent the learned function. Decision trees work by sorting an instance down the tree until it reaches a leaf
node. Each leaf node is labeled with one of the possible values of the target
function and the instance is classified according to that label.

Although there are some techniques designed to translate various learned
function representations into a more human readable form, from a cognitive
modeling perspective, one of the nice properties of decision trees is that
the representation can be highly intuitive. This is in contrast to a neural
network, say, which consists of a bunch of weight assignments that, to the
untrained eye, are not directly useful to look at. Figure 6.2 shows a decision tree that we might obtain for the Jack and Dognap example that we
introduced in Chapter 3.

As we can see, the decision tree is reminiscent of the successor-state
axiom that we wrote down in Chapter 3, Section 2.3. In particular, we can
see that the first question "Is Jack Alive?" just corresponds to a frame

Is Jack Alive (in situation s) ?
    N: Then he will not be alive (in situation $do(a, s)$).
    Y: Is the gun loaded?
        N: Then he will be alive.
        Y: Is the gun aimed?
            N: Then he will be alive.
            Y: Is the action $a = shoot$?
                N: Then he will be alive.
                Y: Then he will not be alive.

Figure 6.2. Simple decision tree.

axiom. The other questions all correspond to the precondition and effect axioms we gave before. We would like an automatic procedure to translate a decision tree into precondition, or effect axioms. The problem with this is that decision trees are propositional, whereas, in general, the axioms of a cognitive model are first-order terms. Therefore, how can we learn first-order logic terms? There are machine learning techniques that have this ability, but they are, in general, more experimental than other machine learning techniques. The topic is therefore beyond the scope of the rather cursory look at learning we have given in this chapter. However, the reader should know that such "analytical learning" techniques do exist and more information can be obtained by consulting the references. Nevertheless, a decision tree can often provide a strong hint as to what a good effect axiom would be.

6.4 Learning Algorithm

Once we have decided on how the learned function will be represented, we still need to decide on which learning algorithm to use. This will depend on the representation and the reader should consult the relevant literature for a guide to the pros and cons of different algorithms.

One of the challenges in using any learning algorithm is to avoid *overfitting*. A decision tree that has one path from root to leaf for each example in the training set is an example of overfitting. It amounts to simply creating a lookup table for all the instances in the training set. For any reasonable training set, the trivial tree would be enormous and thus slow to evaluate. Secondly, when we try to use the trivial decision tree it would only be able to answer queries about examples it had seen before. It would have no ability to extract patterns in the data to generalize and extrapolate what it learned to new examples. That is, overfitting corresponds to learning too much about the peculiar quirks of the training set we happened to use to train the learning algorithm. The problem can potentially arise no matter what representation and learning algorithm we use. It can only be avoided by ensuring that we do not let the learning algorithm run for too long.

Overfitting is a complicated subject in its own right and the interested reader is encouraged to consult some of the given references. However, a simple way to avoid overfitting is to split the training set into two. That is, part of the training set (one quarter, say) is set aside and is called a *testing set*. We can use the testing set to check for overfitting. In particular, we run the learning algorithm on the training set as before. We thus obtain a learned function that will get better and better as we let the learning algorithm run for longer. As the learned function improves, its performance will initially also get better on the testing set. At some point, however, the learned function will start to become overfitted to the training set and this will show up as a downturn in performance on the testing set.

6.5   Discussion

It is important to forewarn the reader that using machine learning techniques successfully will probably require an enormous amount of patience and no small measure of ingenuity. It is not hard to explain why when we consider that we usually do not even expect people to learn so easily. For example, a human learning martial arts is usually not just repeatedly thrown in the ring to fight a seventh Dan black belt trying her hardest and expected to learn anything useful. That is, the novice would be dead, injured, or unconscious before there was opportunity to learn anything at all. The procedure is much more structured with years of practice on isolated skills without a serious opponent even being present. Only after the skill is mastered on its own can any attempt be made to integrate it with other skills. Another important part of the whole process is the explicit natural language instructions, suggestions, and explanations provided by the teacher.

Computer characters are no different. We will usually have to train them on small subsets of their world. The knowledge acquired can then be integrated with other parts of the cognitive model that were perhaps specified manually. The integrated whole can then be used to acquire a new, more sophisticated skill, and so on.

Even if it is possible to easily learn an action selection mechanism, there is still no guarantee that it will result in the best controller. For example, consider playing chess. The day when we build a computer to learn to play chess as well as the best human simply by watching still appears to be a long way off, but suppose for a moment that we could. Consider that, just like the world's best human chess player, this computer would still loose against a computer like Deep Blue that can perform extensive brute force searches. Of course, maybe the learning computer could then learn from Deep Blue, but that is getting too esoteric for the current discussion.

Another interesting issue that comes up when we are selecting a target function is that maybe our target should not be to learn the "best" function at all. That is, maybe we want the computer characters not to win, but to lose well. Of course, most machine learning techniques are not perfect anyway, so we may end up with a suboptimal result simply by accident. In general, however, it is better to be clear about exactly what we are really trying to learn or we might not end up with the correct training set.

6.6 Notes

Much of the text in this chapter was inspired by the work described in [142]. In one of their examples the target function is a human expert Doom player. In another application the target function is a complex rule-based expert system for military flight simulators. In both cases they are able to approximate the target function with a learned function. The authors refer to the technique as "behavior capture" since they are, in effect, able to learn to emulate the target's behavior. They use a well known AI system called SOAR [72]. SOAR has the ability to learn about its own behavior. In particular, it can "chunk" sequences of actions that are used repeatedly in similar situations into one compound action. Next time the character finds itself in an applicable situation, it can execute the compound action without having to decide on all the component actions individually. This means that a character's behavior can get faster with practice.

In this chapter, we concentrated on concept learning. We also briefly touched on analytical learning. Aside from being able to directly produce first-order terms, analytical learning is extremely interesting because it can allow a character to use its prior knowledge to learn from a much smaller training set [95].

There is however an important branch of machine learning that deals with learning without examples. Instead of a training set, we give the character a *reward* function that returns a value in proportion to how well the character achieves some given goal. The character then tries some random actions, some of which result in higher rewards than others. The actions that received higher rewards are then perturbed in some manner and the process is repeated until the process converges to a particular behavior. The process is referred to as *reinforcement learning* [95]. For example, in [139] the reward function is proportional to how far the character travels in some fixed time period of physical simulation. The character initially flails its limbs around randomly and some of these movements happen to result in forward motion. These "successful" motions are then refined (by random perturbation) until the character learns to locomote. There is no guarantee that the character will learn to move in any way that was expected, but it turns out that for various simple examples characters can learn to walk, crawl, and swim. Similar approaches are also described in [123, 60].

For further reading there are literally hundreds of books and thousands of papers on all aspects of machine learning. The two books we used as references for this chapter were [95, 67].

Putting It All Together

In Chapter 5, we mentioned that it is usually more convenient to have the cognitive model represent a character's high-level intentions. The high-level intentions are then filtered down into detailed motion by a predefined deterministic behavior layer. In this chapter, we will run through the details of how this all works out in the context of the theory we have introduced in the preceding chapters. This can often be fairly straightforward, but some additional subtleties can arise. In addition, we will look at the important and related issue of real-time performance.

7.1   A Predefined Behavior Layer

In general, we will want our characters to display both simple and complex behavior. As we mentioned in Chapter 5, it often makes sense to implement the simple low-level behaviors using predefined behaviors. By this we mean that if we can quickly and easily think up (or look up) a few simple stimulus-response rules to implement a behavior then we should go ahead and implement it that way. We also mentioned that for more complex behavior it is often easier to use a more goal-directed approach to specifying behavior.

Therefore, a convenient way to build a cognitive character is to

- Implement the simple behaviors using (deterministic) predefined behaviors.

- Implement the more sophisticated behaviors using (nondeterministic) goal-directed behavior specification techniques. Note that we will usually not restrict ourselves to pure goal-directed behavior, but will use complex actions to help give the character more detailed instructions.

For example, imagine we have a low-level predefined behavior that can make a character go to a specified position. Moreover, it can go to the position in such a way as to avoid colliding into any obstacles that might be in the way. Then, at the higher, cognitive modeling level we can provide a primitive action *gotoPos*. This simplifies the design of the higher level greatly because the character can worry only about deciding where to go and not how to get there. For instance, we can have an effect axiom that states that the effect of going to a particular position is to end up at that position:

$$\text{pos}(do(goto(p)), s) = p.$$

Now, when the character decides it wants to go to a particular position, it just calls the low-level predefined behavior and all the details are taken care of. If we do not take advantage of the predefined behavior, we have to introduce more low-level primitive actions, like *turnLeft*, *goStraight*, etc., and write effect axioms that take into account obstacle avoidance strategies.

The point we wish to convey is that using a low-level predefined behavior system gives us a choice about the level of abstraction we choose for the primitive actions that will be available at the cognitive level. In particular, we can use primitive actions to represent a character's high-level intentions. Of course, if in any particular application we see some advantage to designing the "low-level" behavior using cognitive modeling techniques, then we are perfectly free to do so.

7.2 Interface

Having implemented simple and sophisticated cognitive types of behavior in two different ways we need to interface them so that they can work together. Figure 7.1 shows, diagrammatically, how this can be done.

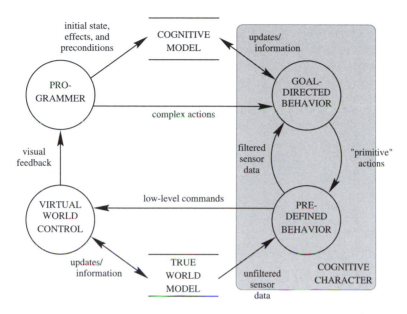

Figure 7.1. Interfacing goal-directed and predefined behavior.

As we have already hinted, primitive actions play a central role in interfacing the two different levels. The idea is that some of the primitive actions are instantiated in the lower level with predefined behavior routines. Whenever the higher cognitive level decides upon an action, it is communicated to the lower level. If a corresponding predefined behavior routine exists, then it is "executed."

The reason that not all primitive actions have corresponding predefined behaviors associated with them is that they are designed to have an effect only at the higher cognitive level. A convenient way to think about it is that all the fluents correspond to the internal state of the character's brain. Therefore, some of the fluents may relate to aspects of the character that are completely internal. For example, a character can be hungry without engaging in any behavior that makes this fact apparent to an external observer. The character might even be able to stop feeling hungry without engaging any sort of visible activity. For example, it could do an action *thinkAbout*(dancing) that causes it to, at least for a while, stop feeling hungry. Of course, many fluents will relate both to the character's internal state and its external world. Moreover, unless we want a character that appears to be insane, it is important that these fluents should bear some correspondence with what is actually going on in the virtual world. Unfortunately, there now appears to be a problem. In particular, if deciding upon some action at the higher level causes some predefined behavior routine to execute, which in turn causes the world to change, then we had better be sure that the corresponding effect axiom captures this change. Otherwise, the character's model of its world will be "out of sync" with what is really going on.

Let's consider a simple example. Suppose we have an action *push*, and a fluent pos that keeps track of the positions of a bunch of bricks in which a character is interested. Suppose the bricks are all stacked on top of each other and the character decides to push the bottom brick. The predefined level then executes the behavior routine that corresponds to the push action and the bricks start to tumble. Suppose the brick movements are derived by a physical simulation. After all the bricks come to rest, how can we be sure that the fluent pos, inside the character's head, is correct for all the new brick positions?

The naïve solution would be to encode all the rules for the physical simulation into the effect axioms, but as we explained in Chapter 1, Section 5, this would have a number of disadvantages.[1] We also explained that the problem is not confined to virtual worlds where we are using physics. Whenever it is complicated to predict the ultimate effect of actions there will be a problem coming up with an effect axiom. For example, we mentioned the often insurmountable difficulties associated with providing effect axioms that capture all the other character's precise reactions to each action.

7.2.1 Sensing

The reader will also recall from Chapter 1 that the way to keep the character's internal representation of its world synchronized is through sensing. In Chapter 4, we introduced the technical apparatus that allowed us to do this. In particular, we introduced the notion of IVE fluents. We recall that IVE fluents are just regular fluents that take on interval values and can be used to represent a character's uncertainty about its world.

To explain further, let's go back to our example with the tower of blocks. The position of block i would be given by some fluent $pos(i, s)$, say. However, to make the example as easy as possible to understand, we will consider just one block and one property of that block; namely its height above the table. We thus introduce the fluent ht to represent the block's height. Next we

---

[1]In some cases it might, however, be reasonable to perform inferences based on approximate physical laws. This is often referred to as *qualitative physics*, and in [70] an example is given on how to discuss physical processes within the situation calculus.

introduce the IVE fluent $\mathcal{I}_{ht}$ to represent what the character *knows* about the height of the block above the table.

The effect axioms for the IVE fluent are trivial. The first one simply states that the character doesn't know the height of the block after a push action:

$$\mathcal{I}_{ht}(s) = \langle v, v \rangle \Rightarrow \mathcal{I}_{ht}(do(\textbf{push}, s)) = \langle 0, v \rangle.$$

More precisely, it states that the character knows the height is somewhere between 0 (assuming the block can't fall off the table) and what it was before it was pushed (this assumes the block wasn't pushed upwards so that it ended up higher up some how).[2]

The second effect axiom states that the character knows the height of the block after sensing it to be the actual height of the block:[3]

$$ht(s) = x \Rightarrow \mathcal{I}_{ht}(do(\textbf{sense}, s)) = \langle x, x \rangle.$$

The effect axiom for the regular ht fluent now just states that ht changes according to an exogenous action *setHt*:

$$ht(do(\textbf{setHt}(x), s)) = x.$$

The exogenous actions are generated by modifying the definition for complex actions. For example, the rule for primitive actions (given in Chapter 4, Section 4) is

$$Do\,(\alpha, s, s') \;\triangleq\; Poss\,(\alpha, s) \wedge s' = do(\alpha, s) \quad \alpha \text{ is a primitive action.}$$

This is modified to

$$Do\,(\alpha, s, s') \;\triangleq\; Poss\,(\alpha, s) \wedge s' = do(\alpha, s)$$
$$\alpha \text{ is a primitive action and } \alpha \neq \textbf{setHt}(x),$$
$$Do\,(\textbf{setHt}(x), s, s') \;\triangleq\; Poss\,(\textbf{setHt}, s) \wedge s' = do(\textbf{setHt}(x), s),$$

where the actual value for x in the argument for *setHt* is determined by the underlying predefined behavior system. For example, it might well be calculated by a physical simulation. The important point is that from the cognitive modeling standpoint, we don't have to care where it comes from.

---

[2]We are, of course, at liberty to add in as much extra computation as we like in order to bound the resulting position more tightly. Or we can be even lazier and simply say the character knows nothing at all, that is $\mathcal{I}_{ht} = \langle -\infty, \infty \rangle$.

[3]In Chapter 4, Section 4 we looked at how to deal with noisy sensors.

Naturally, the *push* action can have effects on other fluents as well. For example, it might cause a completely internal fluent inDanger to become true. This, in turn, can cause the character to decide that a *runAway* action is the appropriate one to take after the *push* action.

The approach using sensing has a number of important advantages:

- By making suitable modifications to the definition of complex actions, we can add an arbitrary number of exogenous actions after various primitive actions. We thus avoid having to formalize any aspect of the domain we consider too troublesome or irrelevant to the process of high-level reasoning. Leaving parts out means that we have to worry about how to keep the character's representation of its world synchronized with its actual world. Fortunately, this can be done through sensing, using IVE fluents to represent the parts about which there might be occasional uncertainty.

- Since we have the option to leave out complicated effect axioms it can be faster, albeit less accurate, to predict the future. Thus, planning can be much faster.

- We can expect much more realistic behavior from our characters as they now function in a way that is more intuitive and appears to be more akin to the way humans and animals behave.

Changing Values

In general, the property of the world that the character needs to sense will be constantly changing. For example, imagine a character that needs to know the speed of an object x. Once again, we introduce two fluents; one for the object's actual speed in the true world model, i.e., $\mathsf{speed}(x, s)$, and another IVE fluent for what the character knows about the object's speed i.e., $\mathcal{I}_{\mathsf{speed}}(x, s)$. From time to time the character will sense the speed, after which it will know the speed and so $\mathcal{I}_{\mathsf{speed}}$ will collapse to the thin interval $\langle \mathsf{speed}(x, s), \mathsf{speed}(x, s) \rangle$. As time wears on, the character will become more uncertain again about the object's speed and this will correspond to the widening of the interval $\mathcal{I}_{\mathsf{speed}}(x, s)$. The situation is depicted graphically in Figure 7.2.

Note that the figure refers to what happens as the character is *executing* actions. When the character is simply thinking about what to do next, it cannot update the $\mathsf{speed}(x, s)$ fluent because if it knew how to do that, it wouldn't have needed to represent its uncertainty about the value in the

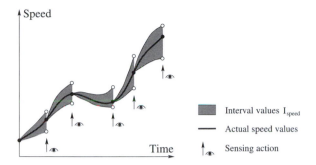

Figure 7.2. Sensing changing values.

first place. It might therefore be better to rename the fluent $\mathsf{speed}(x, s)$ to something more appropriate, like $\mathsf{lastSensedSpeed}(x, s)$, say. Now when the character thinks ahead, the uncertainty about the actual speed will still increase (as it should), but the value of $\mathsf{lastSensedSpeed}(x, s)$ remains constant (as it should). It is also interesting to note that if the actual value of the speed moves outside of its predicted envelope (as represented by $\mathcal{I}_{speed}(x, s)$), then we have a logic of *belief* and not one of *knowledge*, i.e., there are situations occurring now that were not previously considered possible future worlds.

7.3 Rolling Forward

Consider the maze example introduced in Chapter 5. In the example, the character, in effect, has a map of the maze that it can use to plan its path before ever setting foot in the maze. It only needs to execute the plan once it has finished finding a path. Now suppose we have some monsters wandering through the maze in a manner that is unknown to the character. The character can still plan a path but must also keep a look out for monsters. The important point is that the monsters are not marked on the map and so the character can only check for monsters once it is inside the maze. Therefore, the character must first execute some actions to put it inside the maze and then look to see if it can see any monsters approaching. Thus, sensing necessarily entails executing the actions the character has decided upon up until that point.

Another important point is that when a character is planning an action, it can change its mind without influencing its world. This is no longer necessarily the case once an action has been executed. For example, a character may see that a path leads to a dead end and may, in theory, return from whence it came, but in the meantime it may have been spotted by a monster and had its legs bitten off so that it can't go anywhere.

Therefore, we have to decide when the higher cognitive level is going to communicate the required actions to the lower-level reactive system. Communicating actions to the lower level corresponds to committing to those actions. That is, as long as the character is just thinking about what to do at the cognitive level, it can change its mind. At the cognitive level, actions change the value of fluents but nothing in the character's external world is necessarily affected. As long as this is the case, the actions can be "undone" simply by thinking about doing something else. Once the character issues actions to the reactive level they should not be undone because they have caused actual changes in the character's world. In a simulated world, we can technically undo any changes, but this is going down the path of axiomatizing the whole virtual world. In addition, once we add human interaction (as in a computer game), it might become extremely annoying to start undoing actions to which the character previously committed. Imagine you have just defeated a computer character and it decides that it could have done better if only it had done something different earlier on, so it simply keeps resetting the game to that earlier point until it wins! Some of the criteria for deciding to commit to an action sequence are listed below.

- If the character has a specific goal in mind and it comes up with a plan to achieve that goal then it needs to communicate the action sequence to the reactive level so that it can be executed.

- If the character needs to sense the result of an action sequence it must execute the actions first by communicating them to the lower level. When the character does perform a sense action, the reactive level looks up the required values in the graphics database and returns them to the higher level.

- Suppose we are considering an action sequence $a_0, \ldots, a_n$ then, internally, the situation argument for all the fluents is $s' = do(a_n, (\cdots, do(a_0, s_0) \cdots))$. For any large value of n, this situation argument can become unwieldy so the character might want to try committing to at least some prefix of the action sequence.

Once the character has committed and communicated an action sequence to the underlying virtual world, we need to "roll-forward" the fluents. That is, if the current situation is $s' = do(a_n, (\cdots, do(a_0, s_0^{\mathrm{old}}) \cdots))$, then we can

rewrite the initial state to correspond to the current situation s'. We delete
the previous initial state axioms and replace them with ones for which the
fluents take on initial values corresponding to the value of the fluent in the
current situation. So, for each fluent f, we write a new initial state axiom
such that $f(\vec{y}, s_0^{\text{new}}) = f(\vec{y}, s')$. That way, each time after we commit to an
action sequence, we can start "afresh."

Although a character has to commit to any sequence of actions that ends
in a sensing action, it can also be made to commit to any other action we
choose. We simply need to specify the actions to commit to and then when
the character is expanding out complex actions it can check whether the
given action is one to commit to or not.[4]

Another reason we might want a character to commit to an action sequence is that it runs out of time for its deliberations. This takes us to the
interesting issue of real-time performance that we will consider in Section
7.4.4.

7.4 Embedding Goal-directed Behavior

In the first part of this chapter we looked at building goal-directed behavior
on top of predefined behavior. However, it might also be the case that we
want to embed the goal-directed behavior inside some predefined behavior
routine. As a simple example we can imagine that we have a goal-directed
maze-solving module. We can imagine a character that runs around its
world according to some predefined behavior rules. Then, if it happens to
find a map of a maze lying around, it calls up its goal-directed maze-solving
behavior to find a path through the maze. Once the path is established it
remembers it and goes back to its predefined behavior.

7.4.1 Fault Tolerance

As much as we might wish otherwise, the more complex the behavior, the
more likely the character is to fail to achieve it. Using a goal-directed approach this amounts to failing to find a goal situation in the situation tree

---

[4]Conditional planning is where the character does not commit to a sensing action.
It simply makes the rest of its plan *conditional* on the outcome of the sensing action.
Unfortunately, conditional plans quickly suffer from a particularly severe combinatorial
explosion that severely limits their usefulness. Conditional planning is a complicated topic
and the reader is referred to [81, 16] for further discussion.

(see Chapter 5, Section 2.1). If we don't want our character to simply become paralyzed by such a failure we need to give it an alternative strategy. For example, imagine we have some procedure *findGoal* that implements a goal-directed behavior specification. Then, if we embed it in the following complex action, we can achieve a degree of fault tolerance:

$$\text{\textit{findGoal}} \; \S$$
$$\textbf{if } \neg\text{goal}$$
$$(\pi a)\text{Primitive}(a)$$
$$\textbf{else}$$
$$\quad \text{\textit{sense}}$$
$$\textbf{fi}$$

where Primitive is just a predicate that is true for any primitive action a. That is, if the character fails to find a goal, it will just do any possible primitive action. Of course, we might want to choose something more imaginative as the fail-safe, but we hope the basic idea is clear.

In addition, if the fail safe option is not exploiting any of the advanced features of complex actions, then there is obviously no reason to not just use a regular imperative programming language to embed the goal-directed behavior.

We will see some concrete examples of embedded goal-directed behaviors in Chapters 10 and 11. Indeed, we will see goal-directed behaviors that themselves rest upon "low-level" predefined behaviors, embedded in "high-level" predefined behavior. The point we want to convey is that there is a rich chest of tools available to build intelligent computer characters and we can feel at liberty to mix and match as appropriate.

7.4.2 Priority-based Control Systems

Some of the predefined actions will be reflex type actions that happen in response to some immediate and pressing danger. For example, an impending collision should cause a collision avoidance behavior to be instigated as an immediate reaction to the corresponding sensory input. Reflex actions therefore need to be given the highest priority when a character is deciding what to do next. In computing terms, reflex actions should be handled as interrupts. That is, they should be allowed to interrupt other behaviors. A simple way to implement this kind of approach is to assign labels that give a measure of urgency associated with the choice of action. For example, an action that was the result of a predefined behavior that was designated as reflexive will have a value to indicate a high degree of urgency. Thus, in the

Plate I. Cinemasaurus animation.

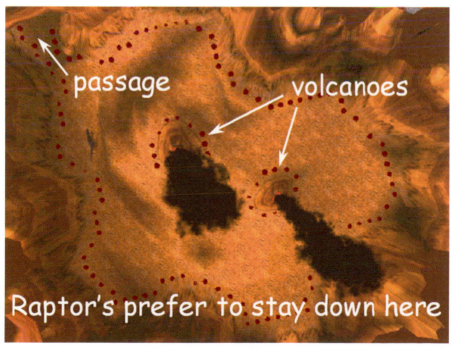

Plate II. Map of prehistoric world.

Plate III. Cognitive models.

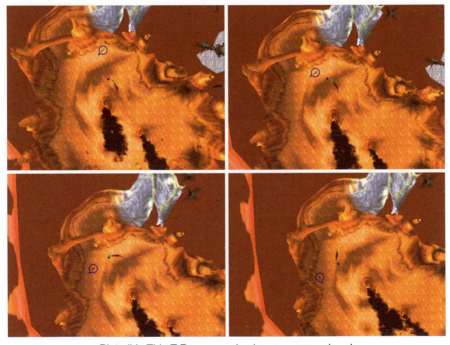

Plate IV. This T-Rex can only plan one move ahead.

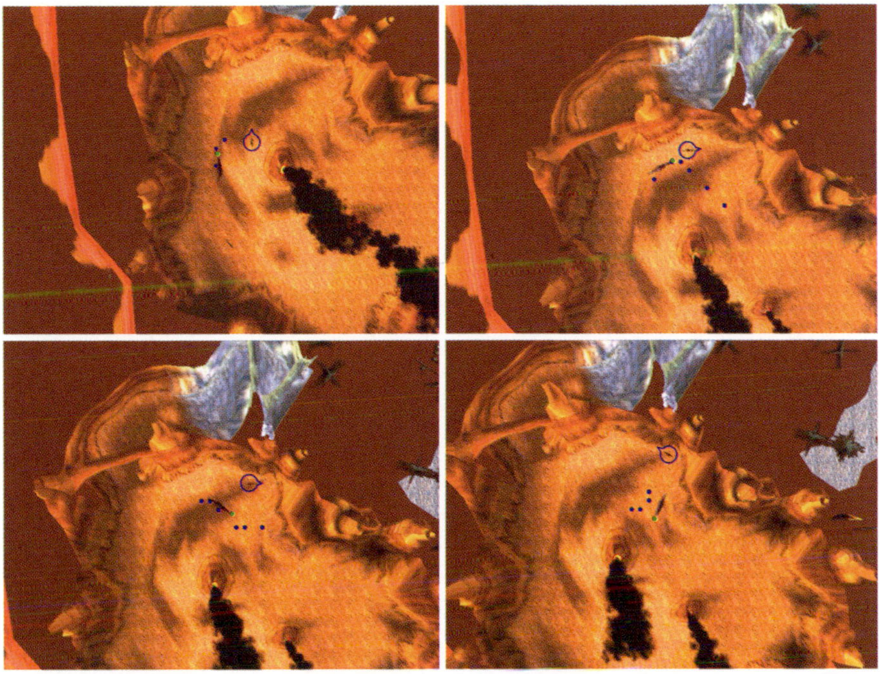

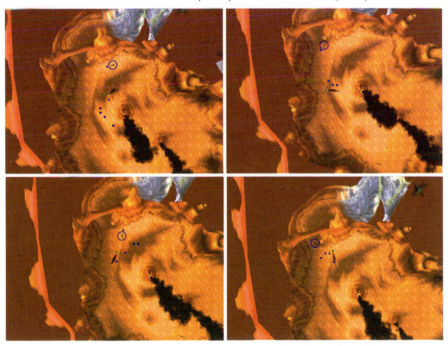

Plate V. This T-Rex can plan up to six moves ahead (Part I).

Plate VI. This T-Rex can plan up to six moves ahead (Part II).

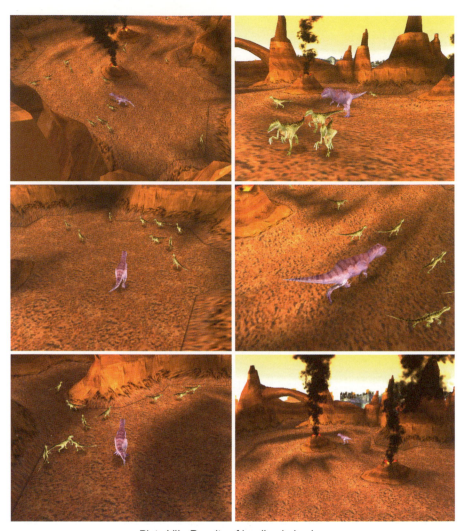

Plate VII. Results of herding behavior.

Plate VIII. Undersea animations.

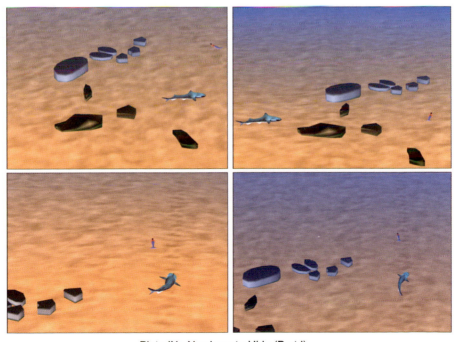

Plate IX. Nowhere to Hide (Part I).

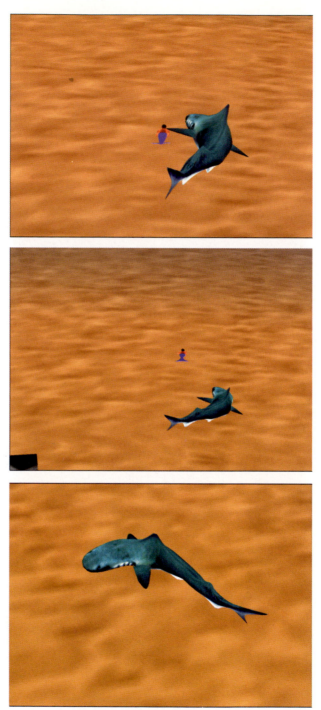

Plate X. Nowhere to Hide (Part II).

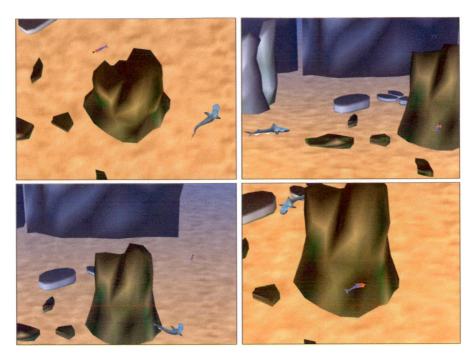

Plate XI. The Great Escape (Part I).

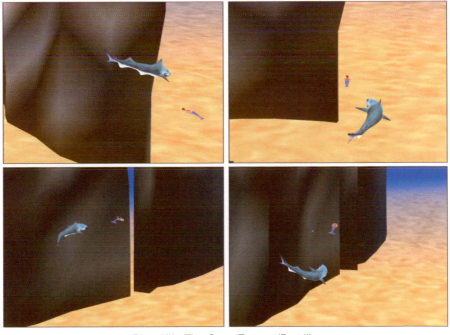

Plate XII. The Great Escape (Part II).

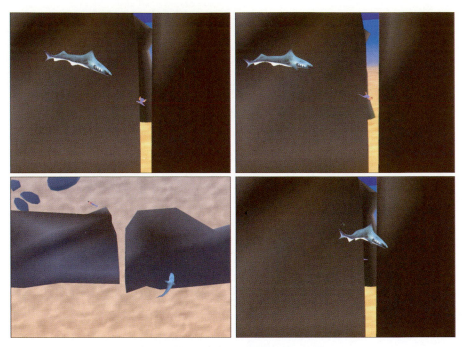

Plate XIII. The Great Escape (Part III).

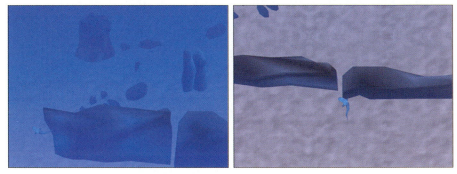

Plate XIV. The Great Escape (Part IV).

case of any conflict, more urgent actions are given priority over less urgent ones.

7.4.3 Subgoals

Sometimes a character's ultimate goal can be easy to define, but we know that it would require such a long sequence of actions that there is little hope of finding the sequence in any reasonable length of time. In such cases it is often possible to think of a sequence of subgoals that would lead to the ultimate goal. This kind of approach is easily implemented using complex actions. There is nothing to stop us, however, from implementing similar ideas in a regular programming language. This might be especially so if we would like to interweave some fault tolerance.

Even if a character could plan out an entire action sequence, it still might not be a good idea to let it try. That is, as we have repeatedly explained, in any reasonably complicated virtual world, the validity of a very long plan is highly questionable. This is because the character's representation of its world and the "true" representation of the world might not be coincident. The longer the action sequence, the more the two will diverge. Therefore, it can also make sense to think of subgoals for the character even if it could manage to come up with a plan to achieve some longer term goal in one shot. In such cases, it is often possible to find a single subgoal, that applied repeatedly, can result in the fulfillment of the ultimate long-term goal. We will see an example like this in Chapter 10.

7.4.4 Real-time Response

A simple set of predefined reactive behavior rules should be fast enough to obtain real-time performance. In many games and animations, however, the bottleneck is the rendering speed so there will often be spare CPU cycles that the character could use to compute more intelligent choices of what to do next. The spare CPU cycles do not even have to be available at the exact point of decision-making. A character can always be busy evaluating what is the best course of action, and then when it needs to act it can be ready to do something intelligent.

An anytime algorithm is an algorithm that can give an answer to a problem "anytime" it is asked, but the longer it gets to compute, the better the answer will be. Therefore, an anytime algorithm is exactly what we want when we talk about real-time performance. That is, the system will never

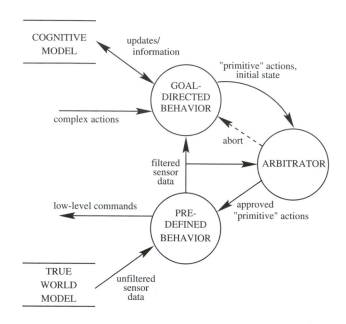

Figure 7.3. Possible system architecture for real-time performace.

have to wait for the character to respond to queries about what it has decided to do because anytime it is asked it will have a response. There are many theoretical issues that can be studied in relation to anytime algorithms, but we will concentrate on what kind of system architecture we can build to support such decision making.

Recall that, in Section 7.4.1, we looked at how a predefined behavior system can make a character's behavior more fault tolerant. In particular, we looked at how it can act as a failsafe for a cognitive layer that failed to find a plan of action. When we consider real-time performance, the cognitive layer can also fail when it can't find a plan *in time*. In such cases the low-level predefined behavior system can provide a response, just as we described in Section 7.4.4. This gives us an anytime style algorithm because the prede- fined behavior level is always ready with some sort of a response, and the cognitive layer is always busy trying to come up with something even better.

For example, Figure 7.3 depicts a fairly simple architecture for real-time performance. The figure is only slightly different from Figure 7.1. In particu- lar, we have modified the predefined behavior module to include an "arbitra- tor." It is the arbitrator's responsibility to ensure that actions are available to the virtual world in time. When the virtual world sends a request to the character for an action, the arbitrator sends a goal to the cognitive level. If the cognitive layer does not respond immediately, then the arbitrator responds with an action from the predefined behavior layer. Note that just as before, even if the cognitive layer does respond in time, the arbitrator can still override it (as in Section 7.4.2) if the predefined behavior layer responds with an action that is labeled as urgent.

If the cognitive layer started reasoning about what to do from scratch each time it got a goal it would hardly ever be able to respond in time. Therefore, it only starts from scratch when it gets a new goal, or if it takes so long that the state of the virtual world has changed too much for its response to be useful. Otherwise, when new goal requests arrive, it just checks that they are the same as before and carries on deliberating. Thus, a goal might arrive eventually for which there is a plan of action ready to use for a response. The cognitive layer is, in effect, acting as a server that is constantly polled by the arbitrator client to see if it has services ready for use. When it does not, the arbitrator goes elsewhere for service. In particular, it settles for lower quality service from the more reliable predefined behavior server.

7.5 Intelligent Flocks

Since each computer character can have its own "brain" there is nothing, in theory, to stop us adding as many characters to a virtual world as we require. However, all these characters reasoning independently could make the code run too slowly. A predefined behavior substrate gives a simple way to implement a version of what is known as *behavior culling*.

In particular, we can use some level of detail measure to cull unnecessary character behaviors. For example, for a few foreground characters we could use a goal-directed approach to control their behavior. The remaining "background" characters could utilize a more reactive approach. Other criteria for culling behaviors could also include notions of crowd membership. Individual characters within a crowd would become more reactive and, at the cognitive level, we could treat the whole crowd or "flock" as a single intelligent entity. We can now give precondition effect axioms and complex actions for the group as a whole. For example, we might specify that the center of the group should be at a specified location. The movement of the individual group members can then be handled by low-level predefined behaviors. It is also possible to use defined fluents that specify the effect of the primitive actions on the individual group members in terms of the center of the group. This would entail having a fluent InGroup that is true whenever the character is part of a group. Either way, the group as a whole can behave in specified ways and perform complicated reasoning tasks.

Unfortunately, this simple strategy won't work so well if we want to control multiple characters in the scene as cooperating individuals. We can still always obtain "emergent behavior." That is, group behavior that arises implicitly from the interaction of the group member's respective behavior rules, and the environment. We might even be able to prove that some desired behavior will emerge (see Chapter 11, Section 5.1). In general, however, our ability to foresee what behavior will emerge depends largely on the complexity of the underlying models, and of course, experimentation.

Beyond this, if we would like some guarantees on how the characters will behave when they are together, we need to add some communication protocol between them. Then they can synchronize with each other, make requests, wait for each other, etc.

7.6 Notes

Instead of emergent group behavior there has been some work on adding additional complex actions to support various kinds of concurrency [78]. There is also a large body of literature on distributed computing in general that is relevant to the topic.

Since we have primarily described learning as a means to acquire a cognitive model in advance (i.e., off-line) we have not discussed it in this chapter. However, we would ideally like learning to happen online. In particular, a learning module could be added to any of the architectures we have described above. It would sit and monitor the character's goal-directed decisions and, as described in Chapter 6, Section 1.3 try to "compile" them into simpler reactive behavior rules.

CML

The mathematical notation we have been using so far has many advantages in terms of clarity and being implementation agnostic. For longer examples, however, it can be hard to follow. Therefore, in this chapter, we will introduce some simpler, easy to read notation, that we will use for the upcoming case studies. We shall refer to the new notation as CML, which stands for Cognitive Modeling Language. CML uses an intuitive English-like syntax for specifying precondition and effect axioms. As a familiar artifice to aid memorization, for complex actions CML falls back on familiar C/C++ style syntax. As we shall see, CML is not a radical departure from the mathematical notation and each CML construct has an obvious and straightforward mapping to the underlying mathematical notation.

To further promote readability, all CML keywords will appear in bold type, actions (complex and primitive) will be italicized, and fluents will be underlined. We may also use various other predicates and functions that are not fluents. These will not be underlined and will usually have names to indicate their intended meaning. Note that "!" denotes negation (not), "&&" denotes conjunction (and), and "||" denotes disjunction (or).

8.1 Precondition and Effect Axioms

As we explained in Chapter 3, Section 2.2, the possibility of performing action a in situation s is specified by a *precondition axiom*. For example, it is possible to drop an object x in a situation s, if and only if a character is holding it:

$$Poss\,(drop(x), s) \Leftrightarrow \mathsf{Holding}(x, s).$$

In CML, this axiom can be expressed more intuitively without the need for logical connectives and the explicit situation argument as follows:

action $drop(x)$ **possible when** $\underline{\mathsf{Holding}}(x)$;

Now let's specify a simple effect axiom that says an object will be broken if it is dropped while we are not sitting down:

$$\neg\mathsf{Sitting}(s) \Rightarrow \mathsf{Broken}(x, do(drop(x), s)).$$

In CML, this can be expressed as follows:

ocurrence $drop(x)$ **results in** $\underline{\mathsf{Broken}}(x)$ **when** $\underline{!\mathsf{Sitting}}$;

The convention in CML is that fluents to the right of the **when** keyword refer to the situation before the action is performed.

Note that we can always give just effect axioms and assume that the syntactic manipulation necessary to turn all the effect axioms into one successor-state axiom for each fluent is done automatically.

In CML notation, because the situation argument is implicit, an initial state is identified with the keyword "**initially**." For example, here is a CML expression that states that initially the cup is not broken:

initially $!\underline{\mathsf{Broken}}(\mathrm{cup})$;

A defined fluent in CML is indicated with the keyword "**defined**" and the defintion appears to the right of a ":=." Just as with regular fluents, anything to the right of a **when** refers to the previous situation. For example, here is a defined fluent UnHappy:

$$\mathsf{UnHappy}(s) \Leftrightarrow \mathsf{Broken}(cup, s) \wedge \mathsf{Sitting}(s)$$

and the corresponding CML:

defined $\underline{\mathsf{UnHappy}} := \underline{\mathsf{Broken}}(\mathrm{cup})\ \&\&\ \underline{\mathsf{Sitting}}$;

In any CML effect or precondition axiom, we can promote readability by introducing auxiliary variables using a "**where**" clause. For example, the following precondition axiom introduces two auxiliary variables d and e.

action *jump* **possible when** <u>distance</u> $< d + e$ **where**
$d = 2 * \text{gapWidth} \;\&\&\; e = \text{hurdleHt}/2;$

8.2 Complex Actions

In Chapter 5, we introduced the theory underlying *complex actions* as a set of recursively defined operators. We recall that any primitive action is also a complex action, and that other complex actions are composed using various control structures. The complete list of operators for specifying complex actions is given in Figure 8.1.

Now lets look at a quick example of a depth-bounded (to n steps) depth-first planner. First, here is the complex action:[1]

$$
\begin{aligned}
&\textbf{proc } \textit{planner}(n) \\
&\quad \text{goal?} \mid \\
&\quad [(n > 0)? \,\mathbin{\raise0.3ex\hbox{$;$}} \\
&\qquad (\boldsymbol{\pi}\; a)(\text{primitiveAction}(a)? \,\mathbin{\raise0.3ex\hbox{$;$}}\; a) \,\mathbin{\raise0.3ex\hbox{$;$}} \\
&\qquad \textit{planner}(n - 1)] \\
&\textbf{end}
\end{aligned}
$$

followed by the corresponding CML code:[2]

```
proc planner (n) {
    choose test(goal);
    or {
        test(n > 0);
        pick(a) {
            primitiveAction(a);
            do(a);
        }
    }
    planner(n − 1);
}
```

---

[1] Adopted from [113].

[2] Notice that because a is a variable we need an explicit **do**. The CML keyword **do** can (optionally) be put in front of any primitive action.

(Primitive Action)
If α is a primitive action then, provided the precondition axiom states it is possible, do the action.
[same syntax in CML i.e., <ACTION>; except we must use an explicit **do** when the action is a variable.]

(Sequence)
$\alpha \,\mathring{,}\, \beta$ means do action α, followed by action β.
[<ACTION> ; <ACTION> ; (note the semi-colon is used as a statement terminator to mimic C)]

(Test)
p? succeeds if p is true, otherwise it fails.
[**test**(<EXPRESSION>)]

(Nondeterministic choice of actions)
$\alpha \mid \beta$ means do action α or action β.
[**choose** <ACTION> **or** <ACTION>]

(Conditionals)
if p α **else** β **fi**, is just shorthand for p? $\mathring{,}$ $\alpha \mid (\neg\, p)$? $\mathring{,}$ β.
[**if** (<EXPRESSION>) <ACTION> **else** <ACTION>]

(Nondeterministic iteration)
$\alpha \,\star$, means do α zero or more times.
[**star** <ACTION>]

(Iteration)
while p **do** α **od** is just shorthand for p? $\alpha \,\star$.
[**while** (<EXPRESSION>) <ACTION>]

(Nondeterministic choice of arguments)
$(\pi\ x)$ α means pick some argument x and perform the action $\alpha(x)$.
[**pick**(<EXPRESSION>) <ACTION>]

(Procedures)
proc $P(x_1, \ldots, x_n)$ α **end** declares a procedure that can be called as $P(x_1, \ldots, x_n)$.
[**void** P(<ARGLIST>) <ACTION>]

Figure 8.1. Complex action operators. Following each definition, the equivalent CML syntax is given in square brackets. The mathematical definitions for these operators is discussed in Chapter 5.

8.3 Discussion

Although we introduced CML as a vehicle of erudition, it is also well suited
to being implemented as a new programming language. In particular, we
have written a Java application that is publicly available to further assist
the interested reader in mastering this novel language [69]. That is, we have
written what amounts to a CML compiler[3]. It is written using the Java
Compiler Compiler (JavaCC) [92] and is freely available online at [69]. The
compiler takes a useful subset of valid CML programs as input and produces
equivalent Prolog programs as output.

There are numerous enhancements that could be made to the CML
compiler. Because of the logic programming connection it was particularly
straightforward to translate CML to Prolog. Ideally, however, the compiler
should generate Java byte code (or at least Java source code) and not Prolog.
The syntax could also be enhanced, perhaps to make it more like natural language. Visual metaphors are a popular way to create finite-state machines,
therefore a more ambitious project would be to create visual programming
paradigms for CML. Because they are so succinct, complex actions are ideally
suited to visual programming. Or we could even go in the other direction. In
particular, we could even take advantage of Java's ability to handle Unicode
characters [Unicode96]. This would result in programs that are syntactically
identical to the theoretical mathematical language.

There are also semantic enhancements that should be made to CML. For
example, in [78], some additional complex actions are described that support
the specification of behaviors in parallel. A nontrivial project would be to
implement these complex actions in CML .

8.4 Notes

CML is not the only programming language available that is based on complex actions. In particular, another implementation, known as Golog, pre-
dates CML and is also available online [57] and is described in detail in
[80, 78]. Golog implements the complex action macro expansion in Prolog by providing an interpreter to expand out Golog terms incrementally at
run-time into equivalent Prolog terms. The connection with logic programming makes Prolog a reasonable choice for implementing concepts based
on logic. For extra-logical notions its value is less clear. Therefore, in our
CML implementation, we perform the macro expansion as a preprocessing

---

[3]See: www.dgp.toronto.edu/~funge/book/.

step. By avoiding the extra overhead of expanding macros on the fly at run-time our compiled programs run much faster.

Although syntactic differences might appear relatively insignificant from an intellectual standpoint, they can be key factors in determining acceptance (even within a research community) of a new computer language. For example, there have been many languages with similar features to Java before but none of them were as popular. Part of the success of Java stems from the way its syntax mimics the well-known syntax of C/C++. The Golog interpreter is written in Prolog and relies heavily on Prolog syntax. This can make programs hard to read for users in animation and computer games who are usually more familiar with standard imperative programming languages. CML supports many of the relaxed formatting conventions C/C++ users are familiar with, such as arbitrary blank spaces, blank lines, tabs, and it supports single and multiline comments. Note also that we are not forced to use ":" as the statement separator, but can use the more usual ";". In Prolog ";" is reserved to mean "or" and thus causes confusion.

For example, in Golog, the precondition axiom mentioned earlier would be written in Prolog as something like

```
poss(act_drop(X),S) :- fl_holding(X).
```

CML automatically rewrites effect axioms into successor-state axioms. In Golog, we would write the successor-state axiom using Prolog as something like

```
fl_broken(X,do(A,S)) :-
  ( A = act_drop(X), \+ fl_sitting(S), !, fail );
  ( \+ (A = act_drop(X)),
    fl_broken(X,S)).
```

As a final comparison, here is the same planner we introduced in Section 8.2 in Golog (adopted from [113]).

```
proc(plans(N),
     ?(goal) #
     ?(N > 0) :
     pi(a,?(primitive_action(a))) : a) :
     pi(n1, ?(n1 is N - 1) :
     plans(n1)))
```

A drawback of sticking with the extra-logical macro expansion semantics is that we limit the expressibility of the language. For example, we cannot quantify over programs. See [35] for a more recent account of complex actions.

Cinematography

The first case study presents an example in which the cognitively enabled character is behind the camera! In particular, we look at an intelligent camera that can use some rules about cinematography to automatically film a conversation. The application is inherently discrete and there is no need to deal with any kind of uncertainty about the ultimate effects of actions. This makes it a particularly gentle introduction to a specific application of cognitive modeling. The camera controller makes minimal use of any planning capabilities. In particular, it only ever plans one step ahead, which means it is extremely fast since the total number of paths through the situation tree is just equal to the number of possible actions. Nevertheless, it demonstrates well how separating out character instruction from the background domain knowledge makes it easier to understand and maintain controllers. It thus demonstrates how cognitive modeling can sometimes subsume conventional behavioral modeling as a limiting case.

9.1 Automated Cinematography

At first, it might seem strange to advocate building a cognitive model for a camera. We soon realize, however, that it is natural to capture in a cog-

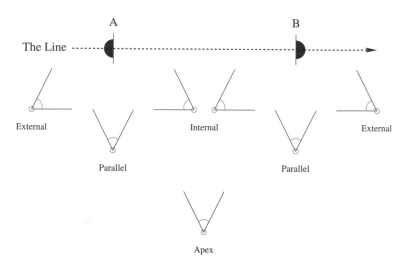

Figure 9.1. Camera placement is specified relative to the "Line" (adopted from Figure 1 of [64]).

nitive model the knowledge of the director and cameraperson who control the camera. In effect, we want to treat all the elements of a scene, be they lights, cameras, or characters as "actors."

To understand what follows, the reader will require some rudimentary knowledge of cinematography. In particular, a film is broken up into a sequence of scenes. Each scene is, in turn, composed of a sequence of *shots*. Each shot typically lasts from a few seconds to a minute and is defined as a portion of film between when a camera was turned on and when the same camera was turned off.

Figure 9.1 shows several different kinds of camera shots. Each shot is defined with respect to an imaginary line. The "Line" can connect two actors, or be in the direction of an actor's motion, or in the direction an actor is facing.

9.1.1 Domain Knowledge

In what follows, we assume that the motion of all other objects in the scene has been computed. Our task is to decide, for each frame, the vantage point from which it is to be rendered.

The precomputed scene is formalized as a lookup function configuration : OBJECT×$\mathbb{N}$ → $\mathbb{R}^n$, which for each object obj, and each frame frameNo returns a list configuration(obj, frameNo) of the n numbers that can completely specify the position, orientation, and shape of the object obj at frame frameNo. To keep track of the current frame number, we introduce the fluent <u>frame</u>, and state that its initial value is zero:

initially <u>frame</u> $= 0$;

The effect axiom for <u>frame</u> just states that a *tick* action causes the frame number to be incremented by one:

occurrence *tick* **results in** <u>frame</u> $=$ k $+$ 1 **when** <u>frame</u> $=$ k;

The defined fluent <u>scene</u> specifies the n numbers that can completely specify the position, orientation, and shape of the object in the current situation:

defined <u>scene</u>(obj) := configuration(obj,<u>frame</u>).

The most common camera placements used in cinematography will be modeled in our formalization as primitive actions. This is a good example of where the term "primitive" is misleading. Low-level camera placement is a complex and challenging task in its own right. Here we shall make some simplifications to clarify our exposition. More realistic equations are easily substituted, but the principles remain the same. In particular, we adopt the standard OpenGL® conventions for camera specification. That is, we specify the camera with two vector-valued fluents: <u>lookFrom</u> and <u>lookAt</u>. Technically, we must also specify an up vector. For most applications, however, we will want up to be constant, pointing along the y-axis, and so for simplicity we shall just fix up to be the vector $(0, 1, 0)$. In addition, we also need to specify the viewing frustum. The standard OpenGL® way of doing this is with a field of view angle, an aspect ratio, a near clipping plane, and a far clipping plane. Once again we make the simplifying assumption that they remain fixed. Despite our simplifications we can still specify a useful range of camera placement actions.

The simplest camera placement action is the *null* action which leaves the camera in its previous configuration. Since it has no effect, there is nothing to write for the effect axiom.

The *raised* action provides a placement relative to the previous camera position, whatever it happened to be. The new camera is further back and higher than the old camera, but has the same orientation as the old camera.

occurrence *raised* **results in**
    <u>lookFrom</u> $= e + k_0 * \widehat{e - c} + k_1 *$ up
when
    <u>lookFrom</u>(s) $= e$ && <u>lookAt</u> $= c$;

where k_0 and k_1 are some suitable constants.

The *fixed* action is used to specify explicitly a particular camera configuration. We can, for example, use it to provide an overview shot of the scene.

occurrence *fixed*(e,c) **results in** <u>lookFrom</u> $= e$ && <u>lookAt</u> $= c$;

A more complicated action is *external*. It takes two arguments, character A and character B, and places the camera so that A is seen over the shoulder of B. One effect of this action, therefore, is that the camera is looking at character A.

occurrence *external*(A,B) **results in** <u>lookAt</u> $= p$ **when**
    scene$(A(\text{upperbody})) = p$;

The other effect is that the camera is located above character B's shoulder. This might be accomplished with an effect axiom such as

occurrence *external*(A,B) **results in**
    <u>lookFrom</u> $= p + k_2 * \text{up} + k_3 * \widehat{p - c}$
when
    scene$(B(\text{shoulder})) = p$ && scene$(A(\text{upperbody})) = c$;

where k_2 and k_3 are some suitable constants.

That completes all the camera placement actions that we will need for this example, but of course there are many others that we could have defined. Some involve performing complicated geometric calculations to obtain the correct position, orientation, and field of view of the camera in order to satisfy constraints on the placement and screen coverage of the protagonists in the final image. Such constraints include cinematographic rules relating to "cutting heights" and occlusion problems. To satisfy them, it is possible that we may even have to resort to moving the original scene around!

9.1.2 Character Instruction

In cinematography, there are many set formulae for filming certain types of action sequences. For example, to film a conversation it is usual to begin with an apex shot that shows all the protagonists and establishes their relative placements. The action usually proceeds by moving to an external reverse shot of the actor who is talking. When the other actor starts to reply, the shot moves to a corresponding shot of that actor. To break up the monotony there are also usually intermittent reaction shots of the actor that is currently listening. We will show how elegantly we can capture this formula using complex actions, but first we must introduce some new fluents.

The fluent $\mathsf{Talking}(A,B)$ is true if a character A is talking to another character B. The effect axioms for $\mathsf{Talking}$ simply state that the fluent becomes true when character A starts talking to character B, and it becomes false when they stop.

occurrence *startTalk*(A,B) **results in** $\mathsf{Talking}(A,B)$;
occurrence *stopTalk*(A,B) **results in** $\overline{!\mathsf{Talking}}(A,B)$;

We shall treat *startTalk* and *stopTalk* as exogenous actions. In terms of an implementation, these exogenous actions can easily be generated automatically. That is, since our characters are situated in a virtual world, any talking must have originally been instigated by the application that we used to generate the configuration function. We can simply modify the macro expansion of the complex actions (as described in Chapter 7, Section 2.1) to look up whether A or B are talking at the frame number given by $\underline{\mathsf{frame}}(s)$. If either of them is talking then the corresponding talk action is generated.

A more interesting fluent is $\underline{\mathsf{silenceCount}}$, which keeps count of how long it has been since a character spoke.

occurrence *tick* **results in** $\underline{\mathsf{silenceCount}} = n-1$ **when**
    $\underline{\mathsf{silenceCount}} = n$ && $!\mathsf{Talking}(A,B)$;
occurrence *stopTalk*(A,B) **results in** $\underline{\mathsf{silenceCount}} = k_a$;
occurrence *setCount* **results in** $\underline{\mathsf{silenceCount}} = k_a$;

Note that k_a is a constant (we used $k_a = 10$), such that the counter will be negative after k_a ticks of no-one speaking. A similar fluent $\underline{\mathsf{filmCount}}$ keeps track of how long the camera has been pointing at the same character:

occurrence *setCount* $\|$ *external*(A,B) **results in** $\underline{\mathsf{filmCount}} = k_b$
    when $\underline{\mathsf{Talking}}(A,B)$;
occurrence *setCount* $\|$ *external*(A,B) **results in** $\underline{\mathsf{filmCount}} = k_c$
    when $!\underline{\mathsf{Talking}}(A,B)$;
occurrence *tick* **results in** $\underline{\mathsf{filmCount}} = n-1$ **when** $\underline{\mathsf{filmCount}} = n$;

where k_b and k_c are constants (we used $k_b = 30$ and $k_c = 15$) that state how long we can continue the same shot before the counter becomes negative. Note that the constants for the case of looking at a nonspeaking character are lower. We will keep track of which constant we are using with the fluent $\underline{\mathsf{tooLong}}$.

occurrence *external*(A,B) **results in** $\underline{tooLong} = k_b$ **when** $\underline{Talking}(A,B)$;
occurrence *external*(A,B) **results in** $\underline{tooLong} = k_c$ **when** $\underline{!Talking}(A,B)$;

For convenience, we now introduce two defined fluents that express when a shot has become boring because it has gone on too long, and when a shot has not gone on long enough. We need the notion of a minimum time for each shot to avoid, MTV cinematography notwithstanding, annoying flitter between shots.

defined $\underline{Boring} := \underline{filmCount} < 0$;
defined $\underline{TooFast} := \underline{tooLong} - k_s \leqslant \underline{filmCount}$; (where k_s is some constant)

The last fluent we shall formally introduce is a fluent $\underline{Filming}$ that keeps track of which character the camera is pointing at.

occurrence *external*(A,B) **results in** $\underline{Filming}(A)$ && $\underline{!Filming}(B)$;

Until now, we have not mentioned any preconditions for our actions. Unless stated otherwise, we assume that actions are always possible. In contrast, the precondition axiom for the *external* camera action states that we only want to point the camera at character A if we are already filming A and it has not gotten boring yet, or if we are not filming A, and A is talking, and we have stayed with the current shot long enough.

action *external*(A,B) **possible when**
    ($\underline{!Boring}$ && $\underline{Filming}(A)$) || ($\underline{Talking}(A,B)$ && $\underline{!Filming}(A)$ && $\underline{!TooFast}$);

We are now in a position to define the controller that will begin with an establishing shot and then move our "cognitive camera" to shoot the character doing the talking, with occasional respites to focus on the other character's reactions. First, let's define a procedure to create the establishing shot (e and c represent suitable vector constants).

proc *establish*
{
    fixed(e,c);
    setCount;
    while ($0 < \underline{silenceCount}$)
        tick;
}

Finally, we can write down the camera controller.

Figure 9.2. Cinemasaurus animation. (See Color Plate I.)

establish;
setCount;
while $(0 <$ <u>silenceCount</u>$)$ {
  pick(A,B) *external*(A,B);
  tick;
}

  As in the maze-solving example of Chapter 5, this specification makes heavy use of the ability to nondeterministically choose arguments. The reader might also like to note that the above camera controller can be encoded as a finite-state machine. See Section 9.4 for an example of an FSM that achieves the same effect as the complex action given above. Notice how in the FSM approach all the domain knowledge and the control information are all mixed up together.

9.2 Implementation

Figure 9.2 shows a few frames from an application that used an implementation of the cognitive camera to automatically film, in real-time, a Tyrannosaurus Rex and a Velociprator "conversing" by roaring at each other. The camera always films the dinosaur that is "talking" unless it talks for too long, in which case it will get a reaction shot from the other dinosaur. The cognitive camera uses essentially the same code as given above, although some of the camera angles are programmed a bit differently. This animation and additional support material is available at: www.dgp.toronto.edu/~funge/book/.

9.3 Discussion

This chapter has hardly begun to scratch the surface of cinematography applications. The reader might like to think about how to implement some of the other common camera motions. A particular challenge would be to implement continuous camera actions, like panning. One could think about doing it using complex actions to repeatedly move the camera by small increments. For example, suppose we have a would-be continuous action *continuousMove*, then we can define this as a procedure something like the following:

```
proc continuousMove {
    while (!Arrived)
        moveALittleBit ;
}
```

Alternatively, we could use the work described in [112] to extend the underlying theory to include support for continuous primitive actions.

Many other interesting issues arise with regard to camera placement. For example, it is common practice in computer animation to create a simulation and then to choose suitable camera placements. In film production the process is not so conveniently partitioned. It is commonplace to reshoot a scene, with the actors in different positions (or even entirely removed from the scene), and pretend that it is the same scene shot from a different angle. The reasons for this approach are both practical and aesthetic. In computer animation we have the option of reshooting the same piece of action from multiple viewpoints. That is, there are no practical reasons to reenact a scene, but it may well be the case that for aesthetic reasons the action needs to be changed depending on the viewpoint. For example, one might imagine a "face the camera if possible" behavior. This is an issue that has not been addressed within computer animation research.

9.4 Notes

The standard text on cinematography is [3]. It provides an informal compilation of formulas, along with a discussion of the situations when a filmmaker might prefer one formula over another. The inspiration for our own work on cinematography (see [47, 46, 48]) comes from two papers on the subject [64, 33]. These two papers use a simple scripting language to implement hierarchical finite state machines for camera control. Note that in [64], the camera placement actions we encode using "primitive actions" are referred to as "camera modules." By way of comparison, we have quoted below the FSM used to describe the same camera behavior as we described in the main text of this chapter.

```
DEFINE_IDIOM_IN_ACTION(2Talk)
    WHEN ( talking(A, B) )
        DO ( GOTO (1); )
    WHEN ( talking(B, A) )
        DO ( GOTO (2); )
END_IDIOM_IN_ACTION

DEFINE_STATE_ACTIONS(COMMON)
    WHEN (T < 10)
        DO ( STAY; )
    WHEN (!talking(A, B) && !talking(B, A))
        DO ( RETURN; )
END_STATE_ACTIONS

DEFINE_STATE_ACTIONS(1)
    WHEN ( talking(B, A) )
        DO ( GOTO (2); )
    WHEN ( T > 30 )
        DO ( GOTO (4); )
END_STATE_ACTIONS

DEFINE_STATE_ACTIONS(2)
    WHEN ( talking(A, B) )
        DO ( GOTO (1); )
    WHEN ( T > 30 )
        DO ( GOTO (3); )
END_STATE_ACTIONS

DEFINE_STATE_ACTIONS(3)
    WHEN ( talking(A, B) )
        DO ( GOTO (1); )
    WHEN ( talking(B, A) && T > 15 )
        DO ( GOTO (2); )
END_STATE_ACTIONS

DEFINE_STATE_ACTIONS(4)
    WHEN ( talking(B, A) )
        DO ( GOTO (2); )
    WHEN ( talking(A, B) && T > 15 )
        DO ( GOTO (1); )
END_STATE_ACTIONS.
```

Low-level camera control is a complex and challenging task in its own right. The interested reader is referred to [22] and [3] as a good starting point.

Prehistoric World

At the end of the last chapter we briefly mentioned a prehistoric virtual world. In this chapter, we will use this prehistoric world to showcase some cognitive characters that autonomously generate intelligent behavior consistent with goal-directed specification by exploiting domain knowledge and reasoning.

10.1 The Prehistoric World

The prehistoric world, comprising a volcanic territory and a jungle territory, is inhabited by a Tyrannosaurus Rex (T-Rex) and some Velociprators (Raptors). It is implemented as a game engine API which runs in real-time on any reasonably up-to-date PC. The dinosaur characters are animated by key framed footprints and inverse kinematics to position the legs onto the ground. To add some physical realism, the body is modeled as a point mass that moves dynamically in response to the leg movements.[1]

Our challenge is to administer enough knowledge to the T-Rex about its world, especially about the predefined behavior of the Raptors, so that the T-Rex knows enough to automatically formulate plans for expelling Raptors

---

[1]See Chapter 2 for a reminder on what these terms mean.

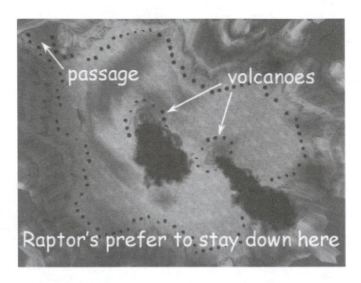

Figure 10.1. Map of prehistoric world. (See Color Plate II.)

out of its volcanic territory into the neighboring jungle territory. To do this, the T-Rex must herd Raptors through a narrow passage that connects the two territories. A stone arch at the northwest corner of the volcanic territory marks the passage. All these features are marked on Figure 10.1.

In Chapter 1, Section 5, we explained why we usually need to discretize the virtual world. For the Prehistoric world it turns out that it is sufficient to use a simple 60×65 regular grid such that each cell is 5 m square (approximately the length of a Raptor). Thus the fluent position refers to the grid cell that a character is in. Just like the maze example of Chapter 5, we also define an auxiliary function *adjacent* that returns the cell that is adjacent to a given cell, in a given direction.

10.2   Effect Axioms

If we glance at Figure 10.2, we can see why the Raptors have good reason to fear the larger, more powerful and highly dangerous T-Rex should it come close. The following effect axiom is used to instruct the T-Rex that the Raptors will become frightened when it approaches them:

occurrence *move*(dir) **results in** Frightened(Raptor(i))
    when position(T-Rex) $= p$ && position(Raptor(i)) $= q$ &&
      $|q - \mathsf{adjacent}(p, \mathsf{dir})| \leqslant \Delta;$

Figure 10.2. Feeding time. (See Color Plate III.)

where Δ is some suitable constant. Another effect axiom tells the T-Rex that less proximal Raptors would also become frightened if it roared, i.e., $\Delta \leqslant \Delta'$.

occurrence *roar* **results in** Frightened(Raptor(i))
when position(T-Rex) $= p$ && position(Raptor(i)) $= q$ && $|q - p| \leqslant \Delta'$;

The next defined fluent heading tells the T-Rex that frightened Raptors will run away from it.

defined heading(Raptor(i)) := dir
where
    (Frightened (Raptor(i)) && dir = opposite(dirRex)) ||
      (!Frightened(Raptor(i)) && dir = dirOld)
when
    relativeDirOfTRex (Raptor(i)) = dirRex && heading (Raptor(i)) = dirOld;

Note that relativeDirOfTRex is a fluent that is easily defined in terms of the relative positions of the T-Rex and Raptor i.

10.2.1 Discussion

The above effect axioms express how the T-Rex *thinks* the Raptors will react to its behavior. In actuality, the reactive controller for the Raptors' behavior consists of about one thousand lines of C code that deals with numerous special cases[2]. For example, it includes code to work out in which direction to turn if the Raptor wants to run away from the T-Rex but there is an obstacle in the way. We can see, therefore, that the T-Rex's cognitive model of the Raptor's behavior is only a crude approximation. The reader might therefore be left wondering if we should not try to make the model more accurate. Perhaps we should include all the relevant C code in the axioms!

Hopefully by now, we have explained why we don't want to go down this road. In Chapter 1, Section 5, we explained some of the disadvantages of making the effect axioms overly complex. In particular, we explained that it makes decision-making slow and gives the character the appearance of being clairvoyant. Moreover, even if we had a completely accurate model of a single Raptor's behavior it would not necessarily tell us very much about the behavior that emerges when there are a whole herd of Raptors to deal with.

Having said this, it may turn out that the effect axioms are too crude to be at all useful. If, as we are testing the cognitive character's behavior, we see it behaving strangely, then an explicit representation of the character's knowledge in terms of actions, effects, and preconditions is nicely suited to debugging. In particular, we can suspend the execution easily and query the character. We can then proceed to ask it various insightful questions about what it "thinks" is going on. Aside from simple queries about what it believes to be the current situation, we can ask it more elaborate questions such as "what if" questions about what it believes will be the effect of various actions in the current situation. This can often quickly reveal important omissions of the effect and precondition axioms.

For example, suppose the T-Rex's roaring does not frighten the Raptors if they are in a group, but that we forgot to tell the T-Rex this fact. If we notice the T-Rex is not behaving effectively, we can ask it to plot the path that it thinks a Raptor will take, and we can then compare this to the actual path the Raptor takes. If we continually find glaring discrepancies, then we can ask the T-Rex some probing questions. For instance, suppose Raptor k is heading east and is north of the T-Rex. The T-Rex thinks to itself that if it roars it will frighten the Raptor and it will change course

---

[2]Animations, source code and additional support material is available at: www.dgp.toronto.edu/~funge/book/

to head north. Unfortunately, because the Raptor is in a group, it keeps on heading east. We quickly spot the result of the T-Rex's mistake, but suppose we cannot figure out why it is getting it wrong. Since the T-Rex has an explicit representation of its knowledge, we can ask it to "explain" its line of reasoning.

It will respond with something like

$$\text{Frightened}(k, s) \land \text{heading}(k, s) = E \land \text{relativeDirOfTRex}(k, s) = S \Rightarrow$$
$$\text{heading}(k, do(\textbf{roar}, s)) = \text{oppositeDir}(S)$$

from which we can immediately see that it made the assumption that Raptor k was frightened in order to arrive at the conclusion that it would head north. We can quickly check the validity of this assumption and see that Raptor k is not actually frightened, from which we can easily deduce our mistake in misinforming the T-Rex. Clearly, characters that do not explicitly represent knowledge about their world could not engage in this kind of dialogue. For example, imagine asking a character that was controlled by a neural network why it did something. All it could reply would be that a certain set of inputs fired, and with the current weight assignments (a long meaningless stream of numbers) in its neural network, this caused a certain output to fire. Such information is next to useless.

10.2.2   Learning Effect Axioms

Another way to avoid human error in giving the T-Rex suitable domain knowledge is to have the T-Rex automatically acquire the knowledge. That is, instead of just writing down the effect axioms, the T-Rex can learn about its world. In particular, we can create a T-Rex that wanders around its world by choosing actions at random. As the T-Rex wanders around moving in various directions and roaring, it notes how the Raptors behave. We'll explain in detail how this works with a simple example. Suppose we define a fluent $\text{RunAway}(i)$ that is true if Raptor i is running away from the T-Rex. To simplify the notation, let's drop the index i, i.e., we'll just consider the case when there is only one Raptor. We also define some other fluents whose intended meaning is given informally by their names. The formal definitions (left as an exercise for the reader) are in terms of the relative placement and orientation of a Raptor and a T-Rex.

The question we want the T-Rex to be able to answer is: Under what circumstances will the Raptor run away? We already know from Chapter 6, Section 1.1 that from a mathematical standpoint, the T-Rex is trying to

RunAway($do(a,s)$)?	Y	Y	Y	N	N	N	hd	6 - hd
FarAway(s)?	Y	Y	N	Y	Y	Y	4	2
Facing(s)?	N	Y	Y	Y	Y	N	3	3
$a = roar$?	Y	Y	Y	Y	N	Y	2	4
RunAway(s)?	Y	Y	N	N	N	N	1	5
Sleepy(s)?	Y	Y	Y	Y	Y	Y	3	3

Table 10.1. A training set with only six instances.

learn about the fluent RunAway in situation $do(a, s)$. A small training set, with only six instances, that the T-Rex can use to learn about a Raptor's behavior is given in Table 10.1.

Each column of the table corresponds to a labeled instance, where the label is given by the value of RunAway($do(a, s)$). The column labeled hd is the *Hamming distance* between the target function and a particular attribute. It gives a simplistic measure of how "good" a particular attribute is at categorizing training instances. The Hamming distance is calculated, for each row, as the number of cases for which the attribute's value disagrees with the label. The value $6 - hd$ is just the number of instances, less the Hamming distance for that row. For each row, we can take the row's value to be the minimum of hd and $6 - hd$. The row with the minimum value is used as the first question to build a decision tree. For example, in the above table, RunAway(s) is the best row, so the first question in the decision tree is:

Is the Raptor already running away?

We should recognize this immediately as a frame axiom, and it should come as no surprise to us that the best indicator of future behavior is current behavior. The other thing we notice, is that for the two instances where the Raptor is running away in situation s, it is also running away in situation $do(a, s)$. If any of the answers to a decision tree question agrees with the target like this, then we are at a leaf node and can stop looking for any more questions down that particular branch. In contrast, if the Raptor is not currently running away, then there is still no clear decision that can be made and so for the other four instances we need to look for another question. Table 10.2 gives the training set for the four remaining instances. This time we can see the T-Rex should pick the question:

Is the Raptor far away?

This question completely characterizes the remaining instances so we are finished.

RunAway($do(a,s)$)?	Y	N	N	N	hd	6-hd
FarAway(s)?	N	Y	Y	Y	4	0
Facing(s)?	Y	Y	Y	N	2	2
$a = roar$?	Y	Y	N	Y	2	2
RunAway(s)?	N	N	N	N	1	3
Sleepy(s)?	Y	Y	Y	Y	3	1

Table 10.2. The training set for the four remaining instances.

The final decision tree is:

Is the Raptor already running away?
    Y: Then it is running away now.
    N: Was the Raptor far away?
        Y: Then it is not running away now.
        N: Then it is running away now.

It is not hard to write down a defined fluent from this tree as follows:

defined RunAway(Raptor(i)) := !FarAway(Raptor(i))
    when !RunAway(Raptor(i));

This is obviously hopelessly simplistic. In addition, since the first question just corresponds to a frame axiom, we can ignore it as the frame axioms will be taken care of when the effect axioms are compiled automatically into successor-state axioms. Unfortunately, we did not obtain a decision tree that mentions any actions and so we can't write down an effect axiom for the *roar* action, as we might have hoped. The reason this occurred is because the training set was so small. With a realistic training set of thousands of instances we will obtain a more useful result.

In addition, we only considered one Raptor. However, even in a real application, this might be a good idea as it makes it easier to learn. That is, with multiple Raptors they can affect each other's behavior (e.g., they change direction to avoid bumping into each other) and the T-Rex can be fooled into thinking it was the cause. Of course, even though the training takes place with only one Raptor present, the resulting cognitive model is still valid when there are multiple Raptors. That is, the T-Rex simply tries to influence them one at a time.

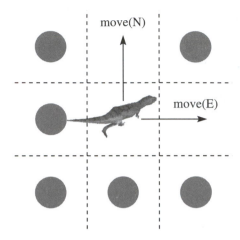

Figure 10.3. T-Rex can only move north or east.

10.3 Precondition Axioms

Using the following precondition axiom (as in the maze example of Chapter 5), we instruct the T-Rex to plan paths that avoid obstacles.

action *move*(dir) **possible when**
    position(T-Rex) = p && Free(adjacent(p,dir));

In fact, the T-Rex can easily map out all the obstacles by exploring its world in a preprocessing step. When it encounters an obstacle, it remembers the obstacle's location in a mental map of its world. This "mental map" is indicated on Figure 10.1. In particular, the red dots indicate obstacle boundaries discovered by the T-Rex. The bounded regions contain volcanoes or rugged terrain over which the T-Rex cannot travel. For example, Figure 10.3 shows a T-Rex that can only move north or east.

10.4 Character Instruction

Given enough patience, skill and ingenuity, it is conceivable that we could successfully program herding behavior using a set of reactive behavior rules. Using goal-directed behavior we can, however, do the same thing with relative ease. Suppose we want to get some Raptors heading in a particular

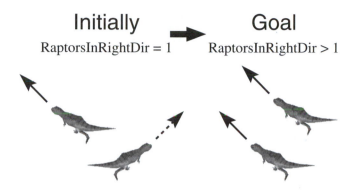

Initially

RaptorsInRightDir = 1

Goal

RaptorsInRightDir > 1

Figure 10.4. Specifying a goal for the T-rex

direction. We simply give the T-Rex the goal of getting more Raptors heading in the right direction than are initially heading that way. Figure 10.4 depicts this graphically. Here is how this goal is specified as a defined fluent:

defined goal := RaptorsInRightDir $= n$ && $n \geqslant n_0 + k$
   when initially $n_0 =$ RaptorsInRightDir;

In particular, the goal is to get *at least* k more Raptors heading toward the goal than are currently heading that way.

    This goal, along with our previous domain knowledge, enables the T-Rex to plan its actions like a good sheepdog. It autonomously plans collision-free paths to maneuver in and around groups of Raptors to frighten them in the desired direction. Notice that this goal will also automatically avoid coming up with any plans that could frighten any Raptors unnecessarily as it plans a path to move toward the errant ones.

10.5 Implementation

The T-Rex is slower and less maneuverable than the Raptors and so it needs to anticipate their positions and move to head them off. Unlike the camera case study, this requires the T-Rex to be able to plan reasonably far ahead. For example, Figure 10.5 shows a T-Rex that can only plan one move ahead. Note that the blue dot (only one in this case) indicates the path planned, the green dot the direction of travel, and the Raptor is circled with a blue circle that also indicates its direction of travel. As expected, all the "reactive

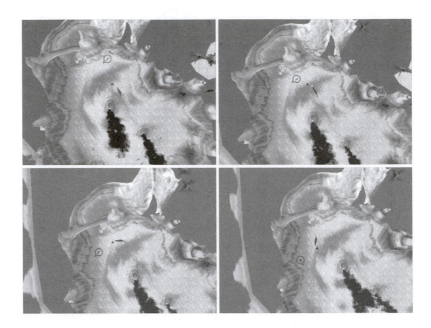

Figure 10.5. This T-Rex can only plan one move ahead. (See Color Plate IV.)

T-Rex" can do is chase the agile Raptors around aimlessly. Only by sheer luck can it eventually chase a few Raptors through the narrow passage under the arch and out of its territory.

In contrast, Figures 10.6 and 10.7 show a T-Rex that can plan up to six moves ahead of its current position. This enables it to anticipate where the Raptors will be far enough into the future for it to get into position ready to frighten them in the correct direction. The dots in the figure show the paths that the T-Rex plans to take. It shows clearly how it continually anticipates the Raptors behavior so it can head them off and get them moving toward the pass. We can let the T-Rex plan even further ahead but this degrades real-time performance. Longer plans are also rarely useful in an unpredictable world about which the T-Rex has only partial knowledge. A better strategy is adaptive herding through periodic re-planning. We can see this replanning on the figure as new paths that the T-Rex comes up with every now and again. By default the T-Rex replans when it has finished executing the current plan, but it can also abort a current plan if necessary. That is, a predefined behavior continually monitors the T-Rex's progress as it executes the plan and can instigate a replan whenever it decides the current plan is out-of-date.

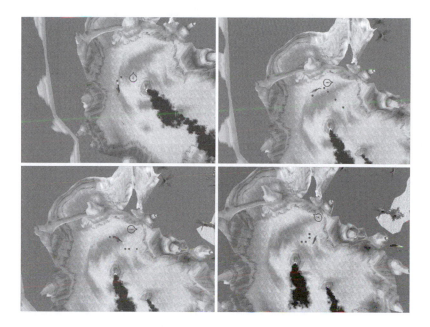

Figure 10.6. This T-Rex can plan up to six moves ahead (Part I). (See Color Plate V.)

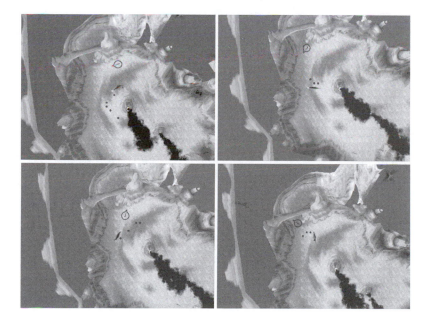

Figure 10.7. This T-Rex can plan up to six moves ahead (Part II). (See Color Plate VI.)

A precondition axiom is designed to tell a character when an action is not possible. In Chapter 5, Section 3.1 we also noted that precondition axioms can be used to prune the situation tree. For example, if the Raptors are too far away then there is no point for the T-Rex to roar as it will have no effect. Unfortunately, if we use a precondition axiom, then the T-Rex could not roar at other times. For example, regardless of how far away any Raptors are, we might want to make the T-Rex give a roar of satisfaction once it has gotten a Raptor through the pass. Therefore, we can define undesirable situations using the fluent <u>Undesirable</u>. These are the antithesis of goals in that they represent situations that, although not illegal, are undesirable. For example, a situation in which the T-Rex roars without anticipating any Raptors changing to head in the right direction is undesirable.

defined <u>Undesirable</u> **after** *roar* := <u>RaptorsInRightDir</u> $= n$ && $n \leqslant n_0$
    when <u>RaptorsInRightDir</u> $= n_0$;

It is easy to modify the herding behavior so that the T-Rex need not consider this or its subsequent situations when searching for appropriate plans. In particular, the complex action *herd*(0,6) uses a breadth-first search to look for plans, between 0 and 6 actions long, that result in herding behavior.[3]

```
proc herd(m,n)
{
    test (m ⩽ n);
    possiblePlan(m);
    choose test goal;
    or plan(m + 1,n);
}

proc possiblePlan(n)
{
    choose test(n = 0);
    or {
        test(0 < n)
        pick(d) move(d);
        ! test(Undesirable);
        possiblePlan(n − 1);
    }
}
```

---

[3] Adapted from [113]

Figure 10.8. Results of herding behavior. (See Color Plate VII.)

Figure 10.8 shows some images from an implementation of the above approach. The pack of reactive Raptors prefer to stay away from the passage under the arch, but the smarter, cognitively empowered T-Rex succeeds in expelling this unruly mob from its territory.

10.5.1   Real-time Performance

To create a robust application that is guaranteed to respond in real-time, the goal-directed behavior described above is embedded in a system architecture not dissimilar to that depicted in Chapter 7, Figure 7.3. The predefined behavior consists of the ability to head toward the nearest Raptor without colliding into anything. Since real-time performance is still possible for plans up to a maximum of six actions long, the predefined behavior is only called upon if the goal-directed behavior fails to come up with anything at all, for example when the errant Raptors are too far away. Note that, even if the T-Rex cannot find a sequence of actions that it believes will get k Raptors heading in the right direction, as long as it makes some partial progress, it should settle for the best it can come up with. It is left as an exercise for the reader to modify the above *herd* procedure to record the best plan found so far.

10.6   Discussion

We have concentrated on endowing the T-Rex with cognitive abilities. There is no reason why we could not similarly endow the Raptors as well. This would allow the animation of much more complex dinosaur behavior.[4] A lone Raptor is no match for the T-Rex, but imagine the following scenario in which a pack of cunning Raptors conspire to fell their large opponent. Through cognitive modeling, the Raptors conceive a strategic plan—the ambush! Based on their domain knowledge, the Raptors have inferred that the T-Rex's size, his big asset in open terrain, would make it much more difficult for him to maneuver within the narrow passage under the arch. The leader of the pack plays the decoy, luring the unsuspecting opponent into the narrow passage. The pack mates, who have assumed their positions near both ends of the passage, rush into it on command. Some Raptors jump on the T-Rex and chomp down on his back while others bite into his legs. Thus the pack overcomes the brute through strategic planning, cooperation, and sheer number. Coordinating multiple Raptors in this way would significantly increase the branching factor in the situation trees of the cognitive models. A solution would be to control them as intelligent flocks (see Chapter 7, Section 5). We could also exploit complex actions to provide a loose script that would specify some key intermediate goals such as the decoy maneuver.

---

[4]See Robert T. Bakker's captivating novel *Raptor Red* (Bantam, 1996).

In this chapter, we also considered the ability to query cognitive characters in order to discover explanations for their actions. In order to do this more effectively, it would be a good idea to provide a convenient language for asking these queries.

10.7 Notes

In [26] some work is described in which the user of a virtual reality simulator tries to herd reactive characters.

Undersea World  11

The undersea world we will describe is entirely physics-based and is inhabited by merpeople, fabled creatures of the sea with the head and upper body of a human and the tail of a fish.[1] Its other inhabitants are predator sharks.

Within the undersea world we will produce complex behavior that would overwhelm naïve goal-directed specification approaches. In particular, we demonstrate how complex actions can be used to provide a loose script for the characters to follow; the animator/programmer provides some of the details of the required behavior while the rest are filled in automatically by the character.

The extremely elaborate physics-based virtual underwater world draws upon numerous techniques all at once and is a good example of "putting it all together." Unlike the other case studies, we will not focus just on the cognitive modeling aspect. In particular, we will take a detailed look at the underlying predefined behavior model, and also the biomechanical and physical models that are used.[2] Presenting a final and complete description of all aspects of this elaborate case study will help draw together all the different threads of this book.

---

[1] "Merpeople" and "merperson" are words we coined as gender neutral terms for what are traditionally referred to as mermaids and mermen.

[2] The reader who is unfamiliar with the terms and concepts we introduced in Chapter 2 may need to refer back to refresh their memory.

11.1   Discussion

As we shall see in Section 11.8, the state of the undersea world after executing an action is an extremely complicated function of muscle activation functions, water force reaction, obstacle location, etc. These are precisely the sort of details that we usually prefer to leave out of the cognitive modeling layer. The fluents will therefore be used to represent the character's intention. Thus, from the character's perspective, what actually occurs within its world is somewhat unpredictable. Typically a character will fix a course of action and then update it in light of any pertinent new information its senses might provide.

For example, later on we introduce a fluent goalPosn, that keeps track of the position to which a merperson *intends* to go. We view the fact that the merperson is trying to get to a particular location as a fact about the world, rather than as an esoteric statement about the merperson's mental state. This is not as peculiar as it might first appear. In the real world a person's inner thoughts might be viewed as somewhat opaque. In our virtual world any such distinction is clearly arbitrary. There is nothing inherently different between peering into our characters' heads to see what their current intentions are and looking up the current rate of flow of the virtual water. Both really are just facts about the virtual world.

Having said all this, problems remain. In particular, the question arises about what to do with fluents that pertain to the character's view of its world. For example, the fluent currPosn could legitimately refer to the merperson's position, or to the position the merperson "thinks" it is in. We choose the former. The latter concept is represented as an interval-valued fluent and the correspondence between the two is maintained by sensing, as described in Chapter 7, Section 2.1.

11.2   Overview

The basic system architecture for a merperson's behavior is the same as in Figure 7.1 of Chapter 7, with some predefined behavior that acts as a low-level behavior system and some goal-directed behavior that acts as a high-level behavior system. We shall refer to these two components, respectively, as the *low-level behavior system* and the *high-level behavior system.* Once again, the standard cognitive modeling term "primitive actions" is somewhat misleading, as some primitive actions, such as "go to position g," may entail nontrivial obstacle avoidance behavior in the low-level behavior system.

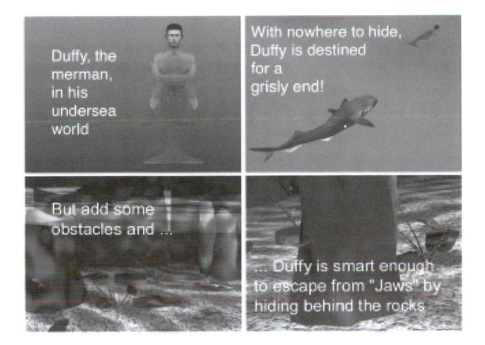

Figure 11.1. Undersea animations. (See Color Plate VIII.)

All the undersea applications revolve around pursuit and evasion behaviors. The hungry sharks try to catch and eat the merpeople and the merpeople try to use their superior reasoning abilities to avoid this grisly fate. For the most part, the sharks are instructed to chase any merperson they see. If they cannot see any merpeople, they go to where they last saw one. If all else fails, they start to forage systematically. Figure 11.1 shows some selected frames from two animations.

11.3 Evasion Behavior

The primary aim of the merpeople is to avoid being eaten by the sharks, but the sharks are larger and faster so they cannot be simply outrun. For example, in Figure 11.2 there are no obstacles/rocks that are large enough for a merperson to hide behind. All the merperson can do is to swim away from the ferocious shark as far and as fast as it can.

As we can see from Figure 11.3, the shark has no difficulty catching and devouring its prey.

Figure 11.2. Nowhere to Hide (Part I). (See Color Plate IX.)

Figure 11.3. Nowhere to Hide (Part II). (See Color Plate X.)

If we add some rocks to the scene, then the merpeople can try to outwit the sharks by finding safe places to hide. This entails giving the merpeople some domain knowledge, and some heuristic knowledge in the form of complex actions.

11.3.1 Domain Knowledge

The primary purpose of the domain knowledge is to define what a "safe place" is. Implicit in this task is defining what a "place" is. We define what a place is by dividing the world up into a set of three-dimensional regions. To avoid a potentially catastrophic combinatorial explosion, it is important to perform the discretization dynamically using a hierarchical data-structure such as the one described in Section 11.7. For now, all we have to know is that each merperson knows about some finite set of regions. In particular, the set of regions the merperson knows about is the set of regions within visual range, plus some noteworthy regions that it remembers from its previous travels. Since the set of known regions is constantly changing, it is represented by a fluent regions.

The merperson then evaluates some subset of these regions to see which one is safest. Which subset it evaluates will be discussed in the next section on complex actions. Since safety is not an absolute notion, we define a function evaluator that assigns a numeric *reward* value to any given region. The particular set of criteria we use to assign the value is not vitally important. It is based on obvious properties of the region, such as its distance from the predator, and whether it is hidden from the predator. Determining whether a region is hidden is also an interesting problem in its own right and we will return to it in Section 11.7.

The next observation is that it is not enough to consider only the reward associated with isolated regions. In particular, we also need to consider the *cost* associated with getting to a given region. For example, suppose the merperson knows about some hidden region, but that to go there directly involves swimming right past a shark. Then, clearly this is not a good region to go to at all. In particular, we have been ignoring any consideration of the path taken to get to a region. Clearly, the path is vitally important since if the shark sees a merperson *en route* to anywhere it will start to pursue it.

There are at least two ways in which we can imagine including support for considering the cost of getting to a region versus the reward associated with getting there. One involves more work for us; the other leaves the work up to the merperson which means slower run-time execution.

- The complicated approach (for us) involves redefining the evaluate function to modify the reward to include extra criteria related to the cost of getting there from the merperson's current location. That is, before all the criteria were related to just the region and the sharks. Now we have to consider factors related to the sharks, the region, and the merperson. For example, from the merperson's perspective, far away regions, regions with obstacles in the way of them, and regions that are in the same direction as a shark should all fair worse. All the extra criteria can make it hard to come up with a fair way to assign values to regions. Taking this route also entails a fair amount of experimentation to see how different value assignments affect the merperson's behavior. This runs against the grain of the cognitive modeling approach somewhat as we can end up with a character whose behavior is related in some obscure way to the assignment of numerical values to regions in space.

- The more elegant approach is to stick with a simple evaluation function and make the merperson use this function to evaluate the cost of a path. For example, the merperson could evaluate a path by adding up the value for each region in the path. The task would then be to find the best path, in the sense that it was the path with the optimal value. Unfortunately, this leads to a computationally expensive combinatorial optimization problem.

In the last chapter, we had a similar problem because, in order to frighten an errant Raptor in the right direction, the T-Rex needed to get to a certain position. However, while it was *en route* it also needed to avoid frightening Raptors that were already heading in the right direction. We therefore chose the evaluation function to be the number of Raptors heading in the right direction and this was evaluated for all *paths* the T-Rex considered. The prehistoric world was subdivided into a two-dimensional grid and all the paths considered were less than six units long. Unfortunately, the undersea world has a *three*-dimensional grid associated with it and we want the merperson to be able to consider goal positions that are quite far away. For these reasons alone, the second option was not feasible, but when we also consider that we wanted an application that would run reasonably fast, even with multiple merpeople, we chose the first option and redefined the evaluate function. Note that this also entails that the "path planning" to get to these regions must be done elsewhere. Fortunately, the low-level predefined behavior layer that we describe in Section 11.8 has the ability to get to specified positions while avoiding collisions.

To keep track of the current regions which have the best valuations we introduce a fluent goalPosn. Another fluent acceptable keeps track of how good the evaluation of a region has to be for it to become a goal position. Here is the effect axiom for the acceptable fluent.

occurrence *setAcceptable*(i,status) **results in**
    (status = panic && acceptable(i) = a_0) ||
    (status = searchRegions && acceptable(i) = a_1) ||
    (status = currPosn && acceptable(i) = a_2) ||
    (status = searchObstacles && acceptable(i) = a_3);

As we shall see in the next section, what counts as acceptable changes according to how desperate to think of somewhere to go the merperson is getting. So, the above effect axiom simply sets what value counts as acceptable to one of the predefined values a_i depending on to where the merperson is currently thinking about going.

A merperson's behavior ends up looking less frenetic if it does not keep changing course wildly. Therefore, a fluent extent keeps track of how far afield a merperson is willing to consider shifting its target location from its current goal position.

occurrence *reset* **results in** extent = 0;
occurrence *expand* **results in** extent = eOld + 1 **when** extent = eOld;

Since most of the work is being done in the evaluate function, the remaining effect axioms are relatively uninteresting. We will assume the reader can, if so desired, easily figure out a suitable effect axiom for any other fluents from the fluent's name and our informal descriptions.

Most of the actions are defined to be always possible. There are, however, some important exceptions. Notably, some pre-condition axioms are referred to later in some of the complex actions. For example, it is possible for character i to pick a goal if it has found some goal positions gs that have worth w that is at least as good as the current acceptable threshold value.

action *pickGoal*(i) **possible when**
    goalPosn(i,w,gs) && acceptable(i) = a && $a \leqslant w$;

11.3.2 Character Instruction

Our first attempt to create a controller for the merpeople using complex actions simply evaluates all the regions and goes to the best one.

```
proc controlAgent(i)
{
    sense(i);
    evalRegions(i);
    pickGoal(i);
}
```

For any reasonably large virtual world this controller requires a merperson to constantly evaluate a huge number of regions. It is therefore too slow to be practical, although, for a single merperson and a small test world, it could quickly provide a working prototype. The next step is to add in more detailed complex actions to act as heuristics so that the controller is applicable to controlling multiple characters in a world consisting of potentially thousands of regions.

The simple, but key, observation we make is that the sharks and merpeople's movements within the undersea world are continuous. Therefore, although there may be occasional discontinuities, the hiding places will also tend to shift around smoothly. That is, there is a lot of temporal coherence that can be exploited by searching for new hiding positions near locations that were recently hiding positions. Trying to get the character to figure out all this for itself would be extremely difficult, so we use complex actions to encode the information as simple predefined heuristics for the merperson to follow without having to think about it.

We can quickly reconfigure and extend the first controller by defining a complex action to progressively expand the number of regions the merperson considers. In particular, all regions that fall within a radius, given by the fluent <u>extent</u>, around the current goal position are considered. If there is no current goal position (for example at the start) then the goal position is simply assigned to be the character's current position.

```
proc searchForGoalPosn(i)
{
    setAcceptable(i,searchRegions);
    star {
        expand(i);
        eval(i);
    }
}
```

Note how we use the **star** construct to specify that a merperson should expand the search region zero or more times. The heuristic that this complex action encodes is that the merperson should begin by considering just a few regions that are close to the current goal and only consider those further afield as a last resort. Like most heuristics, the worst case complexity is unaffected by the above complex action, but on average we should expect the merperson to make decisions much faster than if it always considers every region. In addition, we must not allow the volume in which the merperson searches for suitable regions to expand without limit. Therefore, the following precondition axiom states that the search region can only be expanded provided an acceptable goal has not yet been found, and some predefined limit, maxExtent, has not been reached.

action *expand*(i) **possible when**
  extent(i) = e && $e \leqslant$ maxExtent && ! **possible** *pickGoal* ;

Of course, the more regions a character considers the more likely it is to find a good one. Unfortunately, since the number of regions considered increases exponentially as we use higher values for maxExtent, it is wise to be as conservative as possible. For this reason, we might also want to change the effect axiom for acceptable so that the acceptability threshold is inversely proportional to the extent, the rationale being that, if possible, we want to forestall the more expensive search that will ensue if the more local searches fail.

We can also define some other heuristics. For example, if we think about it for a bit we can see that a merperson is more likely to be able to stay hidden if it can stick close to obstacles. We could encourage the character to think about going to regions near obstacles by altering the evaluate function. Unfortunately, if the regions near the obstacles are currently further away than maxExtent, they will not even be considered. Therefore, we define a new procedure *testObstacles* to explicitly evaluate regions around obstacles. The criteria are more or less the same as for regular regions, but to make the behavior more realistic it is important to worry about whether the merperson would know about a given obstacle or not. That is, it should not head off to a location it cannot see, or has not previously visited.

As the sharks move around, so do the good hiding regions and so it may well come to pass that the merperson finds itself in a safe region by sheer accident. Clearly, the merperson should check for this eventuality before it embarks on any long complicated deliberations. Therefore, the procedure *testCurrPosn* looks to see if the merperson's current location is "acceptable." Notice that, since a merperson begins thinking about regions starting from the current goal position, if the current location is further than extent away it would not otherwise be evaluated at all.

We can now combine the procedures that encode the various search heuristics into one *evade* procedure.

```
proc evade(i)
{
    sense(i);
    choose {
        testCurrPosn(i);
        || searchForGoalPosn(i);
        || testObstacles(i);
        || panic(i);
    }
    pickGoal(i);
}
```

Note that we have as a precondition to *pickGoal* that a good enough goal must have been found. What constitutes "good enough" is maintained by the previously described fluent acceptable. This means the search can stop as soon as we find a good enough position. Note that if all else fails, a merperson will panic. Panicking causes the acceptability criterion, as given by acceptable, to be set to 0 and the best position found so far will be chosen.

11.4   The Great Escape

Now that we have finished defining the *evade* procedure, we can see how it fairs in practice. In particular, we start with the same initial configuration as in Section 11.3, in which the merperson got eaten. This time, the difference is that we add some large rocks to the scene for the merperson to hide behind. To produce a more interesting animation we also instruct the merperson that, whenever it appears reasonably safe to do so, it should make a break for a large rock in the scene. The particular rock to which we want to get the merperson to go offers a narrow crack through which the merperson, but not the larger-bodied shark, can pass. We wanted an exciting animation in which the merperson eventually gets to that special rock with the shark in hot pursuit. The merperson's *evade* procedure should then swing into action, enabling it to evade capture by finding and slipping through the crack. Although we do not know exactly when or how, we have a mechanism to heavily stack the deck toward getting the desired animation. As it turns out, we got what we wanted on our first attempt. If, however, the animation that we desire remains elusive, we can use additional complex actions to further constrain a merperson's behavior all the way down to scripting an entire predefined behavior if necessary.

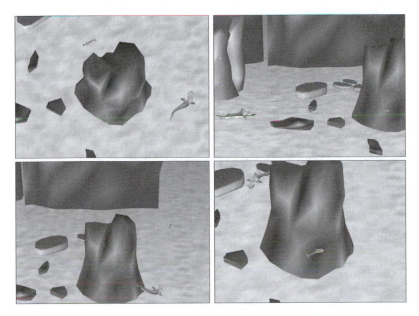

Figure 11.4. The Great Escape (Part I). (See Color Plate XI.)

Figure 11.4 shows some frames from the initial sequence. An intense chase ensues with the shark closely tailing its prey as it circles a big rock. The initial attempts to try to visit the large rock are thwarted as the shark swings back quickly and became too threatening again. Finally, the merperson gets another opportunity and this time makes a break for it. The shark eventually sees the merperson in open water and starts to pursue it. As we can see in Figure 11.5, by the time the merperson makes it to the large rock the shark has almost caught up. The shark continues gaining on the merperson as the pair travel along the side of the rock. Suddenly, the merperson sees a small crack in the rock!

In Figure 11.6, the merperson swims through the crack. The shark tries to follow but the crack is too narrow for it to pass through without risking injury. The merperson seizes the opportunity and the shark is foiled.

In general, the shark chases a merperson if it can see one, otherwise it goes to check where it last saw one. We can see the shark following this behavior pattern as it returns to the crack in the rock where it last saw the merperon.

Finally, in Figure 11.7, the shark gives up and begins to search for the merperson. By the time the shark reaches the other side of the rock, however, the merperson is nowhere to be found.

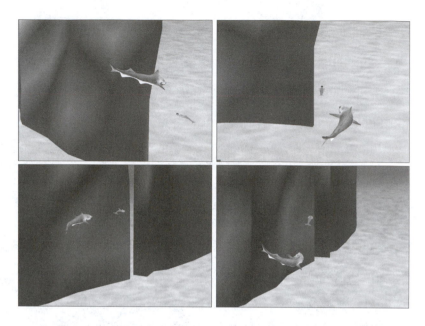

Figure 11.5. The Great Escape (Part II). (See Color Plate XII.)

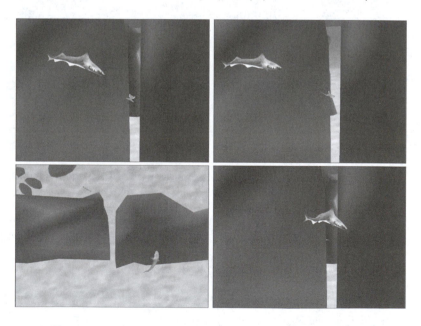

Figure 11.6. The Great Escape (Part III). (See Color Plate XIII.)

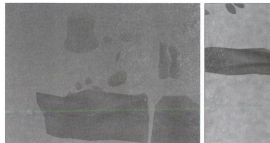 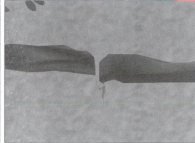

Figure 11.7. The Great Escape (Part IV). (See Color Plate XIV.)

11.5   Pet Protection

Now we will look at creating another action sequence. This time we will use some new complex actions to create some characters with distinct "mersonalities." In particular, let's make some characters brave and others timid. The timid ones cry for help when they are in danger and the brave ones will go to the rescue, provided it is not too dangerous for them. Once the brave ones have attracted the shark's attention, they try to get away themselves.

The small creature (marked with a 'P') in Figure 11.8 is the merperson's pet. It is timid and must be protected by the braver and larger merperson (marked with an 'H'). In the opening sequence, the pet is being chased by a shark (marked with an 'S') and calls out for help. The merperson goes to its rescue. So long as there are multiple prey within range, the shark prefers larger meals. Hence, it gives up on the small pet and starts chasing the merperson.

Figure 11.9 shows what happens now that the merperson has got the shark's attention. The merperson tries to escape and quickly hides behind a rock. The shark immediately discontinues the pursuit and wanders off back to where it last saw the merperson's pet. Once again, the merperson charges to the rescue and the shark again starts to pursue.

However, this time he is too foolhardy and, as we can see in Figure 11.10, is only saved from a grisly end by a lucky near miss that the shark has with an obstacle. Now the merperson swims away from the shark and toward the last known position of his pet. The two of them then swim together and, as in the previous examples, evade capture.

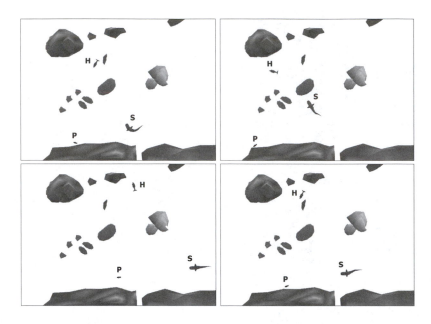

Figure 11.8. Pet Protection (Part I).

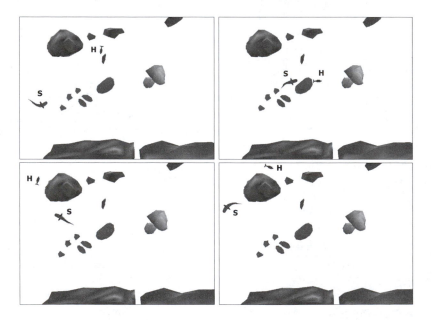

Figure 11.9. Pet Protection (Part II).

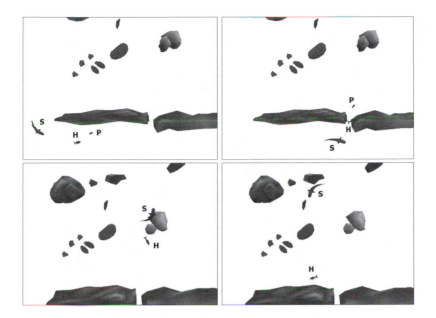

Figure 11.10. Pet Protection (Part III).

11.5.1 Complex Actions

The complex action that controls the pet is nothing special. It simply has the usual evasion behavior, with an additional "call for help" action defined. The hero of the "Pet Protection" piece had a controller based on a complex action as follows:

if ! InDanger(x) && InDanger(y) && isPet(x,y) {
    rescue(x,y)
else
    evade(x)
}

In the last chapter, we showed a simple example of asking a cognitive character to answer a question about its behavior. Now let us look at a more elaborate example. In particular, suppose we have a couple of characters pet and hero, such that pet is hero's pet, i.e. IsPet(hero, pet). Now suppose, in some situation s, we have that the pet is in danger InDanger(pet, s), but that the hero is also in danger, InDanger(hero, s). Then, we want to find out if it is possible that in such a situation the hero will not go to the rescue but will run away. The cognitive character can answer the query with some simple rules of logic and expanding out the specification according to the rules given in Chapter 5.[3]

It is an old adage of computer science that, while important, testing a program can only ever prove the presence of bugs, never their absence. Therefore, another potentially significant aspect of using the situation calculus is the ability to prove properties of our specifications. One could envisage proving the presence or absence of certain (un)desirable traits in the specification of a character's behavior. Moreover, this can be done early on in the software life-cycle, potentially eliminating bugs that would otherwise be costly to rectify later.

$Do\,(\text{if } \neg\mathsf{InDanger}(x) \wedge \mathsf{InDanger}(y) \wedge \mathsf{IsPet}(x,y) \text{ then}$

$\quad rescue(x,y) \text{ else } runAway(x) \text{ fi}, s, s')$

$\triangleq$

$Do\,[((\neg\mathsf{InDanger}(x) \wedge \mathsf{InDanger}(y) \wedge \mathsf{IsPet}(x,y))? \,\substack{\circ\\\circ}\, rescue(x,y)) \mid$

$(\neg(\neg\mathsf{InDanger}(x) \wedge \mathsf{InDanger}(y) \wedge \mathsf{IsPet}(x,y))? \,\substack{\circ\\\circ}\, runAway(x)), s, s']$

$\triangleq$

$Do\,((\neg\mathsf{InDanger}(x) \wedge \mathsf{InDanger}(y) \wedge \mathsf{IsPet}(x,y))? \,\substack{\circ\\\circ}\, rescue(x,y), s, s') \vee$

$Do\,(\neg(\neg\mathsf{InDanger}(x) \wedge \mathsf{InDanger}(y) \wedge \mathsf{IsPet}(x,y))? \,\substack{\circ\\\circ}\, runAway(x), s, s')$

$\triangleq$

$\exists s^*\ [Do\,((\neg\mathsf{InDanger}(x) \wedge \mathsf{InDanger}(y) \wedge \mathsf{IsPet}(x,y))?, s, s^*) \wedge Do\,(rescue(x,y), s^*, s')] \vee$

$\exists s^*\ [Do\,(\neg(\neg\mathsf{InDanger}(x) \wedge \mathsf{InDanger}(y) \wedge \mathsf{IsPet}(x,y))?, s, s^*) \wedge Do\,(runAway(x), s^*, s')]$

$\triangleq$

$\exists s^*\ [\neg\mathsf{InDanger}(x,s) \wedge \mathsf{InDanger}(y,s) \wedge \mathsf{IsPet}(x,y) \wedge s^* = s \wedge Do\,(rescue(x,y), s^*, s')] \vee$

$\exists s^*\ [\neg(\neg\mathsf{InDanger}(x,s) \wedge \mathsf{InDanger}(y,s) \wedge \mathsf{IsPet}(x,y)) \wedge s^* = s \wedge Do\,(runAway(x), s^*, s')]$

$\Rightarrow$

$\exists s^*\ [\neg\mathsf{InDanger}(x,s) \wedge \mathsf{InDanger}(y,s) \wedge \mathsf{IsPet}(x,y) \wedge s^* = s \wedge Do\,(rescue(x,y), s^*, s')] \vee$

$\exists s^*\ [\mathsf{InDanger}(x,s) \vee \neg\mathsf{InDanger}(y,s) \vee \neg\mathsf{IsPet}(x,y) \wedge s^* = s \wedge Do\,(runAway(x), s^*, s')]$

$\Rightarrow$

$[\neg\mathsf{InDanger}(x,s) \wedge \mathsf{InDanger}(y,s) \wedge \mathsf{IsPet}(x,y) \wedge Do\,(rescue(x,y), s, s')] \vee$

$[\mathsf{InDanger}(x,s) \vee \neg\mathsf{InDanger}(y,s) \vee \neg\mathsf{IsPet}(x,y) \wedge Do\,(runAway(x), s, s')]$

$\Rightarrow$

$[\neg\mathsf{InDanger}(\mathsf{hero},s) \wedge \mathsf{InDanger}(\mathsf{pet},s) \wedge \mathsf{IsPet}(\mathsf{hero},\mathsf{pet}) \wedge Do\,(rescue(\mathsf{hero},\mathsf{pet}), s, s')] \vee$

$[\mathsf{InDanger}(\mathsf{hero},s) \vee \neg\mathsf{InDanger}(\mathsf{pet},s) \vee \neg\mathsf{IsPet}(\mathsf{hero},\mathsf{pet}) \wedge Do\,(runAway(\mathsf{hero}), s, s')]$

$\Rightarrow$ \qquad\qquad\qquad (by assumption that $\mathsf{InDanger}(\mathsf{hero},s)$)

$Do\,(runAway(\mathsf{hero}), s, s')$

$\triangleq$

$s' = do(runAway(\mathsf{hero}), s)$

---

[3]Since we are doing straight mathematics now, we revert to the underlying mathematical notation.

So as we can see the hero will not go to the rescue if it is in danger, but will instead run away.

In general such proofs are best conducted by a computer program as they mainly involve lots of substituting definitions. Indeed, this is exactly the process through which the interpreter goes when calculating the appropriate behavior.

Of course, the extent of what we can prove is somewhat limited in our current setting. We have already discussed at some length the undesirability of axiomatizing all the laws of physics that pertain to our undersea simulation. Without such an axiomatization, however, we cannot prove, for example, that a predator will capture a prey from a given initial configuration. The most we could hope for is a proof that it will always *try* to capture a prey in a given situation. This opens up avenues for future research to try and improve on this. In particular, we might consider using qualitative physics and automated proof assistants to enable us prove stronger results.

11.6 General Mêlée

As an extension to behavioral modeling, we can scale our cognitive modeling efforts linearly for a single character in order to create multiple similarly behaved characters. Each character will behave autonomously according to its own unique perspective of its world.

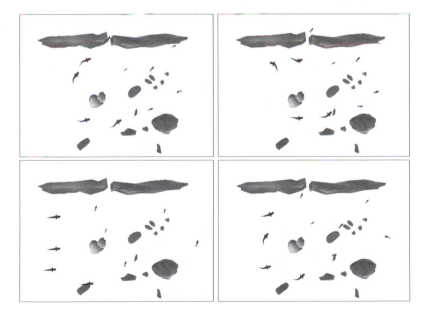

Figure 11.11. General Mêlée (Part I).

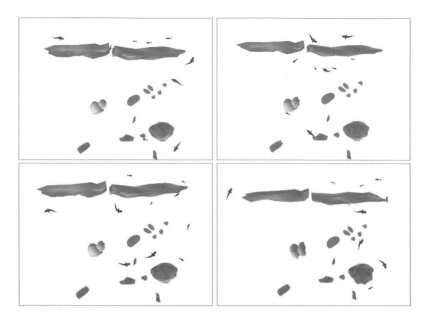

Figure 11.12. General Mêlée (Part II).

Figure 11.11 shows an underwater world containing six merpeople and four sharks. For a given region, the <u>evaluate</u> function takes into account the threat from each visible predator. As the sharks come into visual range the merpeople start fleeing, the ones closest first, then the others.

In Figure 11.12, we can see the *evade* procedure at work as the merpeople head toward the rocks to try and find hiding places.

At the start of this chapter, we promised that for this case study we would give all the gory details. Therefore, for the rest of this chapter we will provide those low-level details. Readers who are already familiar with such techniques can therefore skip the remaining sections without loss of continuity.

11.7   Visibility Testing[†]

One important aspect of our pursuit and evasion example was the ability of the prey to locate hidden regions. The task is nontrivial and a bad solution could result in unacceptably slow execution times. The first observation

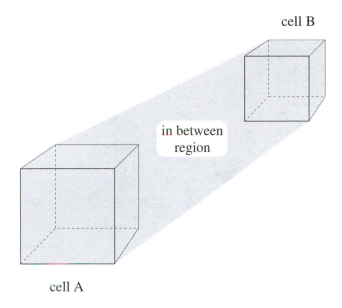

cell B

in between
region

cell A

Figure 11.13. Cells A and B are "completely visible" from one another.

to make is that, if we think of the predators as light sources, the problem of determining regions that are hidden from them is closely related to the rendering problem of fast shadow computation. In our case, the problem is exacerbated by the fact that our "light sources" are moving around.

One possibility is to use OpenGL® and take advantage of specialized graphics hardware to provide a fast solution to the problem. The solution we take however, is based on *octrees*. That is, we can bound the whole scene by a cube. The cube can then be recursively subdivided into eight regions to form a tree-like structure. In theory, whenever we wish to determine the regions hidden from a predator, we check to see which cell the predator is in and then see which cells are obscured by obstacles from that cell. The idea is that, by starting at the top of the octree and working down, we can quickly discard large regions of space as completely visible or completely hidden.

For example, in Figure 11.13, there are no obstacles that interpenetrate the region in between cells A and B. Thus, the pair A, B can be marked as completely visible from one another and, for the purposes of comparisons with each other, need not be subdivided further.

In Figure 11.14, the obstacle completely occludes cells A and B. Thus the pair A, B can be marked as completely occluded from one another and, for the purposes of comparisons with each other, need not be subdivided further.

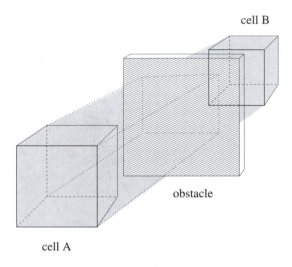

Figure 11.14. Cells A and B are "completely occluded" from one another.

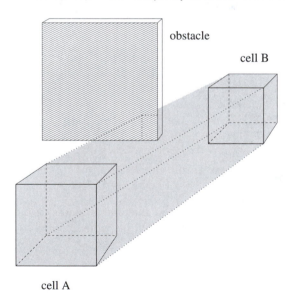

Figure 11.15. Cells A and B are "partially occluded" from one another.

In Figure 11.15, the obstacle partially occludes cells A and B. Thus the pair A, B must be subdivided further to determine complete visibility information. If the smallest allowable subdivision level has been reached then we decide visibility by polling for visibility at each of the vertices. So, in the figure, the pair A, B would be marked as visible.

In practice, subdividing the whole space down to the required fidelity and computing visibility information for all pairs of cells is too expensive. The solution is to make the following observations:

- Characters, especially those in water, will have a limited visual range. They will also have a limited field of view. Therefore, there is no need to compute visibility information for cells beyond a distance, or angle.

- Characters can be given some simple heuristics for finding hidden locations. For example, they can be told that they should only look for cover near obstacles. That is, even if a character is momentarily hidden from a predator when it is in open water, such a location is still far from ideal. It is much safer to seek refuge near obstacles. Thus, visibility information need only be computed within the vicinity of obstacles.

- Approximate visibility information can still be calculated by projecting character locations onto the boundaries of intervening regions for which information is available. By combining these tests with additional simple bounding box/line intersection tests, the reliability of the approximate visibility tests can be enhanced.

- Characters may well visit only small portions of the scene within an animation. It would be wise to provide a coarse evaluation for all obstacles in the scene. To avoid doing lots of unnecessary work, however, we need only compute high fidelity visibility information for regions the characters visit. The calculations can then be cached in a globally accessible database for future reference by any character.

- It is not catastrophic if the odd mistake is made. It enhances realism and the behavior algorithms should be robust enough to avoid disaster if information is unavailable for short periods of time.

Figure 11.16 shows a two-dimensional version of the space partitioning approach we take to visibility testing. Note that we use bounding boxes for the obstacles. This results in "mistakes," as some of the cells which are visible are marked as hidden. A solution to this would be to compute a set of tighter bounding boxes. In general, this would entail computing a

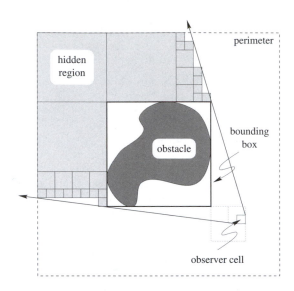

Figure 11.16. Visibility testing near an obstacle.

hierarchical octree of bounding boxes for each obstacle. In practice, the flaw
has little effect since being hidden is only one of the criterion that the prey
use to select suitable goal positions. That is, the erroneously marked cells are
on the periphery of the hidden region and as such the other criteria (such as
distance from the predators, distance from the predators' predicted positions,
size of the hidden region, whether there are hidden regions surrounding
the selected region, etc.) precludes them from being selected as ideal goal
positions in most circumstances. When the prey are in open water far from
any hidden regions they may be selected for short periods of time until more
suitable cells come into range. Again, this is harmless because it does not
affect the general observed evasion strategy. Finally, making mistakes for
borderline cases is extremely realistic.

11.8   Low-level System Implementation[†]

We shall give an overview of the underlying low-level predefined behavior
system. The system consists of a number of subsystems.

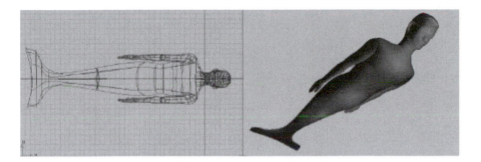

Figure 11.17. The geometric model.

11.8.1 Appearance

The rendering sub-system allows us to capture the form and appearance of a merperson. We use texture mapped, three-dimensional geometric display models with which to "envelope" the dynamics model described in Section 11.8.2.

Three-dimensional Geometric Models

Geometric models for our system can be constructed using any 3D modeler and automatically imported. Aside from the background scenery, we have created a merperson that consists of two unique NURBS surfaces: the body (including the tail); and 16 unique polygonal surfaces: the head, upper arms, lower arms, hands, thumbs and ears, as shown in Figure 11.17. Together they form an articulated figure arranged in a hierarchical tree structure rooted at the merperson's local coordinate system.

The geometric model provides the appearance of the merperson. In order to make it move, an underlying dynamic model is created. The dynamic model (see Section 11.8.2) can be viewed as the "flesh" that moves and deforms over time to produce the locomotion of the merperson. Only the body and tail of the dynamic model actually deform as the merperson swims, the head and limbs move but do not deform. The geometric surfaces are coupled to the underlying dynamic model so that they will move and deform accordingly. This is achieved by associating their control points with the faces of the dynamic model (see Figure 11.18).

For each face in the dynamic model there is a local coordinate system. Each point in the control point mesh (the dotted lines) is then assigned to the nearest local coordinate system and, in the rest state, an offset vector is calculated. (Two example offset vectors are shown in Figure 11.18.)

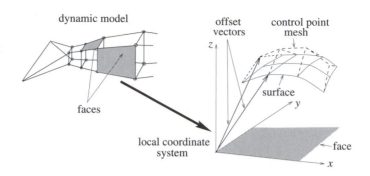

Figure 11.18. Coupling the geometric and dynamic model.

The offset vector is then used to update the control point positions as the underlying dynamic model moves.

In practice, it is necessary to subdivide the faces of the dynamic model into a 4-by-4 grid of patches, each having its own local coordinate system. In this way, artifacts that occur with texture mapping when the offset vectors interpenetrate, are minimized.

Texture Mapping

The next step is to map images onto the geometric display models (texture mapping). We painstakingly created the textures with image manipulation software using scanned-in photographs as our source. The most important step in the texture-mapping process is to derive texture coordinates. The texture coordinates map the digital images of different parts of a merperson onto the corresponding three-dimensional surface. To obtain the texture coordinates we wrote software to stretch the irregular shaped images out into rectangular images.

Once the texture coordinates are determined, the rest of the texture-mapping procedure can be carried out via a simple function call in any commercially available three-dimensional graphics software package that supports texture mapping. Currently we use OpenGL®, which gives interactive animation rates in wire-frame and shaded modes and, for fully textured rendering, gives about 5fps, on any reasonably up-to-date PC.

Texture mapping the merperson's face is especially difficult and we used laser range finder data as our source texture. After some work "fixing up" the model and image the merperson was acceptably aesthetically pleasing. Figure 11.19 shows a closeup of the merperson's face. Note that it consists of

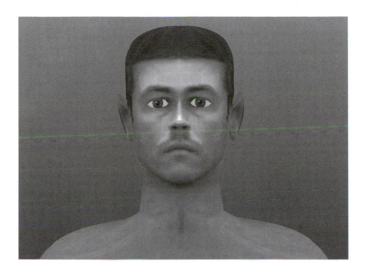

Figure 11.19. Texture mapped face.

eight unique polygonal surfaces. Considerable manual effort was required to ensure the smooth blending of the texture maps for each adjoining surface. Currently we have not attempted any facial animation but our system is ideally suited to its incorporation. It is also worth noting that there are any number of companies that sell and build-to-order fully texture-mapped geometric models.

11.8.2 Locomotion

The locomotion subsystem consists of a biomechanical model that captures the physical and anatomical structure of the character's body, including its muscle actuators, and simulates its deformation and physical dynamics. An interface to the underlying model is provided by a set of abstract *motor controllers*. The motor controllers are parameterized procedures, each of which is dedicated to carrying out a specific motor function, such as "swim forward," "turn left," or "ascend." They translate natural control parameters such as the forward speed, angle of the turn, or angle of ascent into detailed muscle or arm actions. Four frames from an animation of a merperson swimming are shown in Figure 11.20.

The locomotion control problem for physics-based characters is a challenging one. In its full guise, the problem involves the locomotion of hier-

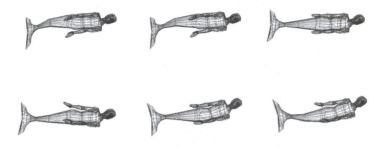

Figure 11.20. A merperson swimming.

archical unstable articulated figures subjected to impulsive forces. A lot of progress has been made in producing physically realistic motion for articulated figures. In addition, there has been impressive progress in solving the locomotion control problem for creatures, like snakes and fish, that can be modeled as deformable bodies.

Deformable Models

Currently, only the body and tail of the merperson deform. The deformable part is shown in Figure 11.21. It consists of 23 point mass nodes and 91 connecting spring and damper units. Each spring and damper unit can deform along one axis. Together they give the body its structure while still allowing it to bend. To prevent twisting and shearing, each face has two

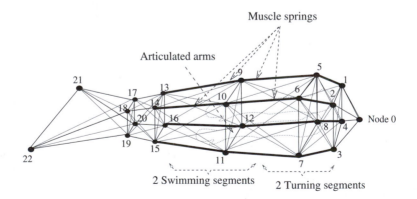

Figure 11.21. The dynamic model.

diagonal units. The bold lines depicted in Figure 11.21 that span the length of the body are active muscles. In total, there are 12 of them and they allow the merperson to deform under its own control. They are arranged in pairs, with two such pairs on each side of the three actuated body segments. The two upper body actuated segments are used for turning while the two lower ones are used for swimming.

We shall now employ the nomenclature of Chapter 2 to explain how the laws of physics are applied to the mass-spring-damper model. The state vector consists of 46 vector quantities which represent the position and velocity of each of the nodes. All the nodes are governed by the same equations so we shall proceed with a study of a single node i. The mass of node i is denoted by m_i and remains constant. The state vector for one node is the position $\mathbf{x}_i(t) \in \mathbb{R}^3$ and the velocity $\dot{\mathbf{x}}_i(t) \in \mathbb{R}^3$. Our aim is to formulate the state equations that will allow us to calculate the acceleration $\ddot{\mathbf{x}}_i(t) \in \mathbb{R}^3$.

The spring-damper units that connect the nodes are the same as the one depicted in Chapter 2, Figure 2.3. We denote the unit that connects node i to node j as s_{ij}, where k^s_{ij} is the associated spring stiffness, and k^d_{ij} the damping factor. The rest length is denoted by p_{ij}. For the active muscles the rest length is a function of time. The activation functions we use were worked out by hand, however, automatic techniques for finding these functions are available.

The vector connecting node i to node j is denoted by $\mathbf{r}_{ij}$, where

$$\mathbf{r}_{ij}(t) = \mathbf{x}_j(t) - \mathbf{x}_i(t).$$

Thus, $r_{ij}(t) = ||\mathbf{r}_{ij}(t)||$ denotes the length of s_{ij} at time t.

Similarly, the relative velocity of node i with respect to node j is denoted by $\dot{\mathbf{r}}_{ij}$, where

$$\dot{\mathbf{r}}_{ij}(t) = \dot{\mathbf{x}}_j(t) - \dot{\mathbf{x}}_i(t).$$

Thus, $\dot{r}_{ij}(t) = (\dot{\mathbf{r}}_{ij} \cdot \mathbf{r}_{ij})/r_{ij}$ denotes the normalized relative speed of node i with respect to node j.

The extension, e_{ij}, of s_{ij} the current length minus the rest length is

$$e_{ij}(t) = r_{ij}(t) - p_{ij}(t).$$

The elastic force, $\mathbf{f}_{ij}$ exerted by s_{ij} on node i can then be calculated using Hooke's law:

$$\mathbf{f}_{ij}(t) \quad = \quad \frac{k^s_{ij} e_{ij}(t)}{r_{ij}} \mathbf{r}_{ij} + \frac{k^d_{ij} \dot{r}_{ij}(t)}{r_{ij}} \mathbf{r}_{ij}$$

Note that there is an equal and opposite force $-\mathbf{f}_{ij}(t)$ exerted on node j.

The set of nodes adjacent to node i is denoted by N_i. The net internal force exerted on node i due to the spring-damper units can then be obtained by summing up the forces exerted by all the spring-damper units connected to nodes in N_i.

$$\mathbf{f}_i^s = \sum_{j \in N_i} \mathbf{f}_{ij}(t).$$

The other source of force on node i is the water force $\mathbf{f}_i^w$. The water is assumed to be irrotational, incompressible, and slightly viscous. We triangulate the faces of the dynamic model. Then, for the sake of efficiency, we approximate the hydrodynamic force on each triangle as

$$\mathbf{f} = \min[0, \, -\mu_w A ||\mathbf{v}||(\mathbf{n} \cdot \mathbf{v})\mathbf{n}], \tag{11.1}$$

where μ_w is the viscosity of the water, A is the area of the triangle, $\mathbf{n}$ is its normal, and $\mathbf{v}$ is its velocity relative to the water. The external forces $\mathbf{f}_i^w$ at each of the three nodes of the triangle are incremented by $\mathbf{f}/3$. Therefore, the total force on a node i is

$$\mathbf{f}_i = \mathbf{f}_i^w - \mathbf{f}_i^s.$$

We are now in a position to give the state equations. They take the form of a set of coupled second-order ordinary differential equations, formulated according to Newton's laws of motion:

$$m_i \ddot{\mathbf{x}}_i(t) = \mathbf{f}_i(t); \qquad i = 0, \dots, 22. \tag{11.2}$$

To simulate the dynamics of the merperson, the differential equations of motion must be integrated over time. This is made difficult because the system is intrinsically stiff. Indeed there are many common scenarios that may cause the equations to become unstable. For example, executing a right turn to avoid an unexpected collision, say, while engaged in a left turn will cause problems. Therefore, to counteract these difficulties, we use a simple, numerically stable, semi-implicit Euler method.

11.8.3 Articulated Figures

In order to provide increased functionality and realism, the merperson has two articulated arms. A researcher may thus begin in the undersea world of nonimpulsive forces and then, for a more challenging problem, have the merperson haul itself out of the water to crawl about on its hands! To date, however, we have concentrated on the movement of the merperson's body instead of the detailed movement of the arms. That is, to simplify the dynamic model and its numerical solution, we do not simulate the elasticity and dynamics of the arms. However, we do approximate the dynamic forces that the arms exert on the body of the merperson to control locomotion.

The articulated arms work by applying reaction forces to nodes in the midsection of the merperson's body, i.e., nodes $N_i, 1 \leq i \leq 12$ (see Figure 11.21). During swimming the arms are simply used in an analogous way to the airfoils of an airplane. Pitch and yaw control stems from changing their orientations $\pi/4 \leq \gamma \leq \pi$ relative to the body. Assuming that an arm has an area A and a surface normal $\mathbf{n}$, and the merperson has a velocity $\mathbf{v}$ relative to the water, the arm force is

$$F_f = -A||\mathbf{v}||(\mathbf{n} \cdot \mathbf{v})\mathbf{n} = -\mathbf{A}(||\mathbf{v}||^2 \cos\gamma)\mathbf{n} \qquad (11.3)$$

(see Equation 11.1) and is distributed equally to the six midsection nodes on the side of the arm. When the arm is angled upward, a lift force is imparted on the body and the merperson ascends, and when it is angled down, a downward force is exerted and the merperson descends. When the arm angles differ, the merperson yaws and rolls.

11.8.4 Perception

The perception subsystem equips a merperson with a set of "on-board" virtual sensors to provide sensory information about the dynamic environment. It also includes a perceptual attention mechanism which allows the merperson to train its sensors at the world in a task-specific way.

11.8.5 Behavior

The behavior subsystem of the character mediates between the perception subsystem and the motor subsystem. It consists of a behavior arbitrator, and a set of behavior routines that implement a repertoire of basic behaviors including "avoiding collisions," "eating," "target following," and "wandering". These primitive behaviors serve a dual purpose. Firstly, they instantiate the "primitive" actions generated by the high-level behavior system. Secondly, as a whole, they constitute the "default" behavior the character exhibits in the absence of commands ("primitive" actions) from the high-level behavior

system. The fundamental function of the behavior arbitrator is to coordinate the primitive behaviors to generate the default character behavior. Arbitration is done by associating differing priorities with different primitive
behaviors. The commands from the high-level behavior system correspond
directly to primitive behaviors and consequently fit elegantly into the behavior arbitration scheme. That is, commands will be executed provided that
no more urgent behavior is judged to be necessary. For example, a character
will head toward a specified location, provided it does not have to avoid a
collision. The behavior arbitrator also controls the focuser which returns required sensory data to the high-level behavior system. At every simulation
time step, the behavior arbitrator activates low-level behavior routines that
input the filtered sensory information and compute the appropriate motor
control parameters to carry the character one step closer to fulfilling the
current intention.

Some "primitive" actions just update the character's model of its world;
the remainder (including all sensing actions) are designated by the user as
actions to be communicated to the low-level behavior system. In our current high-level controllers, the high-level behavior system may select sensing
actions, and, for each character, one nonsensing communicable primitive action every ten frames. The low-level behavior system waits up to a specified
time limit (currently five seconds) for a nonsensing "primitive" action to be
generated. If no such action is forthcoming, it will continue to execute with
the low-level default behavior. Any sensing actions generated in the time
limit will be processed regardless.

Collision Avoidance

The low-level behavior system already enabled our characters to avoid collisions with cylinders. To improve the generality of the system we choose to
implement a potential field approach to collision avoidance.

The idea is that for each point in $q \in \mathbb{R}^3$ we have a force vector $\boldsymbol{F}(\boldsymbol{q}) \in \mathbb{R}^3$
that points the correct direction to travel in order to move toward a goal
position while avoiding any obstacles. The force vector is defined in terms
of a potential function $U : \mathbb{R}^3 \to \mathbb{R}$, such that

$$\boldsymbol{F}(\mathbf{q}) = -\nabla U(\boldsymbol{q}),$$

where $\nabla U(\boldsymbol{q})$ denotes the gradient of U at $\boldsymbol{q}$.

In general, $U = U_-(\boldsymbol{q}) + U_+(\boldsymbol{q})$, where $U_-(\boldsymbol{q})$ is the *repulsive potential*
associated with the obstacles, and $U_+(\boldsymbol{q})$ is the *attractive potential* associated
with the goal point. This, in turn, gives us that $\boldsymbol{F} = \boldsymbol{F}_- + \boldsymbol{F}_+$, where
$\boldsymbol{F}_- = -\nabla U_-$ and $\boldsymbol{F}_+ = -\nabla U_+$.

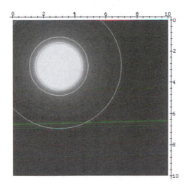 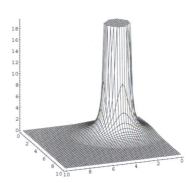

Figure 11.22. The repulsive potential.

To define the repulsive potential, we first define $\rho(\boldsymbol{q})$ to be the minimum distance from the point $\boldsymbol{q}$ to the obstacle. We also define a threshold ρ_0, such that beyond this distance the obstacle has no influence. The repulsive potential we use is now defined, for some constant η, as

$$U_-(\boldsymbol{q}) = \begin{cases} \frac{1}{2}\eta(\frac{1}{\rho(\boldsymbol{q})} - \frac{1}{\rho_0}) & \text{if } \rho(\boldsymbol{q}) \leqslant \rho_0, \\ 0 & \text{otherwise.} \end{cases}$$

The function is chosen to be differentiable for convex objects.[4] It gives us the repulsive force as

$$F_-(\boldsymbol{q}) = \begin{cases} \frac{\eta \nabla \rho(\boldsymbol{q})}{\rho^2(\boldsymbol{q})}(\frac{1}{\rho(\boldsymbol{q})} - \frac{1}{\rho_0}) & \text{if } \rho(\boldsymbol{q}) \leqslant \rho_0, \\ 0 & \text{otherwise.} \end{cases}$$

Note that the gradient $\nabla \rho(\boldsymbol{q})$ is the unit vector that points from the closest point on the obstacle toward $\boldsymbol{q}$.

In the case of multiple obstacles we obtain the total repulsive force at a point by summing the repulsive forces from all the obstacles. In our implementation we also clamp the maximum repulsive force. Also, when we calculate repulsive forces we use a bounding box for the obstacles that is deliberately made slightly bigger than necessary. In particular, the box is grown by an amount proportional to the character's size. This increases realism by allowing smaller creatures to get in closer to an obstacle than a large creature. Moreover, since the sharks are larger, this can be exploited in the specification of the evasion behavior for the merpeople. Figure 11.22 shows a graphical depiction of the repulsive potential around an obstacle.

---

[4]We can always decompose concave objects into a set of convex objects.

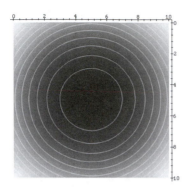 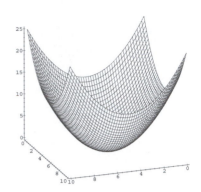

Figure 11.23. The attractive potential.

The attractive potential has a much simpler equation. First, we define $\rho_g(\boldsymbol{q})$ to be the distance from the point $\boldsymbol{q}$ to the current goal position $\boldsymbol{q}$. Then, for some constant ξ, we have that the attractive potential is

$$U_+(\boldsymbol{q}) = \xi\rho_g(\boldsymbol{q}).$$

This gives us that the attractive force is:

$$\boldsymbol{F}_+(\boldsymbol{q}) = -\frac{\xi(\boldsymbol{q} - \boldsymbol{g})}{\rho_g(\boldsymbol{q})}.$$

Note that we must be careful not to divide by 0 at the goal position. Figure 11.23 shows a graphical depiction of the attractive potential around a goal position.

Figure 11.24 shows a graphical depiction of the superposition of the repulsive and attractive potential fields.

It is the case that the goal position can change as a consequence of a new course of action being decided upon by the high-level behavior system. The low-level behavior layer limits the effect that a new goal position may have by imposing a maximum turn angle per time step. In this way the character changes course gracefully, and any momentary oscillation is evened out. For its part, the high-level behavior system preempts many of the traditional problems with local minima by giving preference to goals that have a clear path leading to them. The high-level behavior system is also able to spot when the merperson is not making progress towards its goal. It can then set a new goal, or, depending on the situation, adjust the parameters to

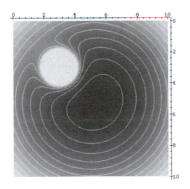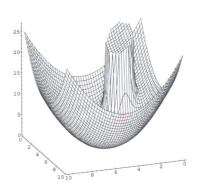

Figure 11.24. The repulsive and attractive potential fields.

the potential field. This is done by making these parameters fluents which can be changed by certain actions. We believe this synergy of a high-level qualitative system monitoring a low-level numerical procedure is a powerful combination. In general, the potential field is mainly used to add a level of robustness. Any collisions that were unforeseen by the high-level behavior system do not result in disaster for the character's well-being.

11.9   Discussion

Ideally, a merperson should learn an evaluation function that assigns value to given regions. This would involve generating a training set that contained the results of numerous experiments on how effective a certain kind of hiding place was at avoiding being eaten. They could also use the path planning approach to selecting regions to go to. This would require a more efficient high-level behavior system. Perhaps one that used stochastic planning techniques or faster, limited models of reasoning.

Currently the merperson's face does not move. This could be amended by using facial animation techniques like those described in [75]. Another interesting enhancement would be to develop a simple "merlanguage." The merpeople could use this language to communicate with each other, for example, they could tell each other about good hiding places they found on their travels. The language could also form the basis of establishing cooperative behavior.

Although we have primarily reserved goal-directed behaviors for the high-level behaviors, the low-level behavior system would also be particularly simple to specify. In particular, the work described in [51] would be well-suited to this task. The challenge would be to make the implementation efficient.

11.10 Notes

The low-level predefined behavior system is derived from a previously available system that is described in [136]. The notable enhancements we made are the ability to import arbitrary geometric models, and a more general collision avoidance mechanism. However, the behavior arbitrator was referred to as an "intention generator." This term may be confusing as its functionality is largely subsumed by the high-level behavior system. In [47] there is some Prolog code that was used to implement an earlier version of the controllers that was used to create the animations described in this chapter. The potential field equations are taken from [74]. Octrees are a standard data-structure used in computer graphics (for example, see [44]).

In [59], a learning technique is described that automatically synthesizes realistic locomotion for physics-based models of animals. This technique specifically addresses animals with highly flexible and muscular bodies, such as fish, rays, snakes, and merpeople. In particular, they have established an optimization-based, multi-level learning process that can sit on top of the locomotion subsystem.

Animations, source code and additional support material is available at: www.dgp.toronto.edu/~funge/book/.

Conclusion

One of the key ideas we have extolled in this book is that knowledge representation can play a fundamental role in attempting to build computational models of cognition. We believe that the way a character represents its knowledge is important precisely because cognitive modeling is (currently) such a poorly defined task. If a grand unifying theory of cognition is one day invented then the solution can be hard-coded into some computer chips and our work will no longer be necessary. Until that day, general purpose cognitive models will be contentious or nonexistent. It would therefore seem wise to be able to represent knowledge simply, explicitly, and clearly. If this is not the case then it may be hard to understand, explain, or modify the character's behavior.

We also do not doubt the ability of skillful programmers to create impressive predefined behavior without using explicit cognitive models. Our hope is that cognitive modeling may assist skillful programmers to work faster, and allow less skilled programmers to be afforded a level of success incommensurate with their ability. Thus, cognitive models should play a role analogous to physical or geometric models. That is, they are meant to provide a more suitable level of abstraction for the task in hand—they are not, *per se*, designed to replace human ingenuity.

The underlying semantics for our cognitive models are grounded in mathematical logic. Admittedly, however, real animals do not appear to use logical reasoning for many of their decision-making processes. Fortunately, we are only interested in whether the resulting behavior appears realistic at some level of abstraction. For games and animation at least, faithfulness to the underlying representations and mechanisms we believe to exist in the real world are not what is important. By way of analogy, physics-based animation is a good example of how the real world need not impinge too heavily on our research. To the best of our current knowledge the universe consists of subatomic particles affected by four fundamental forces. For physics-based animation, however, it is often far more convenient to pretend that the world is made of solid objects with a variety of forces acting on them. For the most part this results in motion that appears highly realistic. There are numerous other examples (the interested reader is referred to [38]).

12.1   AI Accelerator Cards

One of the key catalysts behind the explosion of popularity of computer games has been the hitherto unimagined level of realism afforded by powerful (and inexpensive) three-dimensional accelerator cards. While high quality computer graphics sells computer games, it is the game play that keeps the player's attention. The intelligence of the nonplayer characters contributes heavily to the quality of game play, and yet, most of today's computer game AI engines get no more than ten percent of the CPU time. It is reasonable to wonder, therefore, if AI in computer games and animation would also not benefit from accelerator cards. However, what would be most useful for AI algorithms is a dedicated general-purpose CPU. Therefore, systems with multiple CPUs should make great gaming systems. In the same vein, one can imagine devoting a CPU to physical simulation.

Another key factor in the fast adoption of high-quality of graphics for computer games has been the availability of standardized APIs, e.g., Quick-Draw3D, OpenGL, and Direct3D. Currently the pressure to get games to market, and the budgets available mean that developing robust high-quality AI algorithms are (understandably) not a top priority. A standardized API that could provide some basic functionality for AI algorithms would therefore be extremely helpful. For example, path planning algorithms, learning algorithms, search algorithms, etc., are all well-understood concepts in AI. Game programmers are often too busy to spend the required time to implement these ideas correctly. Moreover, they tend to get reinvented afresh for each new project, and each time with differing degrees of success. What is needed is something like a DirectAI library that is freely available, can be easily extended, and offers advanced features like support for multiple CPUs.

12.2 Robotics

The title of this book emphasizes applications in animation and computer games. The "cognitive modeling" approach we have described grew out of the established and closely related area called cognitive robotics. Unfortunately, the low-level control and vision problems in robotics are so hard that doing any of the more interesting high-level stuff we have been describing is next to impossible. If, however, any readers are interested in robotics then we would particularly recommend that they investigate the use of intervals to represent uncertainty. As we explained in Chapter 4, ours is currently just about the only practical approach for implementing sensing within a logical AI framework.

12.3 Electronic Commerce and Web Avatars

The other major application of autonomous agents is for new software agents that are increasingly being used on the World Wide Web for entertainment and commerce. Anyone hoping to build such an agent would be well advised to spend a moment reflecting on the interesting knowledge representation problems that will arise—problems not unlike the ones we have been considering, and problems that are therefore likely to benefit from some of the approaches we have been considering.

12.4 Other Applications

One aspect of the use of the situation calculus that we could exploit further is the ability to prove properties of our specifications. It seems that the computer industry remains resilient to acknowledging the advantages of proving properties of programs versus testing them. Regardless, it is an idea whose time will no doubt come. The work described in this book will be uniquely poised to capitalize on any such paradigm shift.

In a similar vein, we believe the widespread protection of computer characters as intellectual property may one day become a reality. The problems associated with legal wrangling over copyright infringement could be dispelled easily by recourse to a formalism such as the one used in this book. The advantage to this is, of course, that we would have the opportunity to prove or disprove the alleged similarities.

12.5   Conclusion

Much of the early work in computer games and animation consisted of producing efficient implementations of perfectly good scientific theories, or failing that, approximations to existing theories that still produce realistic looking results. It was not long before difficult unsolved problems, such as the
control problem for physics based animations, presented themselves. For
many aspects of the world, most notably cognitive models, scientific theory
is much less complete and we hope that computer games and animation will
play an integral role, both as a test bed and a driving force, in developing
new ideas.

We have introduced the idea of cognitive modeling as a substantive new
apex to the computer graphics modeling pyramid. Cognitive models go beyond behavioral models by governing what a character knows, how that
knowledge is acquired, and how it can be used to plan actions. To assist
the animator or game developer in implementing cognitive models, we have
described powerful techniques that provide an intuitive way to give a character knowledge about its world in terms of actions, their preconditions, and
their effects. When we provide a high-level description of the desired goal
of the character's behavior, we have described a general, automatic mechanism for the character to search for suitable action sequences. At the other
extreme, complex actions can also serve like a conventional programming
language, allowing us to express precisely how we want the character to act.
We can employ a combination of the two extremes and the whole gamut in
between to build different parts of a cognitive model. It is this combination
of convenience and automation that makes our cognitive modeling approach
such a potentially powerful tool in the arsenal of tomorrow's animators and
game developers.

Bibliography

[1] G. Alefeld and J. Herzberger. *Introduction to Interval Computations.* Academic Press, New York, 1983.

[2] J. Allen, J. Hendler, and A. Tate, editors. *Readings in Planning.* Morgan Kaufmann, San Mateo, CA, 1990.

[3] D. Arijon. *Grammar of the Film Language.* Communication Arts Books, Hastings House Publishers, New York, 1976.

[4] W.W. Armstrong, M. Green, and R.Lake. Near real-time control of human figure models. In *IEEE Computer Graphics and Applications,* 7(6):52–61, June 1987.

[5] F. Bacchus, J.Y. Halpern, and H. Levesque. Reasoning about noisy sensors in the situation calculus. In *Proceedings of the Fourteenth International Joint Conference on Artificial Intelligence: IJCAI '95,* pages 1933–1940, August 1995.

[6] N. I. Badler, J. O'Rourke, and G. Kaufman. Special problems in human movement simulation. In *Computer Graphics Proceedings, Annual Conference Series: SIGGRAPH '80,* pages 189–197, July 1980.

[7] N. I. Badler, C.B. Phillips, and D. Zeltzer. *Simulating Humans.* Oxford University Press, New York, 1993.

[8] N. I. Badler, B. L. Webber, J. Kalita, and J. Esakov. Animation from instructions. In Norman I. Badler, Brian A. Barsky, and David Zeltzer, editors, *Making them move: mechanics, control, and animation of articulated figures*, pages 51–93. Morgan Kaufmann, San Mateo, CA, 1991.

[9] N.I. Badler, B.A. Barsky, and D.Zeltzer, editors. *Making them move: mechanics, control, and animation of articulated figures*. Morgan Kaufmann, San Mateo, 1991.

[10] D. Baraff. Analytical methods for dynamic simulation of non-penetrating rigid bodies. In *Computer Graphics Proceedings, Annual Conference Series: SIGGRAPH '89*, pages 223–232, July 1989.

[11] D. Baraff. Curved surfaces and coherence for non-penetrating rigid body simulation. In *Computer Graphics Proceedings, Annual Conference Series: SIGGRAPH '90*, pages 19–28, August 1990.

[12] D. Baraff. Coping with friction for non-penetrating rigid body simulation. In *Computer Graphics Proceedings, Annual Conference Series: SIGGRAPH '91*, pages 31–40, July 1991.

[13] D. Baraff. Fast contact force computation for nonpenetrating rigid bodies. In *Computer Graphics Proceedings, Annual Conference Series: SIGGRAPH '94*, pages 23–34, July 1994.

[14] D. Baraff. Linear-time dynamics using lagrange multipliers. In *Computer Graphics Proceedings, Annual Conference Series: SIGGRAPH '96*, pages 137–146, August 1996.

[15] D. Baraff and A. Witkin. Dynamic simulation of non-penetrating flexible bodies. In *Computer Graphics Proceedings, Annual Conference Series: SIGGRAPH '92*, pages 303–308, July 1992.

[16] C. Baral and T. C. Son. Formalizing sensing actions: a transition function based approach. In *AAAI '98 Fall Symposium on Cognitive Robotics Working Notes*, 1998.

[17] A. H. Barr, B. Currin, S. Gabriel, and J. F. Hughes. Smooth interpolation of orientations with angular velocity constraints using quaternions. In *Computer Graphics Proceedings, Annual Conference Series: SIGGRAPH '92*, pages 313–320, July 1992.

[18] R. Barzel and A. H. Barr. A modeling system based on dynamic constraints. In *Computer Graphics Proceedings, Annual Conference Series:* SIGGRAPH '88, pages 179–188, August 1988.

[19] J. Bates. The role of emotion in believable agents. *Communications of the ACM*, 37(7):122–125, July 1994.

[20] S. Bergman and A. Kaufman. BGRAF2: A real-time graphics language with modular objects and implicit dynamics. In *Computer Graphics Proceedings, Annual Conference Series:* SIGGRAPH '76, pages 133–138, July 1976.

[21] A. Blake. *Canonical Expressions in Boolean Algebra.* Ph.D. thesis, University of Chicago, 1938. Published by University of Chicago Libraries, 1938.

[22] J. Blinn. Where am I? What am I looking at? In *IEEE Computer Graphics and Applications*, 8(4):75–81, July 1988.

[23] B. Blumberg. *Old Tricks, New Dogs: Ethology and Interactive Creatures.* Ph.D. thesis, MIT Media Lab, MIT, Boston, USA, 1996.

[24] B. M. Blumberg and T. A. Galyean. Multi-level direction of autonomous creatures for real-time environments. In *Computer Graphics Proceedings, Annual Conference Series:* SIGGRAPH '95, pages 47–54, August 1995.

[25] I. Bratko. *PROLOG Programming for Artificial Intelligence.* Addison Wesley, Reading, MA, 1990.

[26] D.C. Brogan, R. A. Metoyer, and J. K. Hodgins. Dynamically Simulated Characters in Virtual Environments. In *IEEE Computer Graphics and Applications*, 15(5):58–69, September/October 1998.

[27] R. A. Brooks. A robot that walks: emergent behaviors from a carefully evolved network. In N.I. Badler, B.A. Barsky, and D.Zeltzer, editors, *Making Them Move: Mechanics, Control, and Animation of Articulated Figures*, pages 99–108. Morgan Kaufmann, San Mateo, CA, 1991.

[28] L. S. Brotman and A. N. Netravali. Motion interpolation by optimal control. In *Computer Graphics Proceedings, Annual Conference Series:* SIGGRAPH '88, pages 309–315, August 1988.

[29] A. Bruderlin and T. W. Calvert. Goal-directed, dynamic animation of human walking. In *Computer Graphics Proceedings, Annual Conference Series:* SIGGRAPH '89, pages 233–242, July 1989.

[30] T. W. Calvert, J. Chapman, and A. Patla. The integration of subjective and objective data in the animation of human movement. In *Computer Graphics Proceedings, Annual Conference Series:* SIGGRAPH '80, pages 198–203, July 1980.

[31] E. Catmull. The problems of computer-assisted animation. In *Computer Graphics Proceedings, Annual Conference Series:* SIGGRAPH '78, pages 348–353, August 1978.

[32] D. T. Chen and D. Zeltzer. Pump it up: Computer animation of a biomechanically based model of muscle using the finite element method. In *Computer Graphics Proceedings, Annual Conference Series:* SIGGRAPH '92, pages 89–98, July 1992.

[33] D. B. Christianson, S. E. Anderson, L. He, D. H. Salesin, D.S. Weld, and M. F. Cohen. Declarative camera control for automatic cinematography. In *Proceedings of the Fourteenth National Conference on Artificial Intelligence:* AAAI '96, 1996.

[34] M. F. Cohen. Interactive spacetime control for animation. In *Computer Graphics Proceedings, Annual Conference Series:* SIGGRAPH '92, pages 293–302, July 1992.

[35] G. de Giacomo and H. Levesque. An incremental interpreter for high-level programs with sensing. In *AAAI '98 Fall Symposium on Cognitive Robotics Working Notes*, 1998.

[36] T. L. Dean and P. Wellman. *Planning and Control.* Morgan Kaufmann, San Mateo, CA, 1991.

[37] J. Denavit and S. Hartenberg. A kinematic notation for lower-pair mechanisms based on matrices. In *ASME Journal of Applied Mechanics*, 22:215–221, June 1955.

[38] D. C. Dennett. *The Intentional Stance.* MIT Press, Cambridge, MA, 1989.

[39] R.C. Dorf. *Modern control systems.* Addison-Wesley, Reading, MA, 1992.

[40] P. Maes (editor). *Designing Autonomous Agents: Theory and Practice from Biology to Engineering and Back.* MIT Press, Boston, 1990.

[41] Herbert B. Enderton. *A Mathematical Introduction to Logic.* Academic Press, New York, 1972.

[42] P. Faloutsos. Physics-based animation and control of flexible characters. Technical report, University of Toronto, 1995. CSRI Technical report 326.

[43] R. Featherstone. *Robot Dynamics Algorithms*. Kluwer Academic Publishers, Boston, 1988.

[44] J. D. Foley, A. van Dam, S. K. Feiner, and J. F. Hughes. *Computer Graphics Principles and Practice*. Addison-Wesley, Reading, MA, second edition, 1990.

[45] J. Funge. In SIGGRAPH '98 course notes (#10, "Hardcore AI for Computer Games and Animation"), July 1998.

[46] J. Funge. Lifelike characters behind the camera. In *Proceedings of Lifelike Computer Characters Conference*, October 1998.

[47] J. Funge. *Making Them Behave: Cognitive Models for Computer Animation*. Ph.D. Thesis, Department of Computer Science, University of Toronto, Toronto, Canada, 1998.

[48] J. Funge, X. Tu, and D. Terzopoulos. Cognitive modeling: Knowledge, reasoning and planning for intelligent characters. In *Computer Graphics Proceedings, Annual Conference Series:* SIGGRAPH '99, August 1999.

[49] M. T. Garrett and J. D. Foley. Graphics programming using a database system with dependency declarations. *ACM Transactions on Graphics*, 1(2):109–128, April 1982.

[50] M.P. Gascuel. An implicit formulation for precise contact modeling between flexible solids. In *Computer Graphics Proceedings, Annual Conference Series:* SIGGRAPH '93, pages 313–320, August 1993.

[51] G. De Giacomo, Y. Lespérance, and H. Levesque. Reasoning about concurrent execution, prioritized interrupts, and exogenous actions in the situation calculus. In *Proceedings of the International Joint Conference on Artificial Intelligence:* IJCAI '97, August 1997.

[52] M.L. Ginsberg and D.E. Smith. Reasoning about action II: The qualification problem. *Artificial Intelligence*, 35:311–342, 1988.

[53] M. Girard and A. A. Maciejewski. Computational modeling for the computer animation of legged figures. In *Computer Graphics Proceedings, Annual Conference Series:* SIGGRAPH '85, pages 263–270, July 1985.

[54] J. A. Goguen and G. Malcolm. *Algebraic Semantics of Imperative Programs*. MIT Press, Cambridge, MA, 1995.

[55] H. Goldstein. *Classical Mechanics*. Addison-Wesley, Reading, MA, second edition, 1980.

[56] M. Green. Using dynamics in computer animation: Control and solution issues. In N. I. Badler, B. A. Barsky, and D. Zeltzer, editors, *Making Them Move: Mechanics, Control, and Animation of Articulated Figures*, pages 281–314. Morgan Kaufmann, San Mateo, CA, 1991.

[57] Cognitive Robotics Group. A golog interpreter in eclipse prolog. www.cs.toronto.edu/ cogrobo/gologinterpreter, 1998.

[58] The Cognitive Robotics Group. `www.cs.utoronto.ca/~cogrobo`. Contains copies of numerous relevant papers, April 1996.

[59] R. Grzeszczuk and D. Terzopoulos. Automated learning of muscle-actuated locomotion through control abstraction. In *Computer Graphics Proceedings, Annual Conference Series: SIGGRAPH '95*, pages 47–54, August 1995.

[60] R. Grzeszczuk, D. Terzopoulos, and G. Hinton. Neuroanimator: Fast neural network emulation and control of physics-based models. In *Computer Graphics Proceedings, Annual Conference Series: SIGGRAPH '98*, pages 9–20, July 1998.

[61] J. K. Hahn. Realistic animation of rigid bodies. In *Computer Graphics Proceedings, Annual Conference Series: SIGGRAPH '88*, pages 299–308, August 1988.

[62] S. Hanks and D. McDermott. Temporal reasoning and default logics. Technical report, Yale University, 1985. Computer Science Research Rept. No. 430.

[63] B. Hayes-Roth, L. Brownston, and E. Sincoff. *Directed Improvisation by Computer Characters*. Available as KSL technical report KSL-95-04, Stanford University, CA.

[64] L. He, M. F. Cohen, and D. Salesin. The virtual cinematographer: A paradigm for automatic real-time camera control and directing. In *Computer Graphics Proceedings, Annual Conference Series: SIGGRAPH '96*, pages 217–224, August 1996.

[65] E.C.R. Hehner. Boolean formalism and explanations. In *International Conference on Algebraic Methods and Software Technology*, July 1996.

[66] J. E. Hopcroft and J. D. Ullman. *Introduction to Automata Theory, Languages, and Computation*. Addison-Wesley, Reading, MA, 1979.

[67] A. Hutchinson. *Algorithmic learning*. Oxford University Press, New York, 1994.

[68] P. M. Isaacs and M. F. Cohen. Controlling dynamic simulation with kinematic constraints, behavior functions and inverse dynamics. In *Computer Graphics Proceedings, Annual Conference Series:* SIGGRAPH '87, pages 215–224, July 1987.

[69] John Funge, www.cs.toronto.edu/~funge/cml. *CML Compiler Applet*, 1997.

[70] T. Kelley. Reasoning about physical systems with the situation calculus. In *Common Sense 96, Third Symposium on Logical Formalizations of Commonsense Reasoning*, Stanford, CA, 1996.

[71] Y. Koga, K. Kondo, J. Kuffner, and J. Latombe. Planning motions with intentions. In *Computer Graphics Proceedings, Annual Conference Series:* SIGGRAPH '94, pages 395–408, July 1994.

[72] J. E. Laird and P. S. Rosenbloom. The evolution of the soar cognitive architecture. In T. Mitchell and D. Steier, editors, *Mind Matters: A Tribute to Allen Newell*. Lawrence Erlbaum Associates, Mahwah, NJ, 1996.

[73] J. Lasseter. Principles of traditional animation applied to 3D computer animation. In *Computer Graphics Proceedings, Annual Conference Series:* SIGGRAPH '87, pages 35–44, July 1987.

[74] J. C. Latombe. *Robot Motion Planning*. Kluwer Academic Publishers, Boston, 1991.

[75] Y. Lee, D. Terzopoulos, and K. Waters. Realistic modeling for facial animation. In *Computer Graphics Proceedings, Annual Conference Series:* SIGGRAPH '95, pages 47–54, August 1995.

[76] J. Lengyel, M. Reichert, B.R. Donald, and D.P. Greenberg. Real-time robot motion planning using rasterizing computer graphics hardware. In *Computer Graphics Proceedings, Annual Conference Series:* SIGGRAPH '90, pages 327–335, August 1990.

[77] Y. Lespérance, H. Levesque, F. Lin, R. Reiter D. Marcu, and R. Scherl. Foundations of a logical approach to agent programming. In *Working Notes of the IJCAI '95 Workshop on Agent Theories, Architectures, and Languages*, August 1995.

[78] Y. Lespérance, H.J. Levesque, and R. Reiter. A situation calculus approach to modeling and programming agents. In A. Rao and M. Wooldridge, editors, *Foundations and Theories of Rational Agency*. Kluwer, New York, 1999.

[79] H. Levesque. A completeness result for reasoning with incomplete first-order knowledge bases. In *Proceedings of Sixth International Conference on Principles of Knowledge Representation and Reasoning (KR'98)*, June 1998.

[80] H. Levesque, R. Reiter, Y. Lespérance, F. Lin, and R. Scherl. Golog: A logic programming language for dynamic domains. *Journal of Logic Programming*, 31:59–84, 1997. Special issue on Reasoning about Action and Change.

[81] H.J. Levesque. What is planning in the presence of sensing? In *Proceedings of the Thirteenth National Conference on Artificial Intelligence:* AAAI '96, August 1996.

[82] F. Lin and R. Reiter. Forget it! In Russ Greiner and Devika Subramanian, editors, *Working Notes of AAAI Fall Symposium on Relevance*, November 1994.

[83] Fangzhen Lin and Raymond Reiter. State constraints revisited. *Journal of Logic and Computation*, Special Issue on Actions and Processes, 4(5):655–678, 1994.

[84] M. C. Lin. *Efficient Collision Detection for Animation and Robotics.* Ph.D. thesis, Department of Electrical Engineering and Computer Science, University of California, Berkeley, December 1993.

[85] Z. Liu, S. J. Gortler, and M. F. Cohen. Hierarchical spacetime control. In *Computer Graphics Proceedings, Annual Conference Series:* SIGGRAPH '94, pages 35–42, July 1994.

[86] N. Magnenat-Thalmann and D. Thalmann. *Synthetic Actors in Computer-Generated Films.* Springer-Verlag, New York, 1990.

[87] S. Mah, T.W. Calvert, and W. Havens. Nsail: Behavioural animation control using constraint-based reasoning. In *Proceedings of Graphics Interface '94*, pages 200–207, May 1994.

[88] J. McCarthy. Epistemological problems of artificial intelligence. In *Proceedings of the International Joint Conference on Artificial Intelligence: IJCAI '77*, pages 1038–1044, 1977.

[89] J. McCarthy and P. Hayes. Some philosophical problems from the standpoint of artificial intelligence. In B. Meltzer and D. Michie, editors, *Machine Intelligence 4*, pages 463–502. Edinburgh University Press, Edinburgh, 1969.

[90] Sheila A. McIlraith. *Towards a Formal Account of Diagnostic Problem Solving*. Ph.D. thesis, Department of Computer Science, University of Toronto, 1997.

[91] M. McKenna and D. Zeltzer. Dynamic simulation of autonomous legged locomotion. In *Computer Graphics Proceedings, Annual Conference Series: SIGGRAPH '90*, pages 29–38, August 1990.

[92] C. McManis. Looking for Lex and Yacc for Java? You don't know Jack. *JavaWorld*, 1, December 1996. Written before the name change from Jack to JavaCC.

[93] D. Metaxas and D. Terzopoulos. Dynamic deformation of solid primitives with constraints. In *Computer Graphics Proceedings, Annual Conference Series: SIGGRAPH '92*, pages 309–312, July 1992.

[94] G. S. P. Miller. The motion dynamics of snakes and worms. In *Computer Graphics Proceedings, Annual Conference Series: SIGGRAPH '88*, pages 169–178, August 1988.

[95] T. M. Mitchell. *Machine Learning*. McGraw Hill, New York, 1997.

[96] M. Moore and J. Wilhelms. Collision detection and response for computer animation. In *Computer Graphics Proceedings, Annual Conference Series: SIGGRAPH '88*, pages 289–298, August 1988.

[97] R. C. Moore. A formal theory of knowledge and action. In J. R. Hobbs and R.C. Moore, editors, *Formal Theories of the Commonsense World*, pages 319–358. Ablex, Norwood, NJ, 1985.

[98] R. E. Moore. *Interval Analysis*. Prentice Hall, Englewood Cliffs, NJ, 1966.

[99] R. E. Moore. *Methods and Applications of Interval Analysis*. SIAM, Philadelphia, 1979.

[100] B. A. Nayfeh. Using a cellular automata to solve mazes. *Dr. Dobb's Journal*, February 1993.

[101] V. Ng-Thow-Hing. A biomechanical musculotendon model for animating articulated objects. M.Sc. thesis, University of Toronto, 1994.

[102] J. T. Ngo and J. Marks. Spacetime constraints revisited. In *Computer Graphics Proceedings, Annual Conference Series:* SIGGRAPH '93, pages 343–350, August 1993.

[103] A. Pentland and J. Williams. Good vibrations: Modal dynamics for graphics and animation. In *Computer Graphics Proceedings, Annual Conference Series:* SIGGRAPH '89, pages 215–222, July 1989.

[104] Ken Perlin and Athomas Goldberg. IMPROV: A system for scripting interactive actors in virtual worlds. In *Computer Graphics Proceedings, Annual Conference Series:* SIGGRAPH 96, pages 205–216, August 1996.

[105] J. Pesonen and E. Hyvonen. Interval approach challanges Monte Carlo simulation. In *IMACS/GAMM International Symposium on Scientific Computing, Computer Arithmetic and Validated Numerics:* SCAN '95, 1995.

[106] C. B. Phillips and N. I. Badler. Interactive behaviors for bipedal articulated figures. In *Computer Graphics Proceedings, Annual Conference Series:* SIGGRAPH '91, pages 359–362, July 1991.

[107] C. Pinhanez, K. Mase, and A. Bobick. Interval Scritps: a Design Paradigm for Story-Based Interactive Systems In *Proceedings of CHI'97*, March 1997.

[108] J. Pinto and R. Reiter. Reasoning about time in the situation calculus. In *Annals of Mathematics and Artificial Intelligence*, 14(2–4), Festschrift in Honor of Professor Jack Minker, 1995.

[109] J. C. Platt and A. H. Barr. Constraint methods for flexible models. In *Computer Graphics Proceedings, Annual Conference Series:* SIGGRAPH '88, pages 279–288, August 1988.

[110] M. H. Raibert and J. K. Hodgins. Animation of dynamic legged locomotion. In *Computer Graphics Proceedings, Annual Conference Series:* SIGGRAPH '91, pages 349–358, July 1991.

[111] R. Reiter. The frame problem in the situation calculus: A simple solution (sometimes) and a completeness result for goal regression. In Vladimir Lifschitz, editor, *Artificial Intelligence and Mathematical Theory of Computation: Papers in Honour of John McCarthy*, Academic Press, Boston, 1991.

[112] R. Reiter. Natural actions, concurrency and continuous time in the situation calculus. In *Principles of Knowledge Representation and Reasoning: Proceedings of the Fifth International Conference (KR'96)*, November 1996.

[113] R. Reiter. *KNOWLEDGE IN ACTION: Logical Foundations for Describing and Implementing Dynamical Systems*. www.cs.toronto.edu/~cogrobo, 1999.

[114] C. W. Reynolds. Computer animation with scripts and actors. In *Computer Graphics Proceedings, Annual Conference Series:* SIGGRAPH '82, pages 289–296, July 1982.

[115] C. W. Reynolds. Flocks, herds, and schools: A distributed behavioral model. In *Computer Graphics Proceedings, Annual Conference Series:* SIGGRAPH '87, pages 25–34, July 1987.

[116] H. Rijpkema and M. Girard. Computer animation of knowledge-based human grasping. In *Computer Graphics Proceedings, Annual Conference Series:* SIGGRAPH '91, pages 339–348, July 1991.

[117] S. Russell and P. Norvig. *Artificial Intelligence: A Modern Approach*. Prentice Hall, Englewood Cliffs, NJ, 1995.

[118] R. Scherl and H. Levesque. The frame problem and knowledge-producing actions. In *Proceedings of the Eleventh National Conference on Artificial Intelligence:* AAAI '93, 1993.

[119] R. J. Schilling. *Fundamentals of Robotics: Analysis and Control*. Prentice Hall, Englewood Cliffs, NJ, 1990.

[120] B. Selman and H. Kautz. Knowledge compilation and theory approximation. *Journal of the ACM*, 43(2):193–224, 1996.

[121] S. Shapiro, Y. Lespérance, and H. Levesque. Goals and rationality in the situation calculus – a preliminary report. In *AAAI Fall Symposium on Rational Agency*, 1995.

[122] K. Shoemake. Animating rotation with quaternion curves. In *Computer Graphics Proceedings, Annual Conference Series:* SIGGRAPH '85, pages 245–254, July 1985.

[123] K. Sims. Evolving virtual creatures. In *Computer Graphics Proceedings, Annual Conference Series:* SIGGRAPH '94, pages 15–22, July 1994.

[124] J. Snyder. Interval analysis for computer graphics. In *Computer Graphics Proceedings, Annual Conference Series:* SIGGRAPH '92, pages 121–130, July 1992.

[125] J. M. Snyder, A. R. Woodbury, K. Fleischer, B. Currin, and A. H. Barr. Interval method for multi-point collision between time-dependent curved surfaces. In *Computer Graphics Proceedings, Annual Conference Series:* SIGGRAPH '93, pages 321–334, August 1993.

[126] Pedagoguery Software. GRAFEQ. www.peda.com.

[127] S. N. Steketee and N. I. Badler. Parametric keyframe interpolation incorporating kinetic adjustment and phasing control. In *Computer Graphics Proceedings, Annual Conference Series:* SIGGRAPH '85, pages 255–262, July 1985.

[128] A. J. Stewart and J. F. Cremer. Beyond keyframing: An algorithmic approach to animation. In *Proceedings of Graphics Interface '92*, pages 273–281, May 1992.

[129] J. E. Stoy. *Denotational Semantics: The Scott-Strachey approach to programming language theory.* MIT Press, Cambridge, MA, 1977.

[130] Meng Sun and E.Fiume. Technique for constructing developable surfaces. In *Proceedings of Graphics Interface '96*, pages 176–185, May 1996.

[131] Symbolic Dynamics Inc., Mountain View, California, USA. *SD/Fast User's Manual*, 1990.

[132] E. Ternovskaia. Interval situation calculus. In *Proceedings of ECAI '94 Workshop Action and Change*, 1994.

[133] D. Terzopoulos and K. Fleischer. Modeling inelastic deformation: Viscoelasticity, plasticity, fracture. In *Computer Graphics Proceedings, Annual Conference Series:* SIGGRAPH '88, pages 269–278, August 1988.

[134] D. Terzopoulos, J. Platt, A. Barr, and K. Fleischer. Elastically deformable models. In *Computer Graphics Proceedings, Annual Conference Series:* SIGGRAPH '87, pages 205–214, July 1987.

[135] D. Terzopoulos, X. Tu, and R. Grzeszczuk. Artificial fishes with autonomous locomotion, perception, behavior, and learning in a simulated physical world. In *Artificial Life IV: Proceedings of the Fourth International Workshop on the Synthesis and Simulation of Living System*, pages 17–27, July 1994.

[136] X. Tu. *Artificial Animals for Computer Animation: Biomechanics, Locomotion, Perception, and Behavior.* Ph.D. thesis, Department of Computer Science, University of Toronto, Toronto, Canada, January 1996. Winner of the ACM 1996 ACM Doctoral Dissertation Award.

[137] X. Tu and D. Terzopoulos. Artificial fishes: Physics, locomotion, perception, behavior. In *Computer Graphics Proceedings, Annual Conference Series:* SIGGRAPH '94, pages 43–50, July 1994.

[138] J. Tupper. *Graphing Equations with Generalized Interval Arithmetic.* M.Sc. thesis, Department of Computer Science, University of Toronto, Toronto, Canada, January 1996.

[139] M. van de Panne and E. Fiume. Sensor-actuator networks. In *Computer Graphics Proceedings, Annual Conference Series:* SIGGRAPH '93, pages 335–342, August 1993.

[140] M. van de Panne, E. Fiume, and Z. Vranesic. Reusable motion synthesis using state-space controllers. In *Computer Graphics Proceedings, Annual Conference Series:* SIGGRAPH '90, pages 225–234, August 1990.

[141] M. van de Panne, R. Kim, and E. Fiume. Virtual wind-up toys for animation. In *Proceedings of Graphics Interface '94*, pages 208–215, May 1994.

[142] M. van Lent and J. Laird. Behavior capture: Motion is only skin deep. In *Lifelike Computer Characters '98*, October 1998.

[143] B. Von Herzen, A. H. Barr, and H. R. Zatz. Geometric collisions for time-dependent parametric surfaces. In *Computer Graphics Proceedings, Annual Conference Series:* SIGGRAPH '90, pages 39–48, August 1990.

[144] P. Wavish and M. Graham. A situated action approach to implementing characters in computer games. *Applied AI Journal*, 10(1):53-74. 1996.

[145] J. Wilhelms. Using dynamic analysis for realistic animation of articulated bodies. In *IEEE Computer Graphics and Applications*, 7(6):12–17, June 1987.

[146] A. Witkin and M. Kass. Spacetime constraints. In *Computer Graphics Proceedings, Annual Conference Series:* SIGGRAPH '88, pages 159–168, August 1988.

[147] A. Witkin and W. Welch. Fast animation and control of nonrigid structures. In *Computer Graphics Proceedings, Annual Conference Series:* SIGGRAPH '90, pages 243–252, August 1990.

[148] Victor Ye. *A Rule-based Approach to Animating Multi-agent Environments*. Ph.D. thesis, Department of Computer Science, University of Brighton, Brighton, England, April 1996.

[149] D. Zeltzer. Motor control techniques for figure animation. In *IEEE Computer Graphics and Applications*, 2(9):53-59, 1982.

[150] R. Ziegler. *Character Animation using Transformation Based Linear Dynamics*. M.Sc. thesis, Department of Computer Science, University of Toronto, Toronto, Canada, January 1997.

Index

This book is dedicated to Prof. M. Selick.